Lecture For Every One

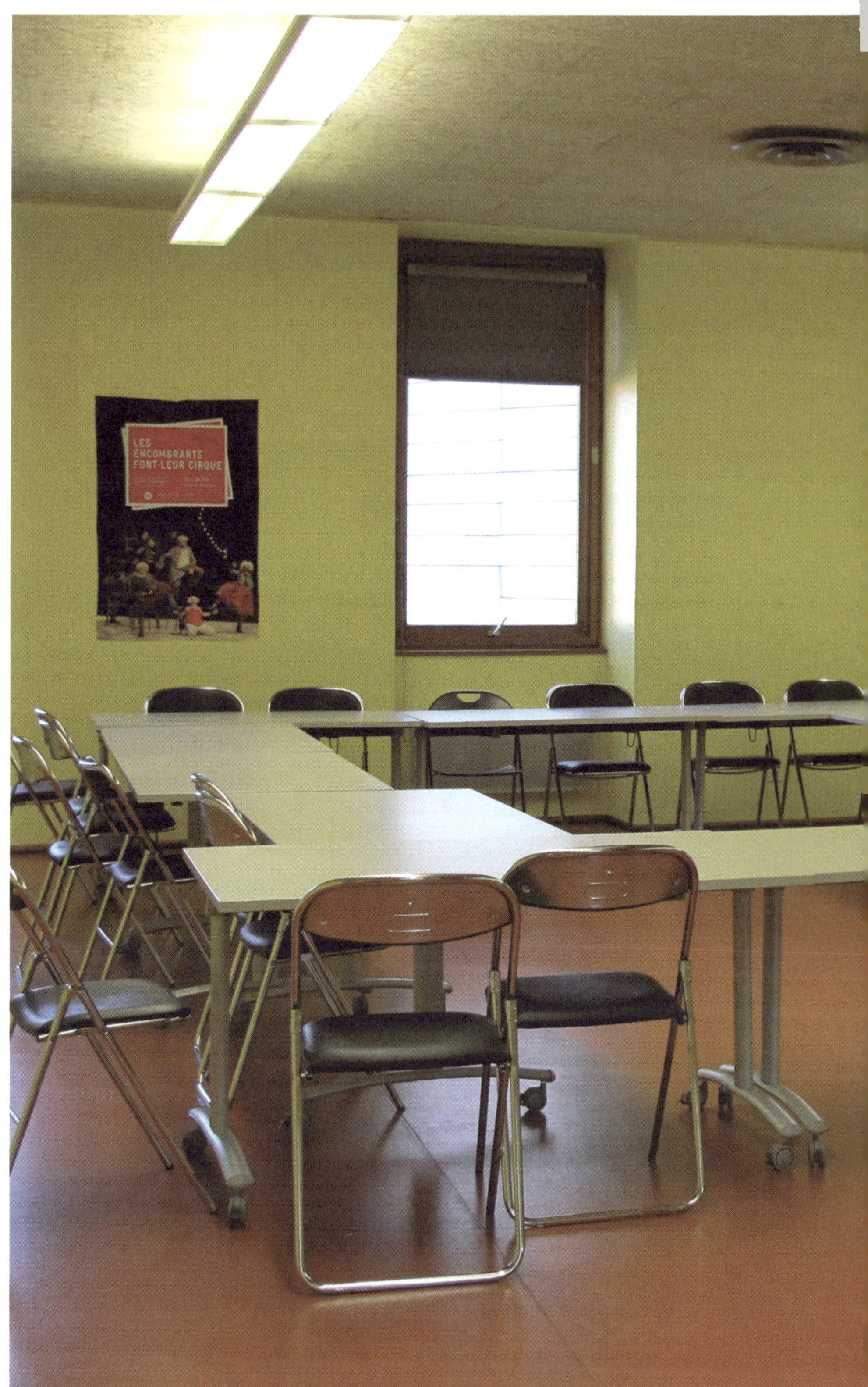
LES
ENCOMBRANTS
FONT LEUR CIRQUE

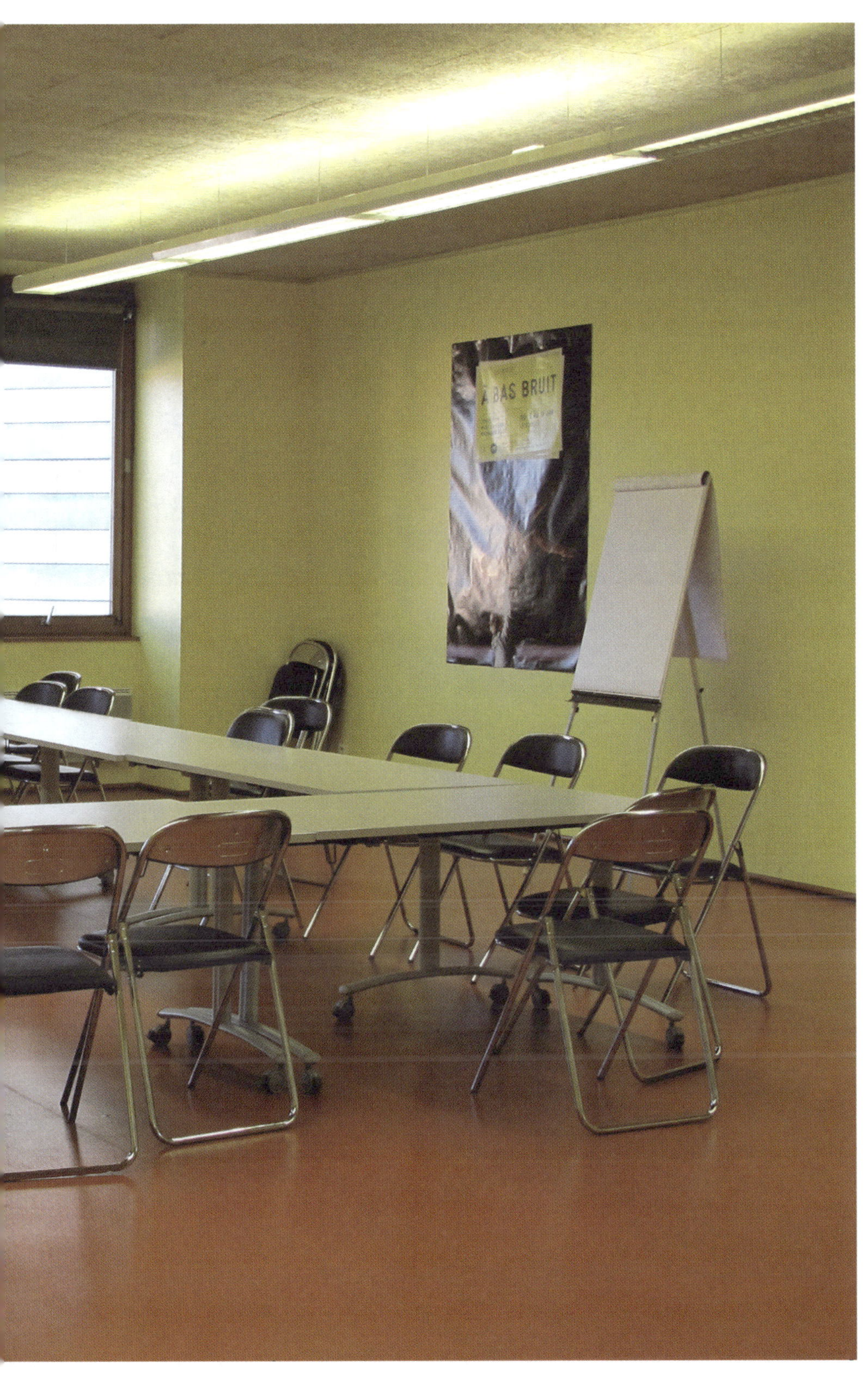
À BAS BRUIT

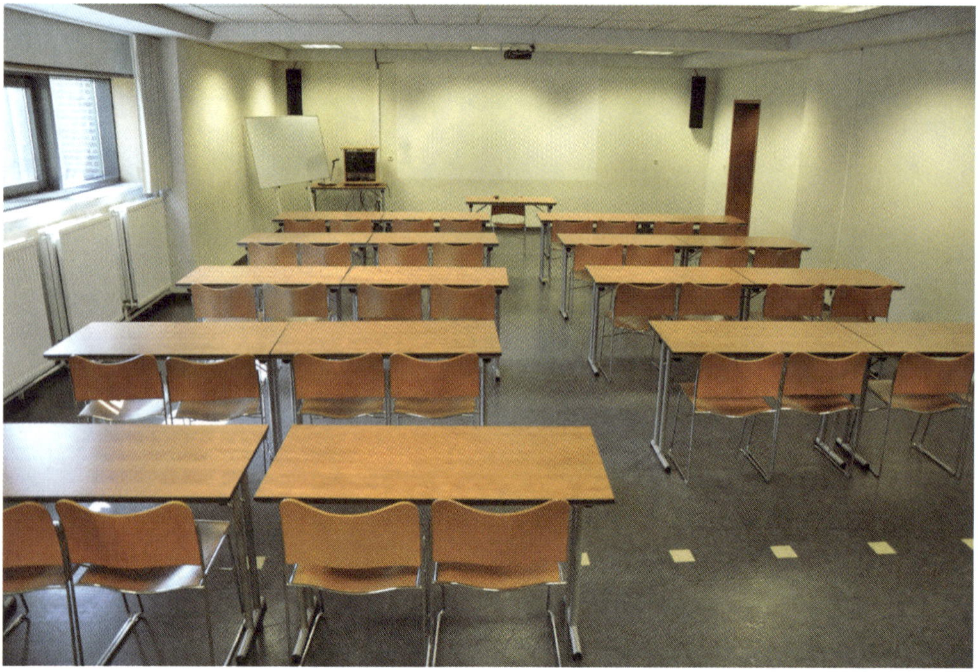

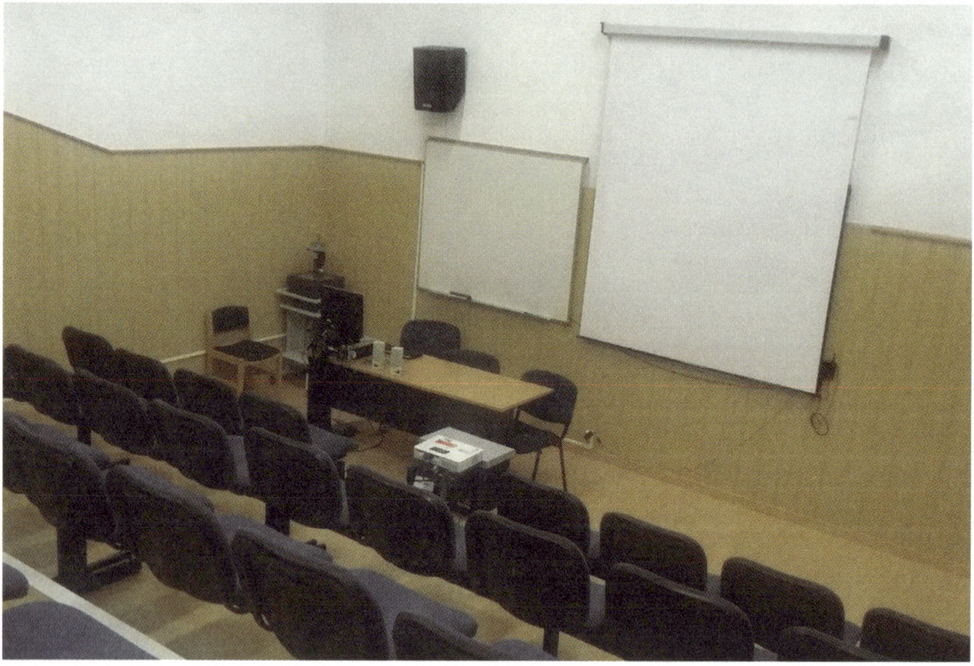

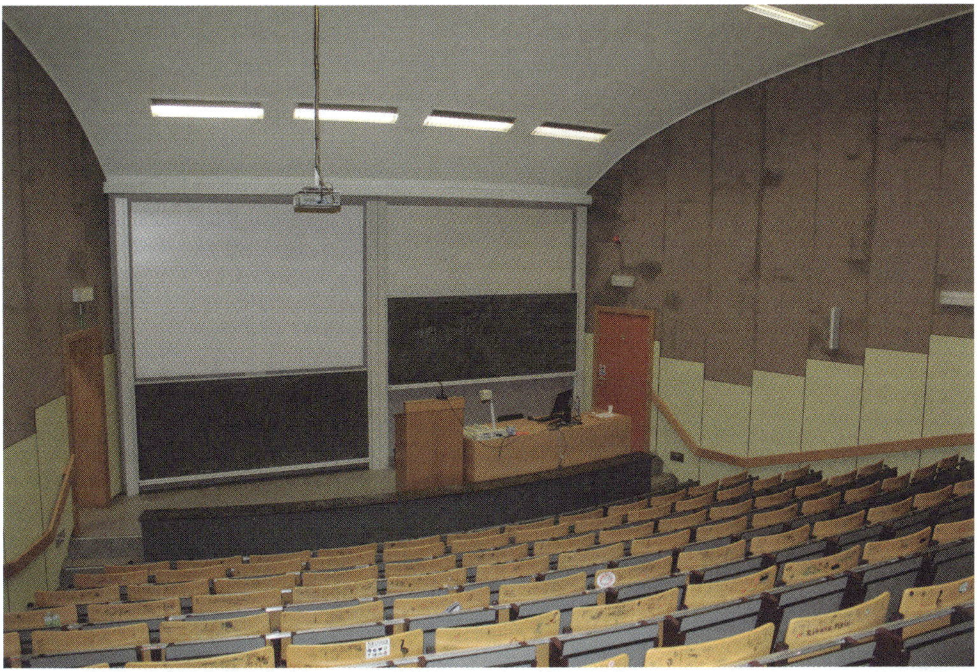

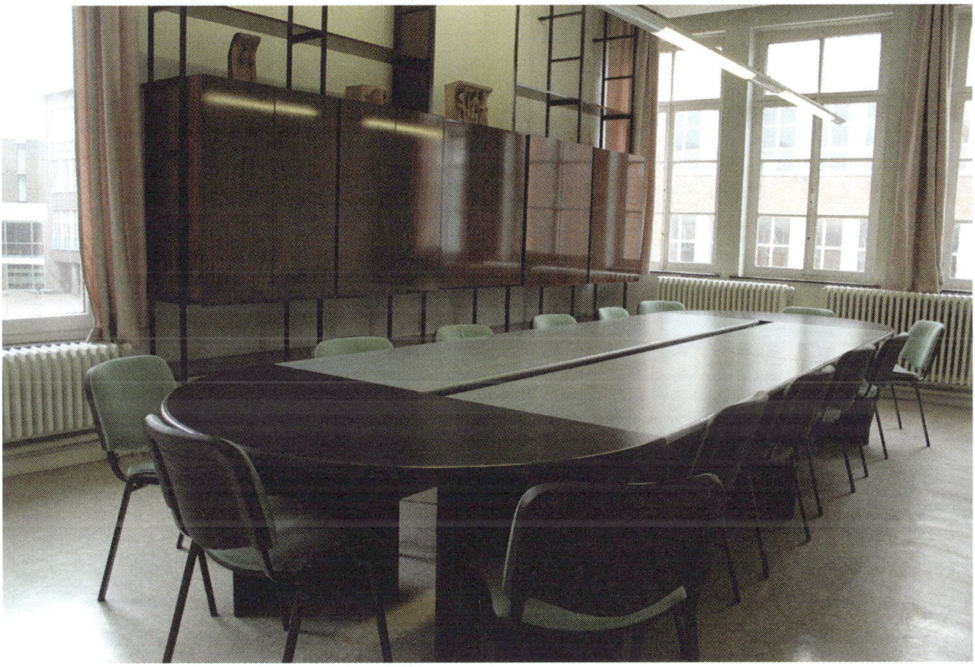

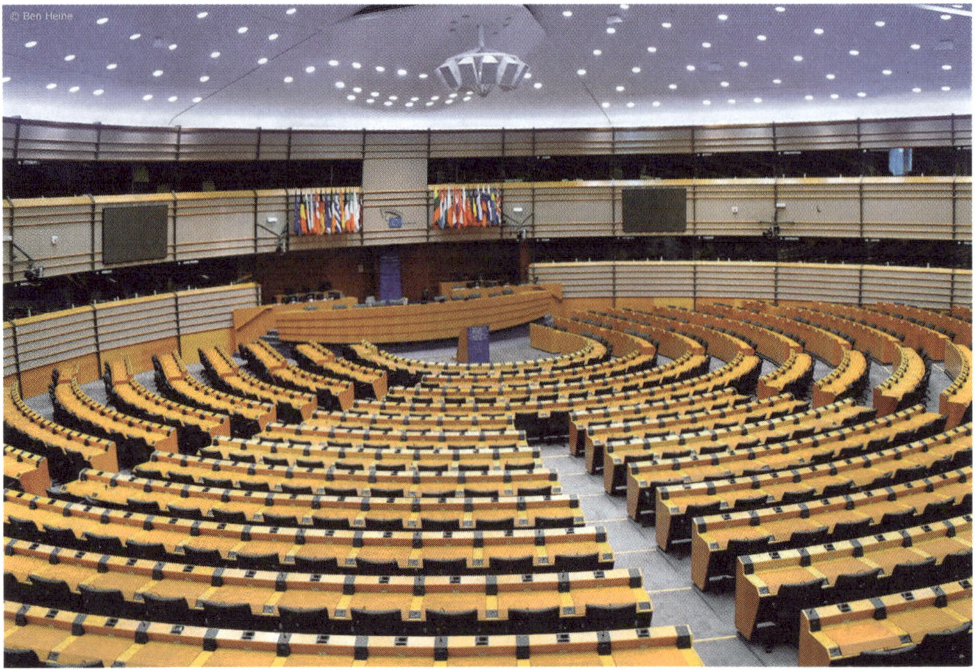

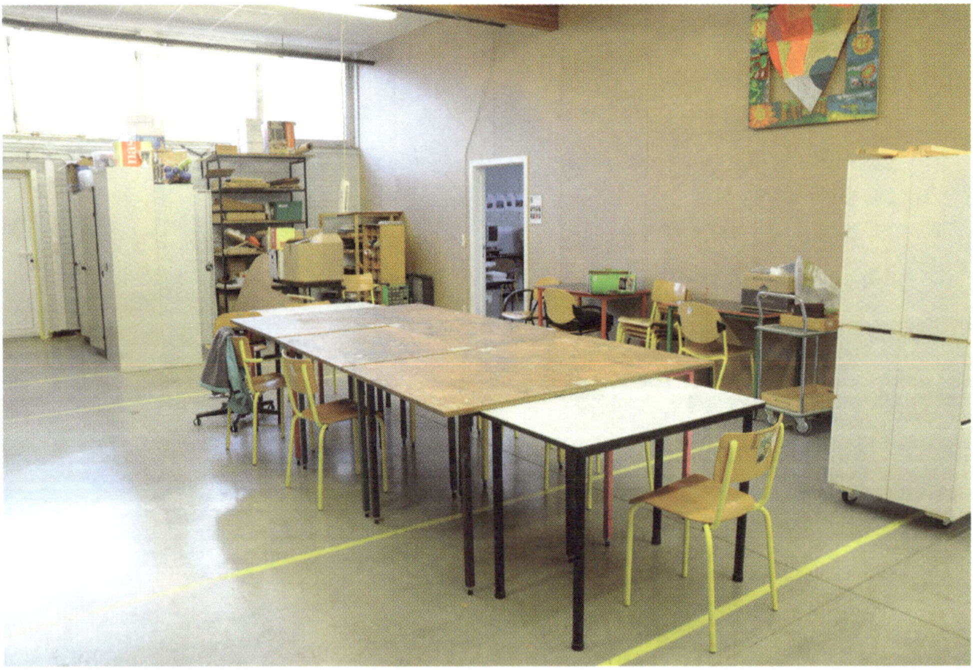

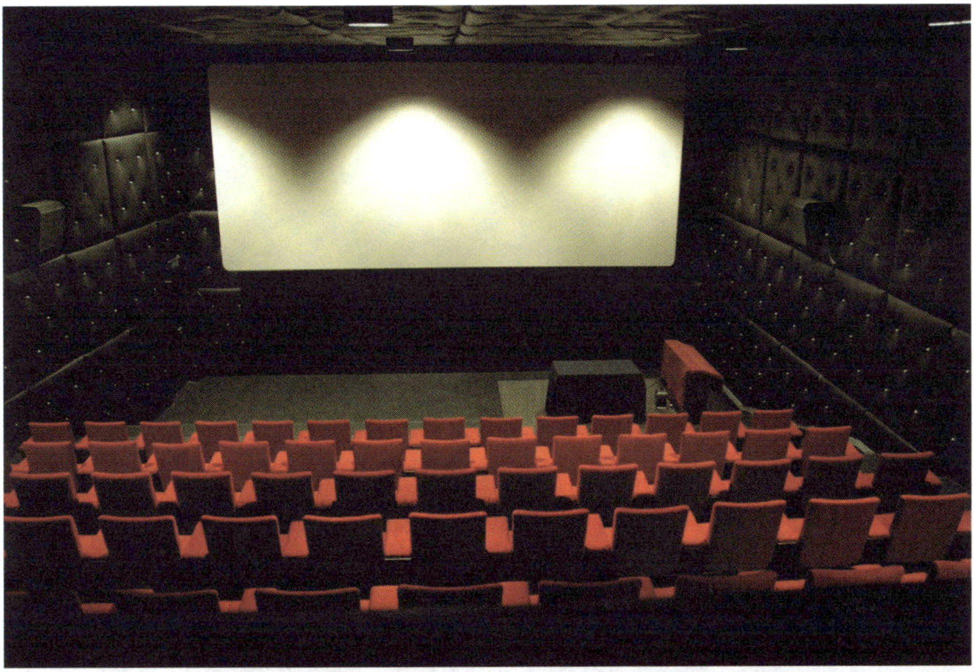

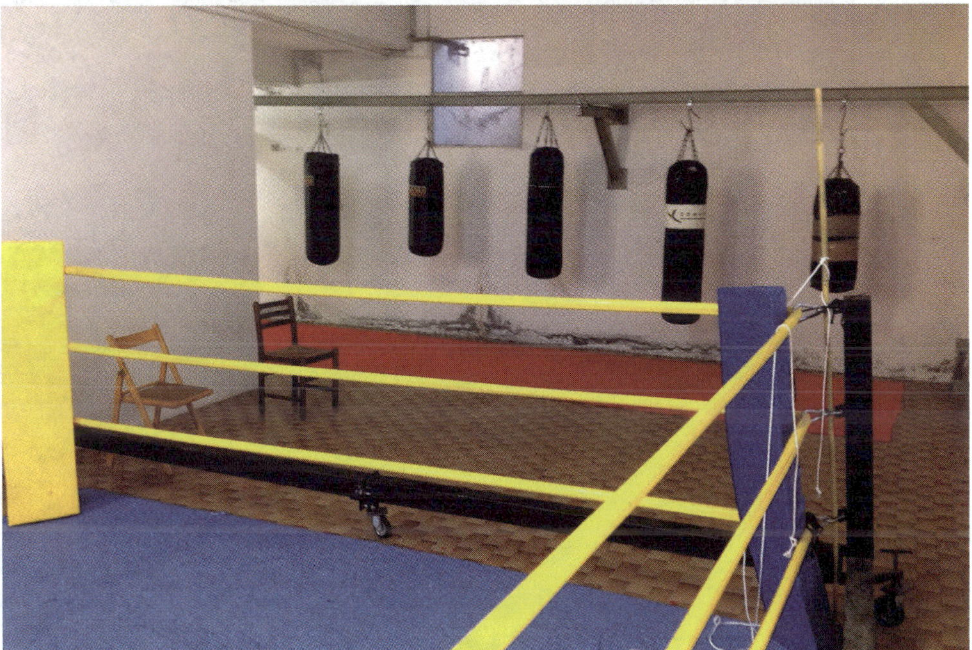

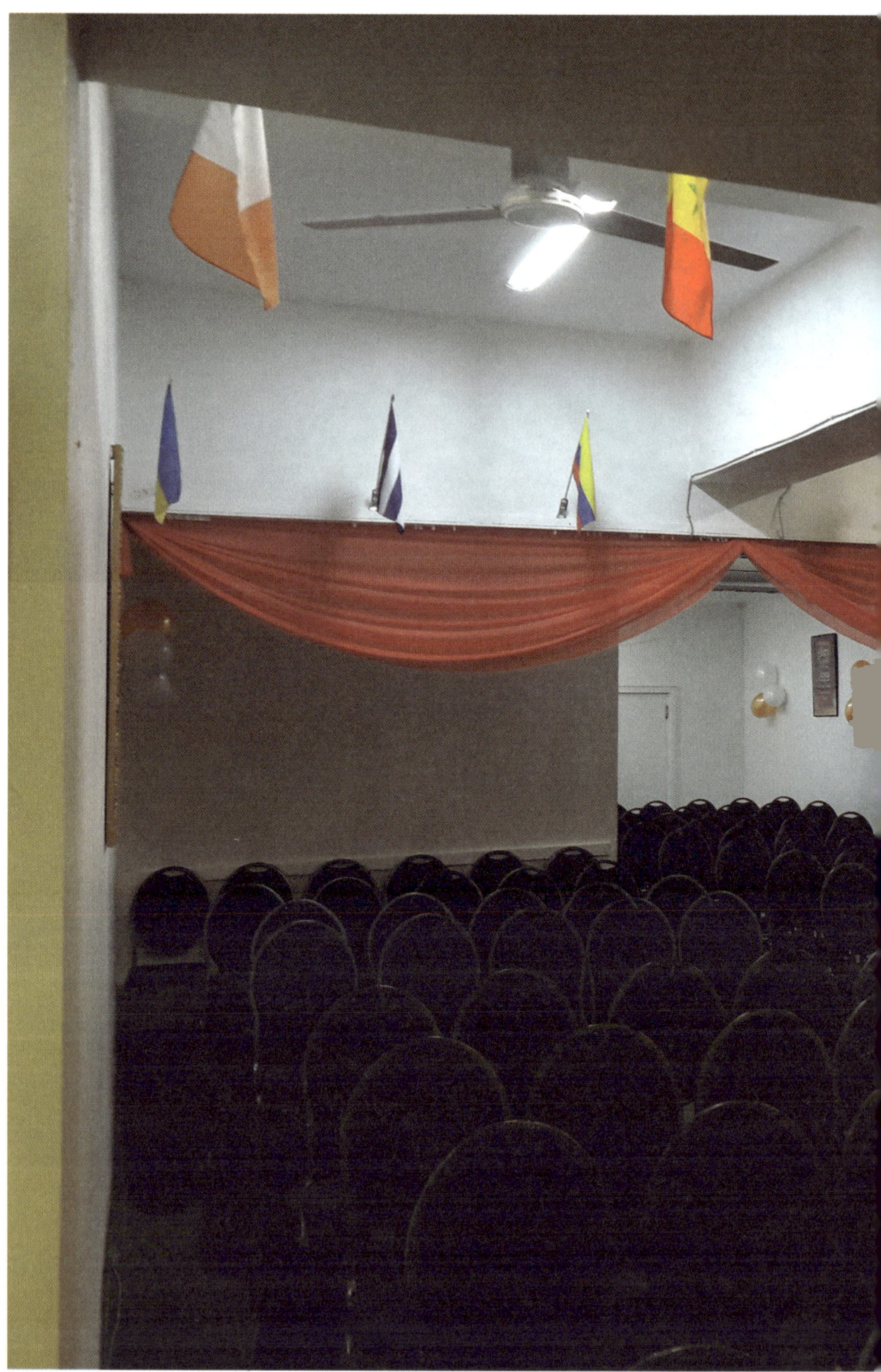

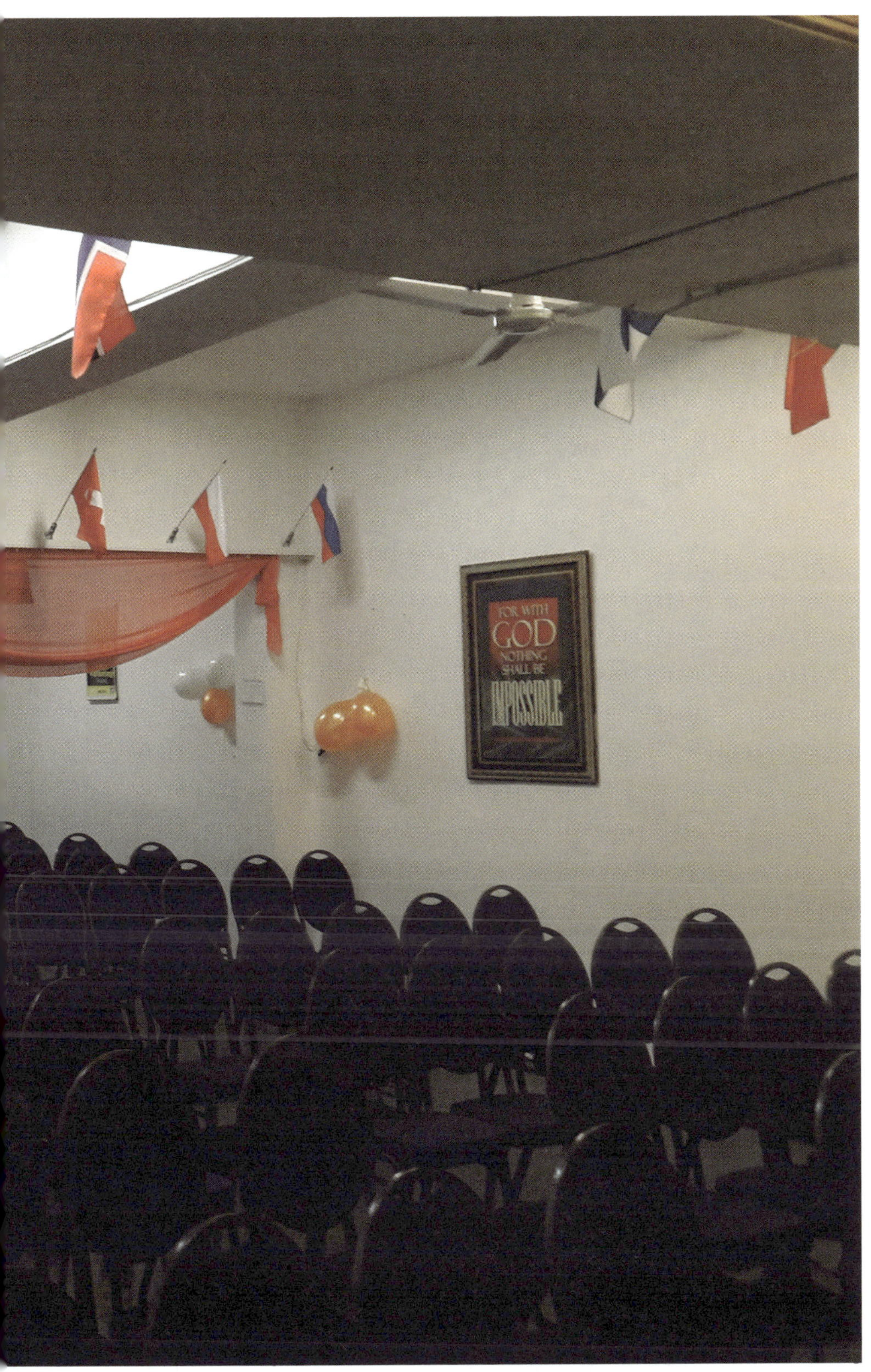
FOR WITH
GOD
NOTHING
SHALL BE
IMPOSSIBLE

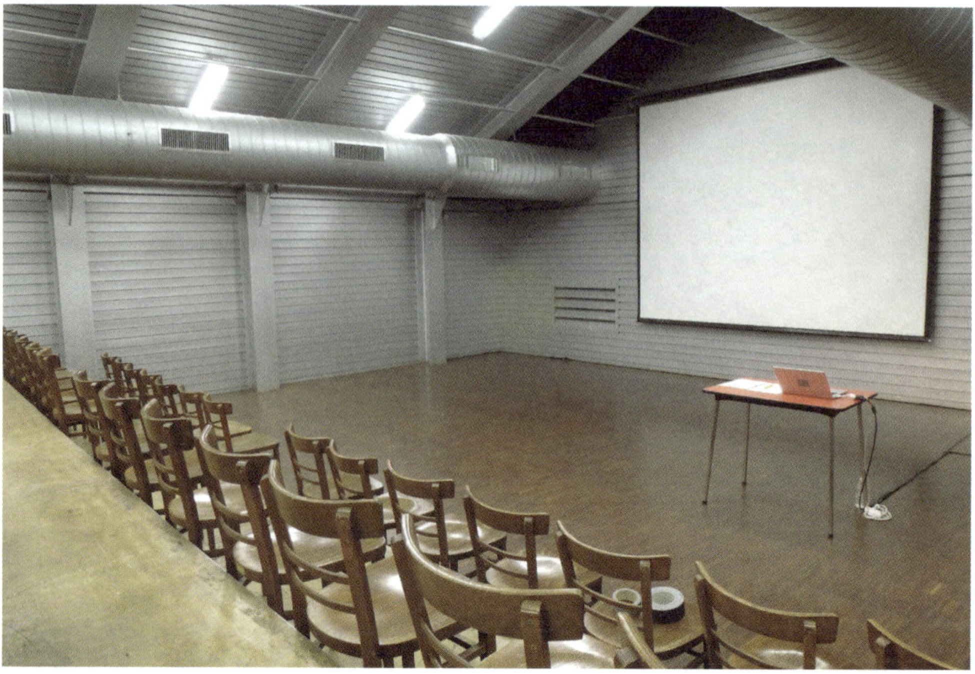

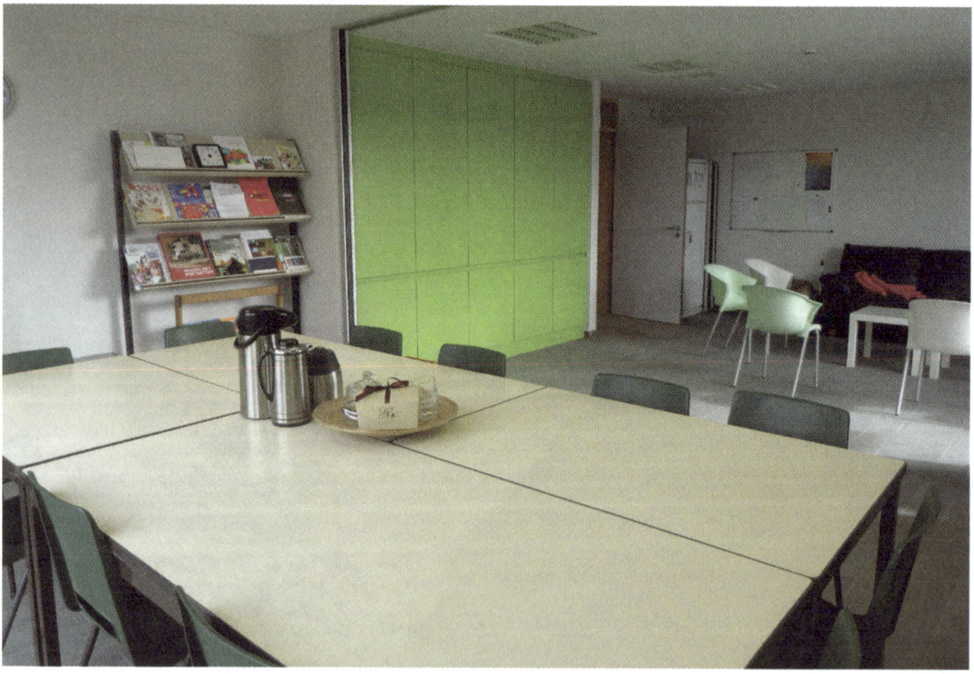

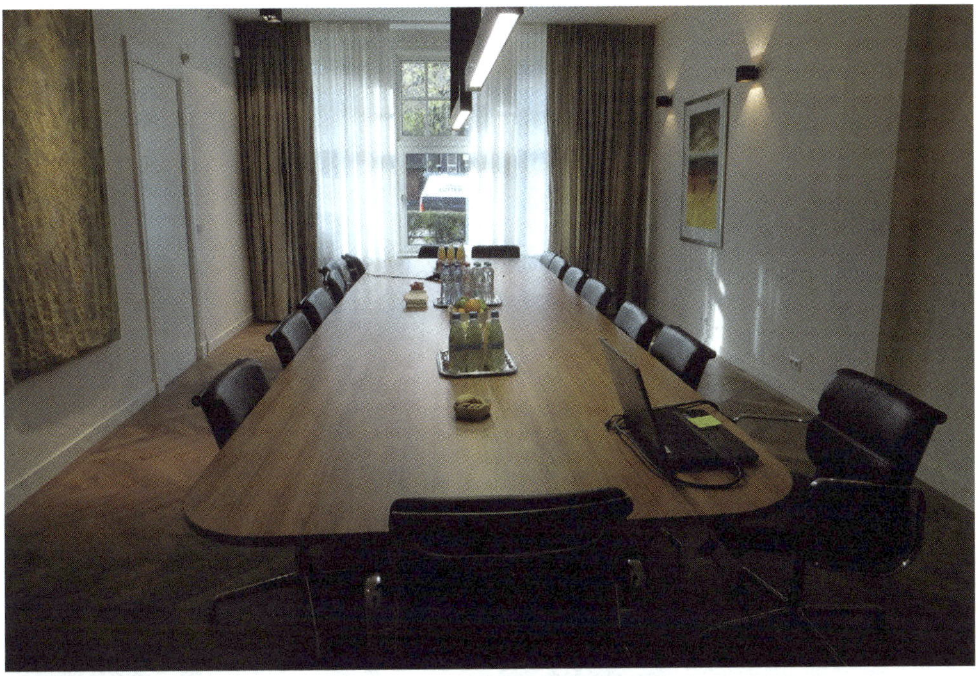

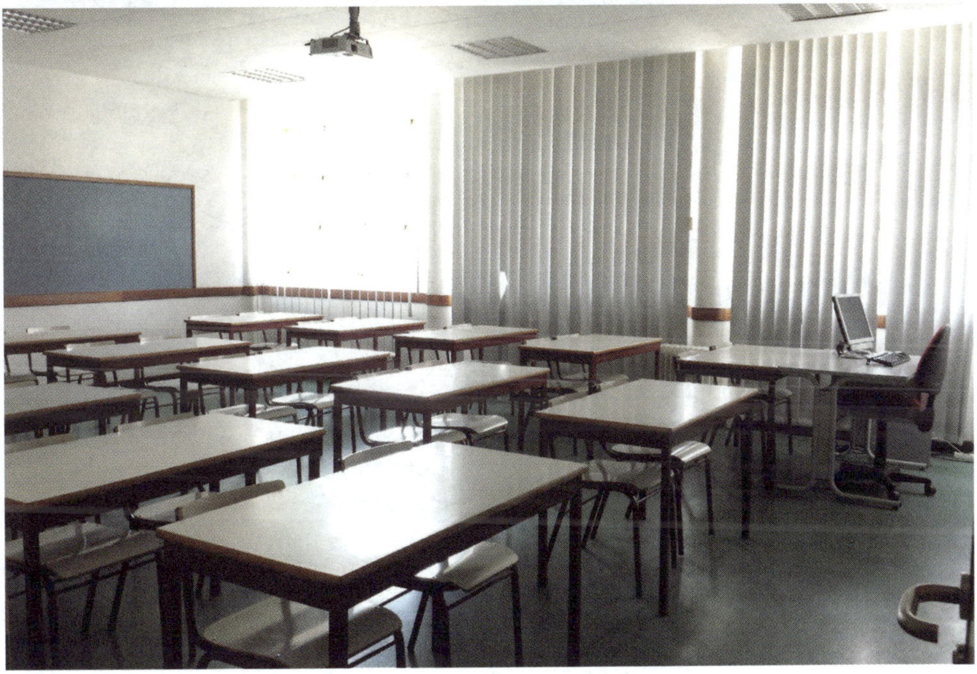

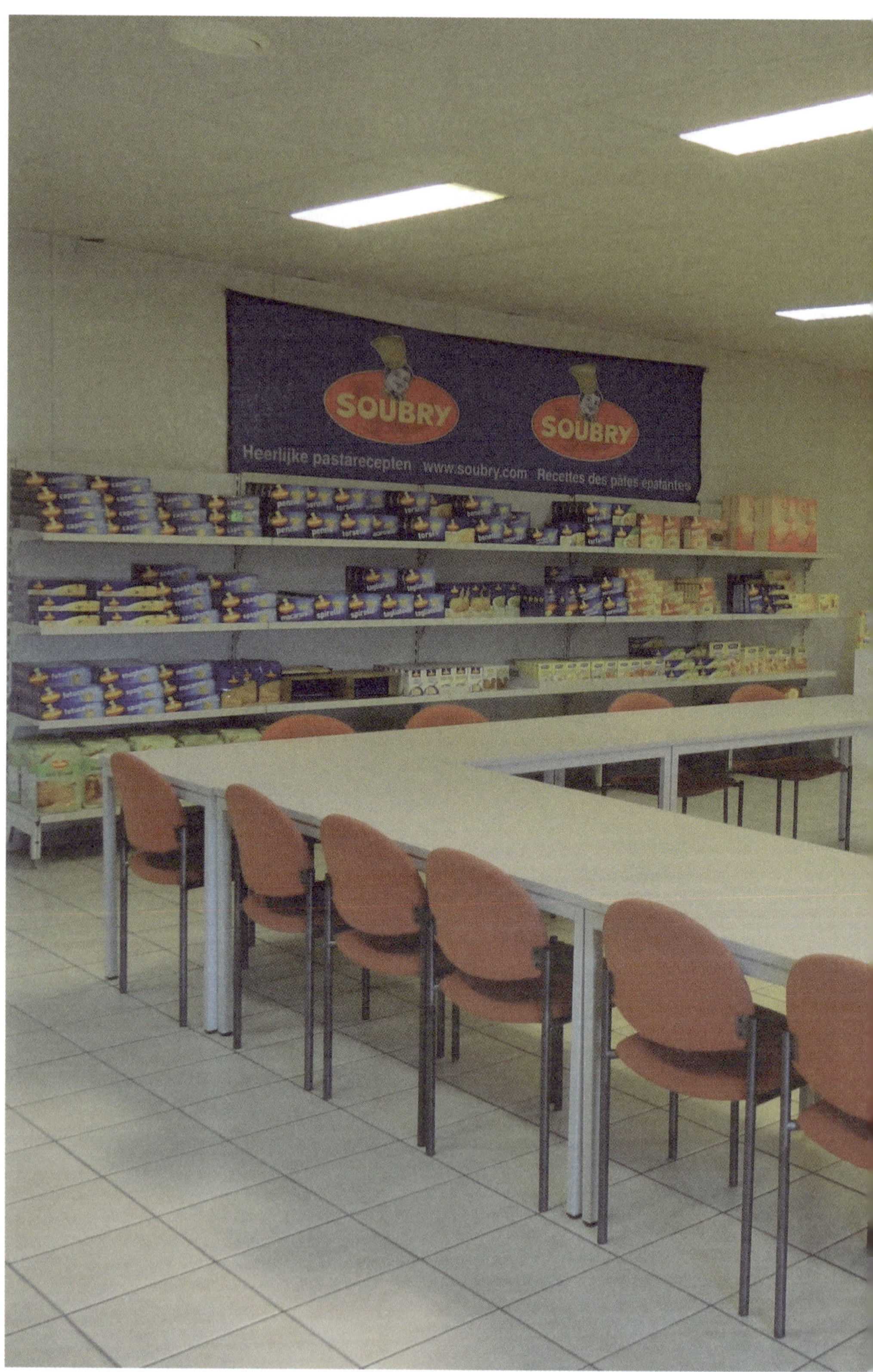
SOUBRY
SOUBRY
Heerlijke pastarecepten www.soubry.com Recettes des pates epatantes

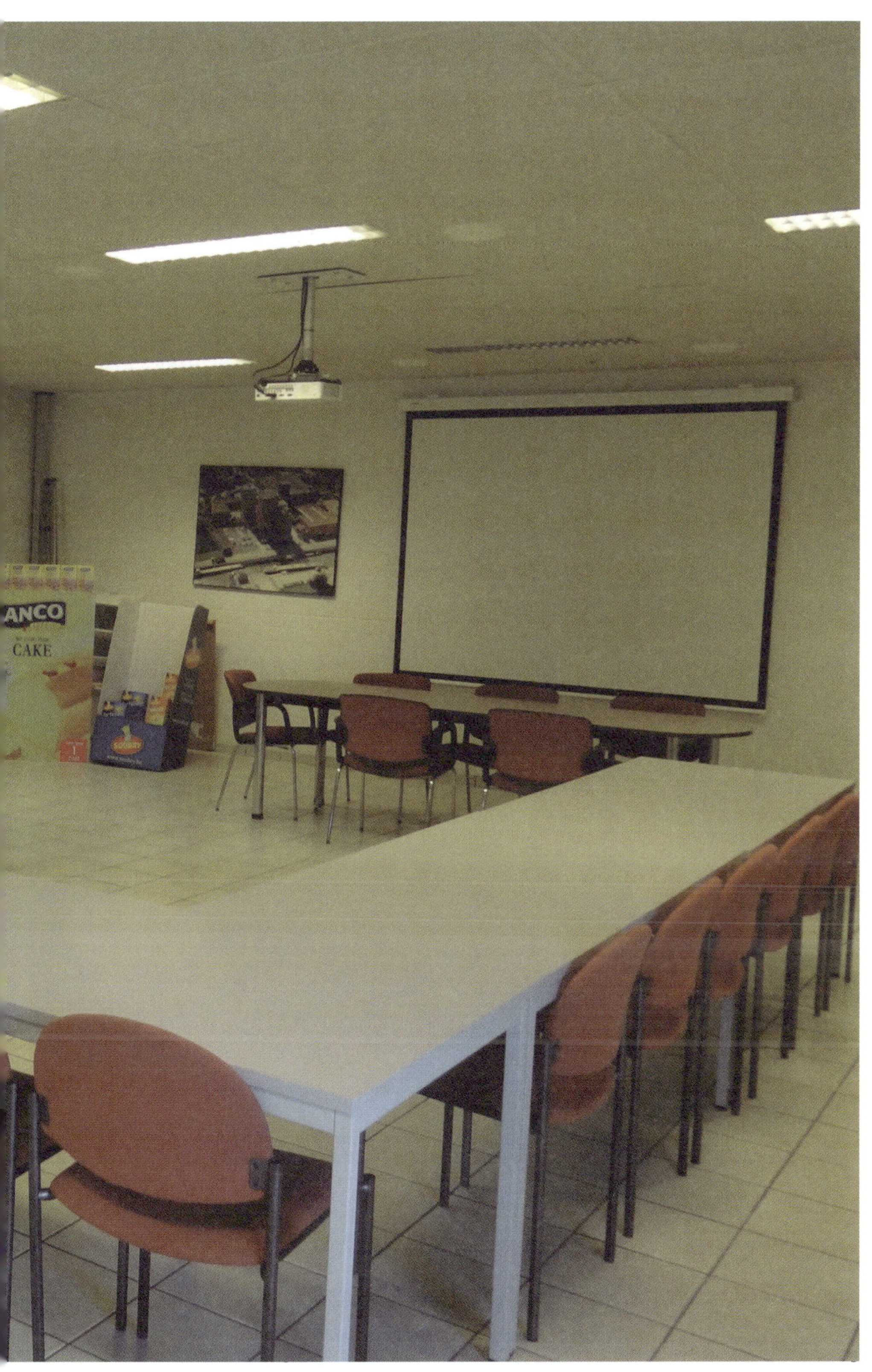
ANCO
CAKE

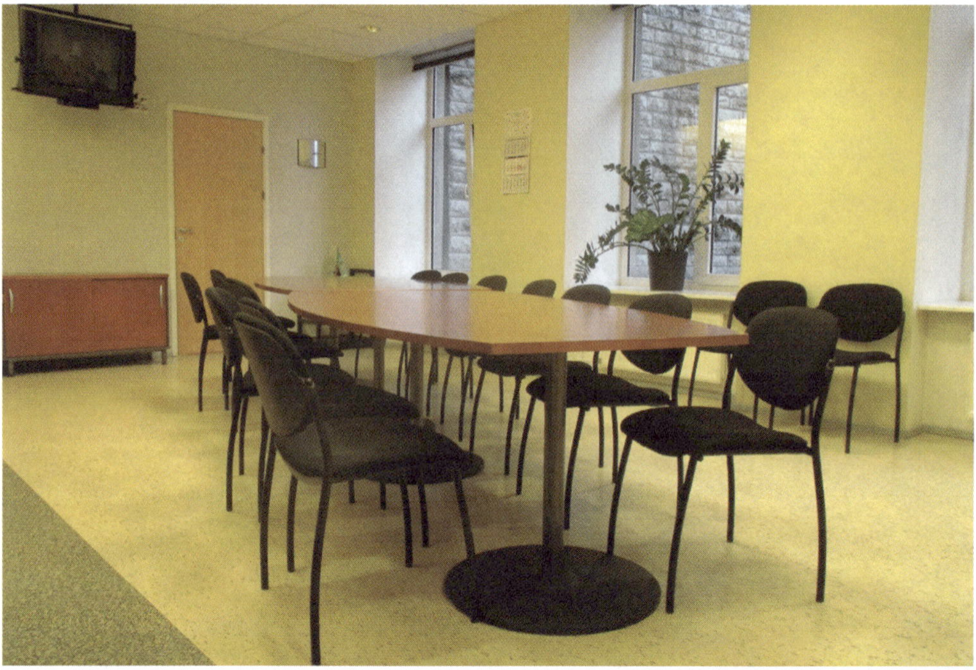

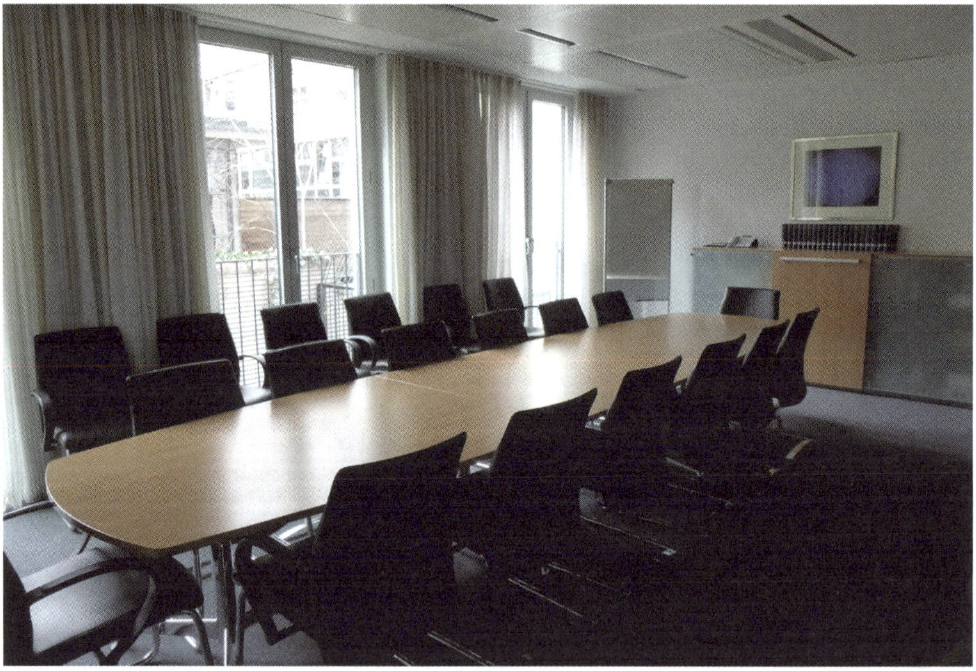

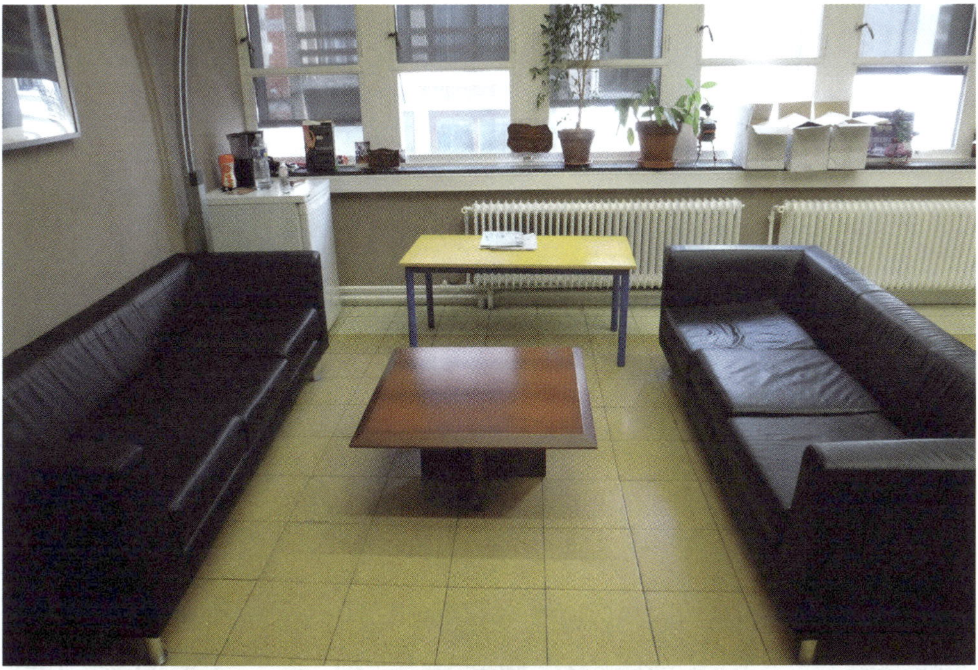

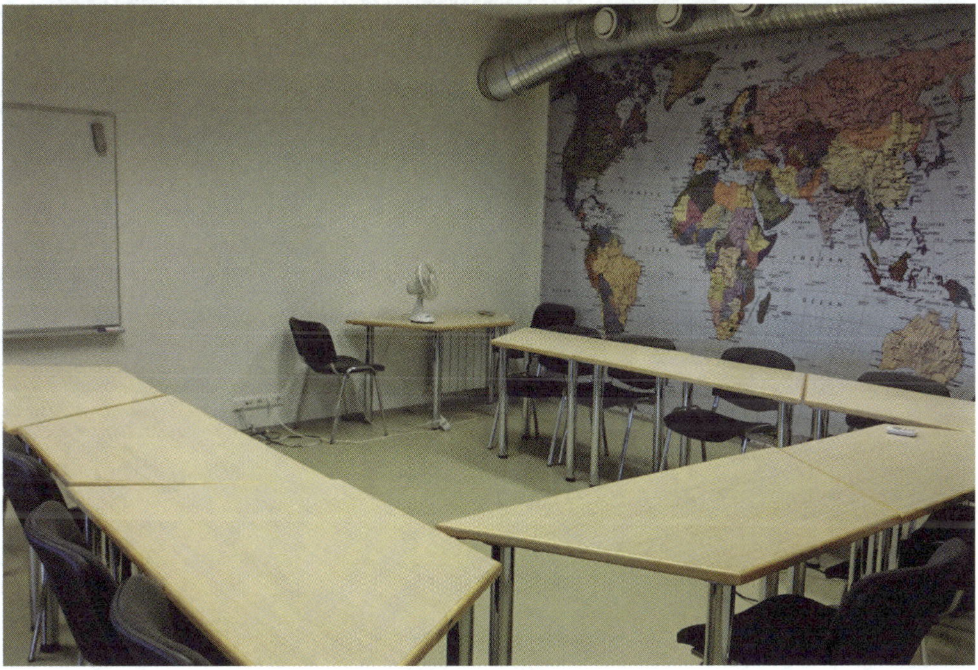

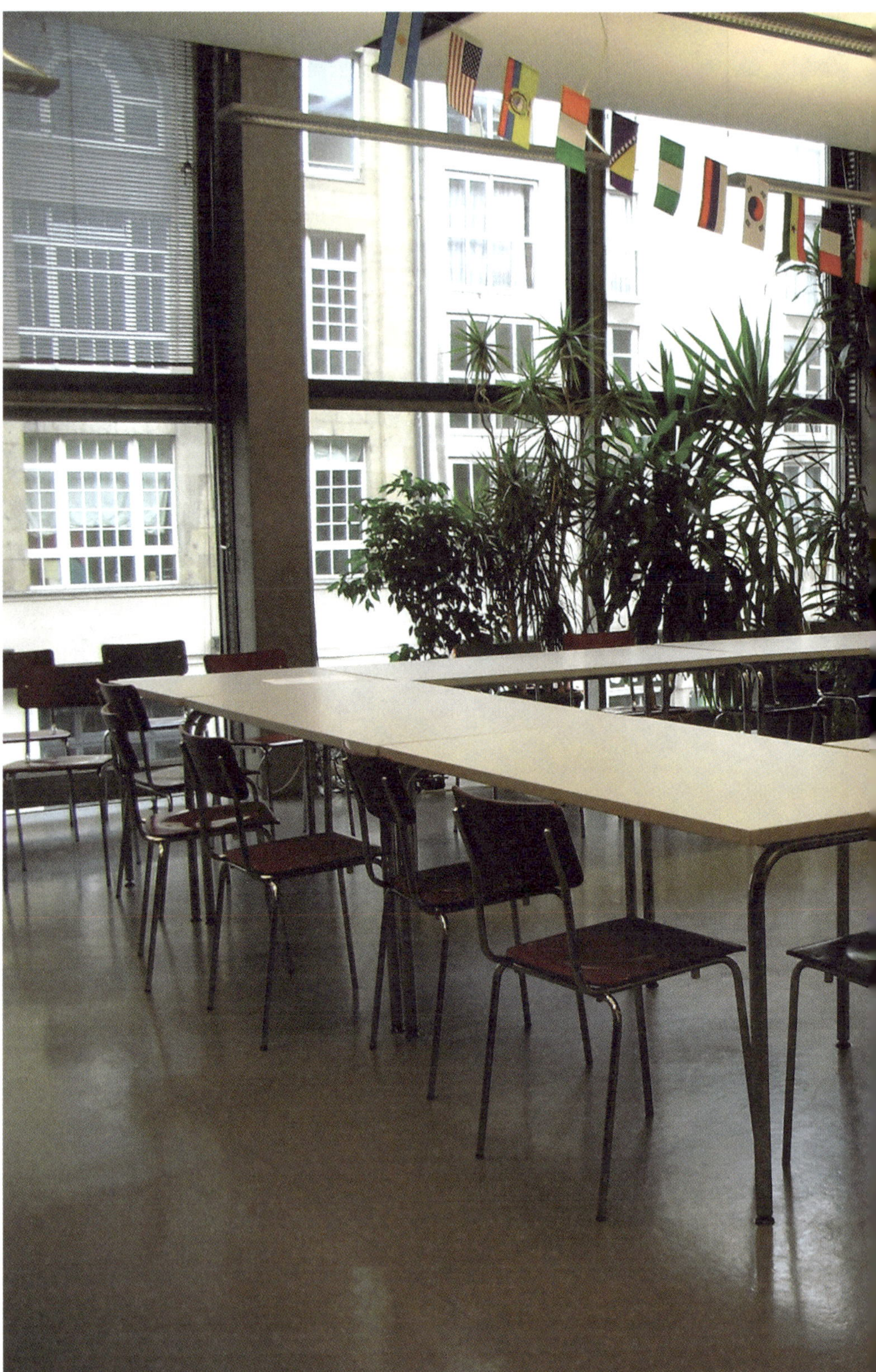

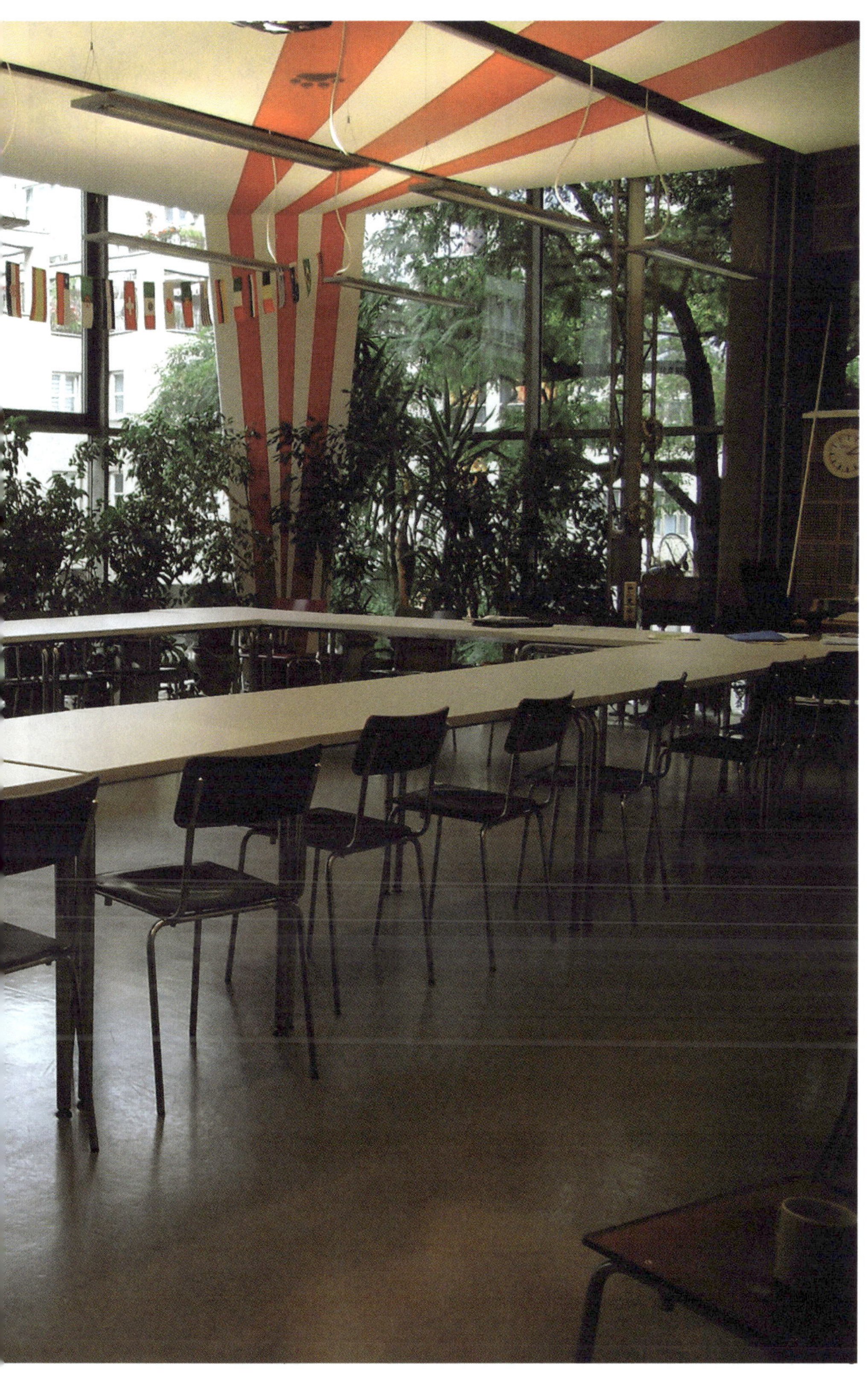

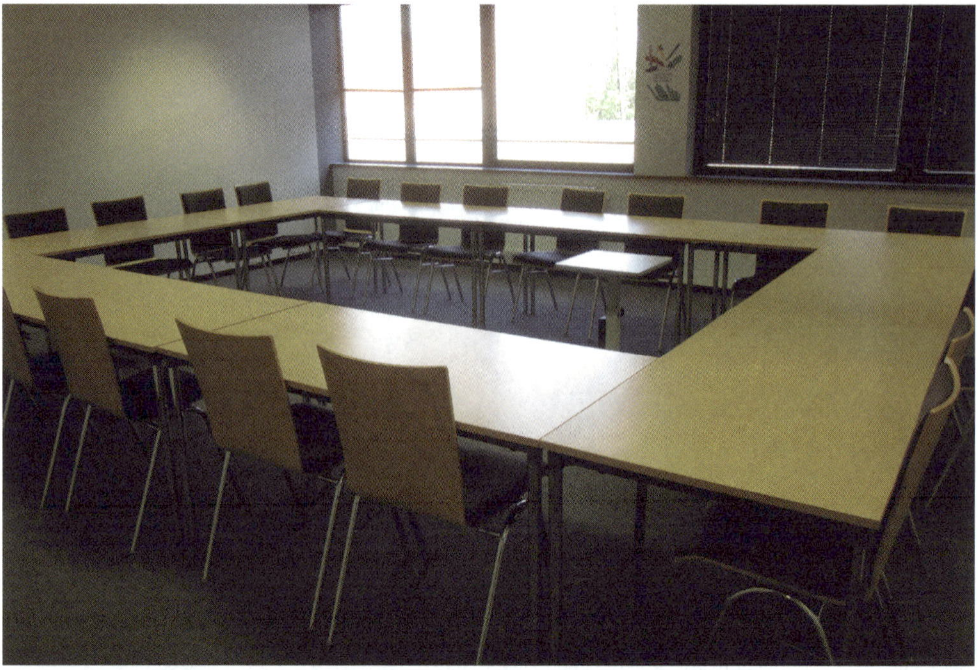

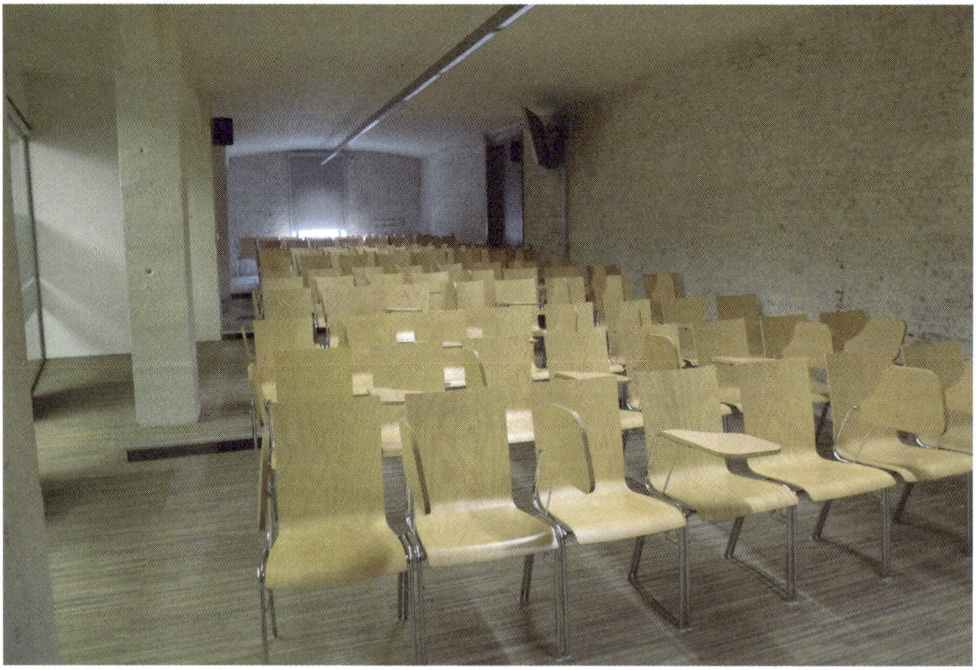

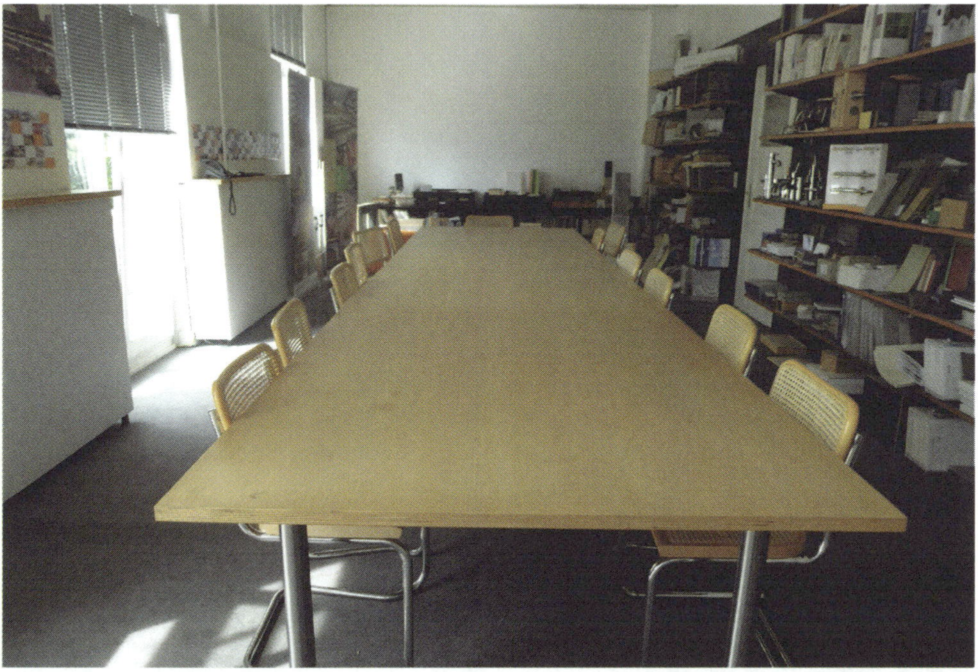

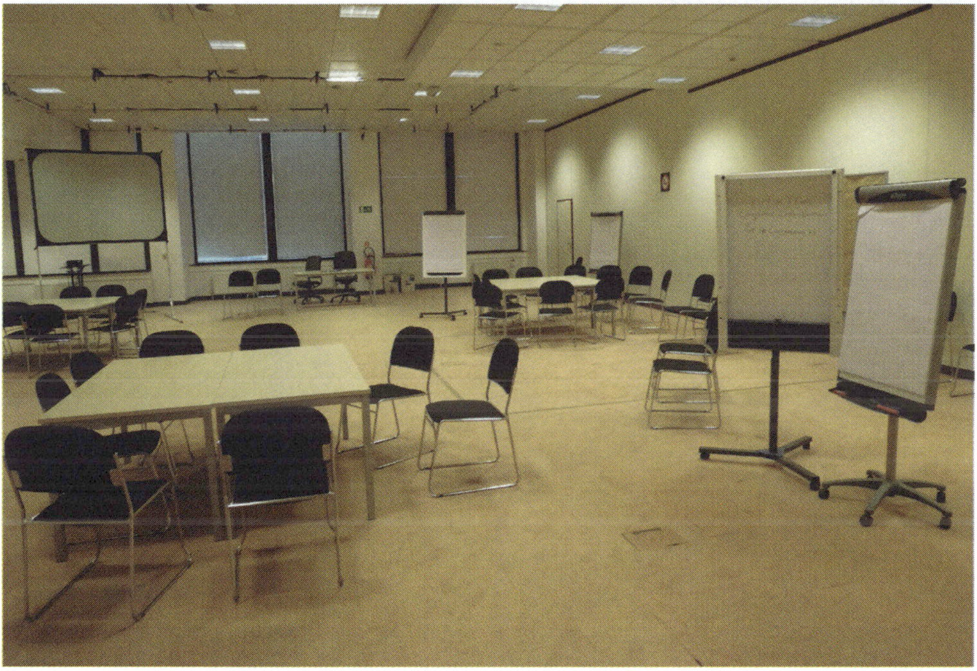

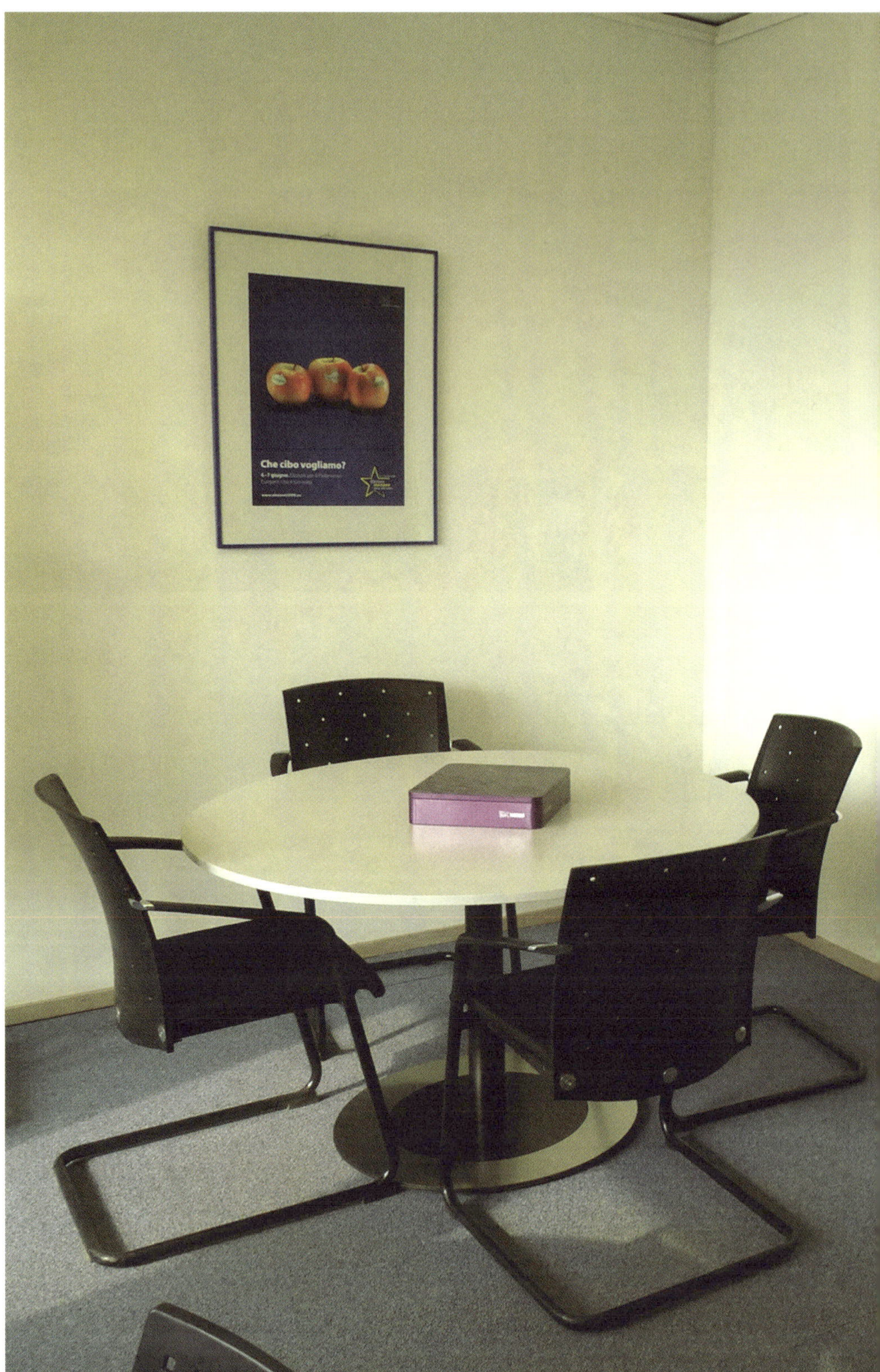
Che cibo vogliamo?

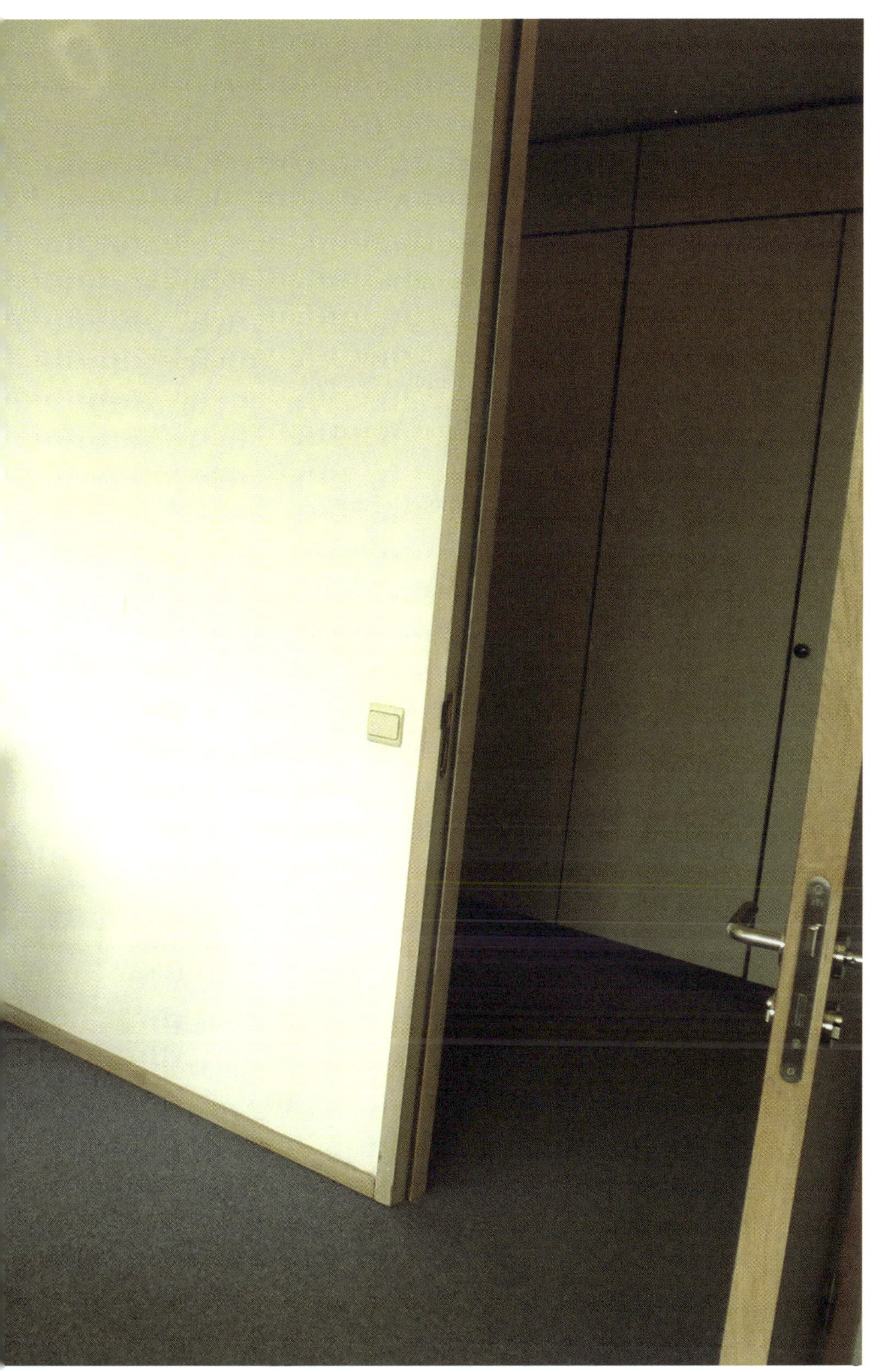

Table of contents

'Living
alone.
Living with others.
Here we are.'

Is it possible, in an increasingly atomized society undergoing constant and transformative 'crises', to address people collectively in ways other than through laws and regulations, simplistic political messages, mainstream media and advertisements?

Lecture For Every One is a text of about 15 minutes that I, or another performer, say on many different occasions where people are gathered together for a specific purpose. It could be a private or professional situation, or something in-between. One very important aspect of the project is that I invite myself to these places. Most of the time only one person in the group knows that I'm coming. For the others, my appearance at their meeting is totally unexpected. So with this lecture I'm kind of an intruder: I enter, I give the lecture, and I leave right away. I personally perform LFEO in English and Flemish, but the text exists in several languages by now. Altogether we did the lecture in about 300 different places.

LFEO is in an attempt to speak 'freely', with a gesture that addresses both the individual and the collective. It considers our contemporary (Western) society as a co-creation of 'every-one'. LFEO is a personal and an artistic gesture, a simple but strange object that enters a certain homogenous environment consisting nevertheless of individuals. In each of these situations, Lecture For Every One uses exactly the same words. [1]

Between 2013 and 2020, LFEO spread throughout Europe—for the most part, invisibly. This invisibility was one of the conditions of its existence. The only visible element of our passages were the photographs taken by the assistant who accompanied the performer in all the meeting rooms and spaces. Now and then an eyewitness also went along and wrote an account of her or his experience. The photos and the eyewitness reports were posted on an LFEO website, which still functions as a memory for the project today. For a very long time these were the only public traces of the project. Ninety percent of the work remained invisible: the strategies we had developed to get into all these places; the feedback we received after we had carried out our surprise attack; the project's artistic and political implications; the emotional and visceral memories of those who experienced it live; and so on.

This book is an attempt to unlock this specific expertise, to answer unanswered questions; a moment to step back into a multilayered, lively and polyphonic memory; an opportunity to collect the unspoken experiences, reflections and associations surrounding LFEO—in artistic but also in political, philosophical, aesthetic and logistical terms. Like the lecture itself,

[1] Texts taken from public presentations of the project and the LFEO website: www.lectureforeveryone.be

which is an amalgam of different kinds of text, this book is a hybrid of textures, voices and perspectives.

More than documentation, I hope this book can be a catalyst, a beginning rather than an end.

As I write this, LFEO is getting a second new beginning: together with a group of Brussels teenagers, we're writing a new lecture for every one, in the year 2020, which the teenagers themselves will deliver as a surprise at different closed meetings. In this way, the project will be passed on to a young generation: what do they want to say in a text addressed to every-one, and at what places do they want to do it?

My deepest thanks to the many people, to every-one, who in one way or another contributed to LFEO over the years, and to all those who contributed to this publication.

'We are before.'

Brussels, 21 January, 2020

Where does an artwork begin and where does it end?

I didn't fully understand what I had signed up for when Sarah invited me to help with this book. First, I received more than 200 pages of writing. Later that week, more followed. The various forms of documentation surrounding Lecture For Every One seemed overwhelming and at times even obsessive. Sarah had said, 'If it's OK with you, I'll just send you everything. Let me know how it reads'.

To this day, I have never witnessed LFEO, which I assume made me enough of an outsider to read these texts with fresh eyes. Somewhat strangely, I did know about the project long before I got to know Sarah and before she invited me to be a reader of the collected material. I knew about the lecture because other people would mention it—people who had heard the lecture or, like me, had heard *about* the lecture. Hearsay is sometimes enough to create one's own idea of what an artwork is like. The reading of the written documents added to these projections or, as some collaborators of LFEO describe it in this book, to my own fictions of what this lecture is and what it could be.

When experiencing a work of art, we often only see a glimpse, just that which is presented to us. The work behind and around it is mostly invisible. Of course, there are the *making-ofs* and the *behind the scenes* to satisfy our curiosity about how things are made. But in the case of LFEO, I am unsure if this book can be described in such a way. It is hard to know how the book will function, how it will be read and what it will do to other readers. And surely, there is excitement in not knowing.

As this book doesn't signify the end of LFEO, but rather a marking of a certain period in time, the text is ordered according to a cyclical logic: at the core of the book you will find the lecture itself as a written text, and around it you will discover pictures, memories, reflections, and information on the logistics; even a DIY guide on how to make your own LFEO. Maybe the logic of this book is an attempt to illustrate how seven years of stories and conversations trace back to one simple text—words once performed for and shared with thousands of listeners. And now shared with you, the reader.

This is the first time that Sarah's LFEO is published as a text available to anyone, not only to a performer reading it out loud, or an audience taken by surprise. What happens to language when it is transmitted from spoken word (as performance) to written page (as book)?

As I dug my way through all the texts Sarah had sent, I somewhat reluctantly avoided reading the actual lecture, holding off until I had read everything else. I found pleasure in imagining all these people in meeting rooms and all the different ways people had been involved in LFEO—the producer always wearing the same dress when trying to convince someone to host the project, the director of a vehicle company crying in the background, the programmer discovering (in a city he knows so well) a fencing club behind a little door. The more I read, the more it felt like circling the source while discovering the surrounding landscape, and finding lots of different paths to the centre—or as Sarah describes it in her correspondence with Sarah Vanagt, to an 'empty centre where reality is, and life'.

As long as I had never experienced LFEO, it held a kind of aura for me. Working on this book, I started to wonder if that aura would disappear. But so far, it hasn't. Maybe the aura of LFEO doesn't come from the text itself, or from the performance of it. Rather it comes from the people and places and situations and thoughts and conversations LFEO has set in motion so far. Or as Daniel Blanga Gubbay puts it, 'It's not the sound itself but what it generates in the echoes'. In those echoes, seven years of people trying to meet.

Brussels, 28 January, 2020

The fictions we carry around with us

Joe Kelleher

-7

Joe Kelleher is a Professor and the Head of Department of Drama, Theatre and Performance at the University of Roehampton. He wrote this text for the evening programme of Kunstenfestivaldesarts 2013, after a long conversation he had with Sarah Vanhee. March 2013, London.

At the time of writing I have not experienced—neither seen nor heard—Sarah Vanhee's Lecture For Every One. I haven't even read the text of the lecture. To this extent I am in the same situation as those who might invite Vanhee—or accede to her offer to invite herself—to their annual general meeting, their monthly sales conference, their weekly support group, or their once-in-a-lifetime investiture or wedding party or leaving do. As such, her performance comes onto the horizon as a sort of promise: but a promise of what? I imagine how it might be if Vanhee were to bring the lecture into the kind of environment I am familiar with, a university committee meeting, say, where—whatever else we might be to ourselves and to each other during the rest of our lives: thinkers, teachers, writers, activists, friends, or opponents—on these occasions we focus our otherwise chaotic and multiform selves into forms of distributed and coded rationality, with more-or-less identifiable interests and modes of bureaucratic capability. Who, or what, would Vanhee be in those circumstances? A stranger in the room? A representative of some other part of the institutional apparatus, proposing *her* strangeness as an item on *our* agenda? What would she say? How might she act? And how should we respond? Would we do what such gatherings are supposed to do: debate the issue—whatever the issue turns out to be—then make a note in the minutes and commit ourselves to a point of action? What sort of action—what sort of decision—might Vanhee's intervention call-on us to take, if any?

What I do know is that Vanhee has already been working in this territory of the carefully measured—but at the same time radically uncertain—promise of the human encounter. Her 2010 book *The Miraculous Life of Claire C* recounts a series of meetings with strangers, conducted through emails and on park benches in Amsterdam, with the intention of re-populating an unfinished novel with the 'real life' that the novel evokes. The book is self-consciously clever. It is also touching in what it says about the quality of accidental intimacy being part of the texture of life in all of our cities. Like much of Vanhee's work—for example, the ongoing project *Untitled,* which involves individual members of the public visiting another individual's home for a personal tour of the self-accumulated art that is kept there—the book speaks of the hopeful, but also uncertain ways that the fictions we carry around with us, and carry ourselves around in, are able to slip in and out of reality at any moment. As if, indeed, the promises we make to our imaginations might at any moment be called to account by the world those very promises are drawn from, with who-knows-what consequences.

My own first encounter with Vanhee's work was in the theatre, at a performance of *Turning Turning (a choreography of thoughts)* in 2011, where Vanhee and two fellow-performers presented a particular, virtuosic practice; a way of speech, to put it simply, which involved the performers speaking whatever came into their mind as quickly as they could, in turn, for a fixed period of time. It is a performance in which words and images—a countless number of both—swirl and refract randomly like oil splashed onto the pool of thought. It is a work that has the strange effect of seeming to promise us everything and anything, while leaving us with something else that is also more than that 'everything': the singularity, the fragility of the individual person, the bare actor, as it were, attempting to think, attempting to speak. If, however, *Turning Turning* was about a very particular provocation of attention, putting the activity of thinking itself into play and having it acted-out in public for spectatorial consumption, Lecture for Every One promises a different sort of relationship to thinking. Indeed, I imagine the Lecture more as a coaxing to action—or at least a call to activity—which it does by functioning as a sort of placeholder: for other people's thoughts, for other people's considerations, or just for other people's fifteen or twenty minutes of stopping-time, of rest from the machine, and of ethical recuperation. Something 'for' everyone, however we might take it. But then, what is at stake in that 'for'?

When discussing some of the ideas behind Lecture for Every One, Vanhee talks about the ancient Greek concept of *parrhesia,* or 'free speech', in the sense of words spoken in public in a way that puts the speaker at risk, speech that takes on the fear of truth-telling—in relation to power, in relation to strangers—speech, we might say, that puts the truth itself at risk. It goes without saying, there is nothing simple—and nothing too direct either—about free speech conceived in this way. As Foucault remarked in his late lectures on *parrhesia,* what is at stake is not 'the disclosure of a secret that has to be excavated from the depths of the soul', but rather 'the *relation* of the self to the truth or to some rational principle'. That indirection is only likely to be exacerbated when Vanhee translates her lecture, conceived largely for non-arts spaces, to the rather specific public space of the theatre, as she will be doing at the Kunstenfestivaldesarts this spring. Perhaps, though, the peculiar promise of Lecture for Every One has also to do with driving a line between a gesture conceived, on the one hand, very simply and directly indeed—'it should be possible', she tells me, 'it's basically just a person who says some things, a person who speaks to other persons'—and, on the other hand, as something altogether *difficult.* As Vanhee herself points out, the very title of her lecture —leaving aside the self-evident element of hubristic ambition—is an equivocation: can a lecture for 'everyone' be at the same time a lecture for every 'one'? What kind of relationships, between individuals and the collective, between citizens and strangers, between natives and foreigners, between oneself and one's several other selves and all one's significant and insignificant others, would be at stake in that distinction?

Another writer who addressed, as she put it, 'the difficulty of the difficulty' around the question of 'how to represent the aporia between everyone and every "one"', was the philosopher Gillian Rose. Rose's concerns—not unlike those of Vanhee, who spoke to me about Rousseau's social contract, or the challenge of engaging the 'rational egoist' identified by Hobbes, in the interests of the common good—are with the politics of citizenship, or as Rose refers to it, the questions of love and the state. What distinguishes Rose's thoughts is the way her critique of what she calls spurious universals—ethical, religious, and legal values that tend to be imposed and maintained through violence and exclusion—leads not to an outright rejection of such values, but rather to the ever-to-be-repeated, ever-to-be-renewed performance of an 'aporetic universalism', an indefatigable trying again—at love, at justice, at truth, at care—that takes place in the 'broken middle' of all of our equivocations. Rose's own examples refer to the likes of Rosa Luxemburg and Hannah Arendt; for Vanhee, too, Arendt's thoughts on the potentiality but also the fragility of the 'space of appearance' that comes into being wherever people 'are together in the manner of speech and action', has been crucial to her work on the Lecture. It is the sort of thinking that seems to borrow something from a theatrical way of understanding the world. And the sort of considerations—practical considerations, we might say—that Rose discusses in relation to the performances that take place in the broken middle—philosophical, artistic, and political performances—have to do with dilemmas such as those of authors and actors: what it means, for instance, to speak with one's own voice, or to act or perform in one's own name, when one is heard by others as a stranger, or when one's own name is at the same time a sort of pseudonym. The work of love and the violence of the situation tend to go hand in hand.

Vanhee takes up the thread of love and violence when we meet to talk. 'For me', she says, 'this problem of the stranger is very important; the stranger, not as something that should be repelled or embraced, but as something that fundamentally changes us, something viral that cannot but transform you. It has something almost brutal, and I like this brutality.' When discussing her own role in the Lecture, as an actor, a persona; as another sort of aporetic performance, a way of registering—alongside the simple 'possibility' referred to earlier of a person speaking to other people—she also speaks about the accompanying degrees of 'impossibility' inherent in the project. She is there, she suggests, in the places she is invited into, as 'the clown, the stupid one, maybe a "nobody" or an "everybody", as one element of this "being amongst". It's a tricky role, because I cannot speak about "we" at that moment; there is no "we" I can speak of. And at the same time I cannot speak about "you" either, because there is no "you" that I know. Consequently, I can only speak of myself. But I cannot speak of myself as an example.' If not an example, I suggest to her, then perhaps in her role—as an intruder, a guest, a messenger, a parasite, an analyst, or a visiting functionary from some other worldly reality that by its very existence draws attention to the contingent structures and boundaries of the situation into which she arrives—she also brings a potentiality to the situation that was always already there. A sort of elasticity: not quite in the sense of a situation expanding of its own accord, priding itself on its capacity to accommodate—and it may be tame and incorporate—the foreign element, the stranger, but rather the lecturer herself, as *part* of the situation, for as long as she is there, bringing that elasticity herself, and then... taking it away. An elasticity of the imagination, let's call it, which takes perhaps its most telling risk—to recall the earlier topic of *parrhesia*—when it takes on the banality, the everydayness, the ubiquity of fear. 'A great deal of our imagination', Vanhee says to me, 'is being filled with fear. Fear asks so much of the imagination. How, then, to address the imagination in another way than by filling it with fear? I think about the society we live in as a fiction we decide to believe in. One of the questions I put to myself in this project is what kind of other fiction would I find interesting to believe in? What *other* images come with that? What other languages come with that?'

So much promise, so much that *could* be promised, and imagined. But promising can also be a sort of trap. As Vanhee herself allows: 'It is not *the* lecture for everyone; it is just a lecture, for every one.' It makes a difference. 'I think, anyway, that it will not be enough', she says, 'because when I say "lecture for every one" to you, you have a dream about it. I do too. But this can never be that. It's not a dream speech, it's actually quite unspectacular.' I say to her that I was imagining it might be unspectacular. Something, in the absence of the event, is taking shape. We return to the question of the performance as a placeholder: for the imagination of the stranger element, for something yet unspoken, unthought-of, undone; for something yet to come into appearance, if only some fleeting contribution to the struggles of the broken middle and the work of love. 'It probably has a lot to do with love', Vanhee says, 'where love is keeping that space open for whatever comes in, even if you never know what it will be. The perverse thing is, of course, that people don't "give" me that space; basically, I take it. I put them in the situation of having given me that space, so there is something very forceful about it. I don't know if it will stay this way but in the text, as it is now, I also say "thank you for giving me the time to speak in the coming fifteen minutes". But they didn't decide to give me that. There's something violent in it.'

A meeting table, a woman reading out 'something' from a sheet, a handful of adult men and women listening

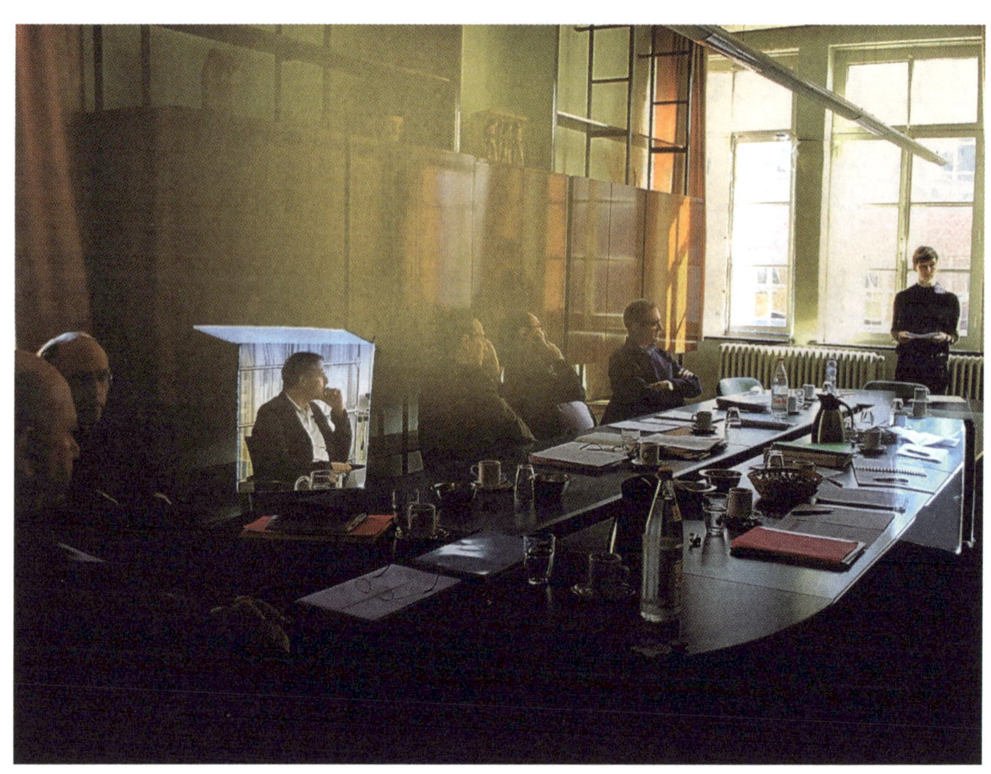

Sarah Vanagt is a Belgian film-maker. On the basis of a long-term exchange about their work, Sarah Vanhee invited Vanagt to have an email exchange about Lecture For Every One.

Hi Sarah, 07.10.2019

When you invited me to react to your LFE and in doing so to engage in a dialogue with you or with the text, I first set to work on the pictures. I looked for a long time at the photos that document all the past lectures in countless European cities. Then I began cutting into them. I simply made viewing holes in order to be able to look from one head to another, perhaps because I know you're so attached to the word or the concept EVERYONE and perhaps even more to the word pair MANY ONE. I seemed to have made a common head.

There's something strange about these photos. There is clearly a recurrent pattern: we see a (generally oval) meeting table, a (changing) woman who is reading out 'something' from a sheet that she holds in her hands, and a handful of adult men and women who are listening. I can't detect a single emotion on the faces of the listeners, which doesn't necessarily mean that nothing is moving them within. In fact I think that a lot is happening simultaneously in those collected heads. I think that for them it must have been a very confusing experience: something that must have conjured up both admiration and inner resistance.

I want to start this email discussion with a question that I've also often been asked during Q&As after a film screening: 'How did you get the idea?'

It's a question I often have to answer hesitantly. I say that it's a combination of a meeting, a memory, a painting, an article in a newspaper, something like that. There's rarely *one* specific source, or *one* clear starting point. And now I find myself asking you the same question, 'How in God's name did you get the idea of intruding in meeting rooms to "deliver" that text—which is so vulnerable—unexpected and uninvited?'

I look forward to your answer and attach some see-through heads.

Sarah Vanagt

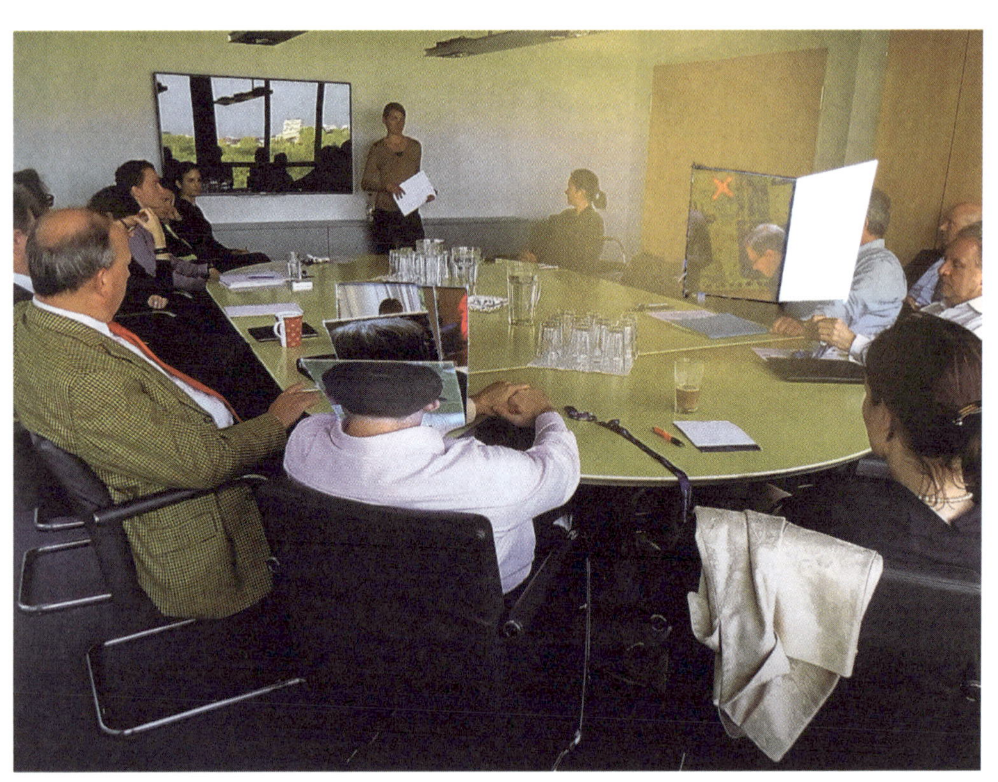

Hi Sarah, 08.10.2019

Thanks for your email and the pictures.

So much to think about all at once—my head's now like one of those little flaps under which there are several little windows.

Viewed this way, the heads are exchangeable. So many heads and bodies in so many meeting rooms. Are they the same table, the same cups, the same coffee everywhere?

When I talk about EVERYONE, I spell it EVERY ONE. Hence: LFEO. With LFEO I wanted to address both everyone and every one.

And in all those similar-looking meeting rooms I met EVERY ONE. In the beginning I literally address the people's faces and bodies. And I talk about 'faces that do not give themselves away'. But they generally did, gradually, during the lecture, as if slowly that standardized meeting mask was peeled off and another face appeared in its place. That wasn't something that I experienced as an image really, but rather as an emotion, an affect. As if I myself —also exchangeable for another woman—were dissolving slightly in order to come into contact with what lurked under those faces. One time a woman came up to me after a lecture and told me something very personal, and then she looked up at me and said: 'But you see all that, no? You know all that?'

As if I could see through them.

But no, I can't. I've often had to conclude that we can't read faces. Not in that way.

But that experience, the experience of connecting what is beneath the skin, I think that that was one of the initial principles. In fact I prefer to use the word 'belief'.

In 2012 when I started the project, I wanted to choose to believe that connection is possible. Connection on the basis of our humanity. I wanted to choose to believe that we are all part of the system, but that we also co-create that system.

I'd had rather enough of the intellectual debates in the so-called progressive art world about neoliberalism fragmenting society and driving communities apart. It sometimes seemed as if the only thing we agreed on was that magic capitalism was the enemy and that it paralyses us all. In other words: an excuse never to do anything. We could never agree on how we should come together because we were in fact inherently cynical. The cynicism was couched in elegant words that are difficult to understand, for sure. What we opposed was clear, but never quite what we were for. The instance where collectivity may perhaps be possible, 'the public' that came to performances or exhibitions, for instance, was also won over to what would be said. To me, this de-politicized the space of art completely. Preaching to the converted.

I thought at the time that it would be a lot more interesting to confront those so-called political works with a public that wasn't convinced in advance. And also, that there are already so many places where people come together one way or another. That only a single gesture is necessary to turn them into a 'public'. A 'public' not as a herd of culture consumers but as a group of people who come together for a moment, a moment that can potentially be a political moment, by addressing them in a way that is different to the way they are used to being addressed within that meeting.

I also wanted to do that on the basis of my own experience that I can talk to every one. I'm not an artist who is interested in other artists. I'm interested in people. If, for instance, I had a certain idea or judgement about people working in advertising, I always found it a relief to speak to someone like that, to understand who that person, is, why they do what they do. At the time I often found the art world to be arrogant, so I would be even more arrogant in an attempt to address 'every one'.

Describing all this now again, it strikes me that I was really young and naive at the time. But it also strikes me that the art world has changed, or else I got to know a different art world.

Most projects take shape slowly, the way you describe it, you actually don't know when and where a work really emerges. I think it was only after the premiere that I understood what my performance *Oblivion* (2015), for instance, was about.

The situation was very different with LFEO: I simply *got* the idea for LFEO, in this precise form. It literally came over me. I woke up too early one morning, worrying about everything I believed was wrong in society and thinking that I wanted to do something that would potentially have an impact. I imagined that I believed that we were all human beings—that I was tired of cynicism—that I was tired of art that preaches to the converted, of the idea that there is no more being-together, that there are so many people who come together on a daily basis but are not necessarily together for that matter—that I would like to go to these meetings to talk about being-together, without for that matter having to agree. And that I would call it 'lecture for every one'. And that that was a very arrogant thought, but at the same time naive: that it would just be someone coming to talk to them. And what hubris to think that I could ever write such a text. But that I wanted to try anyway, to find a language that every-one understands. And so there I lay in my bed, having given birth to the idea of the lecture for every one and I was afraid of it but at that time already I couldn't go back. And yes, it was such a big, such a violent idea almost that it made me feel quite vulnerable too.

I can really feel a certain emotion when I look at those pictures of those meeting rooms.

Warm wishes,
Sarah Vanhee

Hi Sarah, 08.10.2019

Reading your email just now, I really saw you lying in your bed that morning, with an angry gaze. It was as if the inspiration for the LFEO was reborn at that moment, *while* I was reading your email. You write that you can't read thoughts *(gedachten)*—you actually wrote faces *(gezichten)*—neither can I. But reading your email, I suddenly had the feeling that I could linger in your head for a moment, so that I suddenly also found that the LFEO was at once vital and frightening. The wonder of language…

Funny (or typical?) that I had simply omitted the most important letter in the abbreviation of LFEO. The O of everyONE. The O of the oval table.

I also wrote that you or the other performer read out the text from a sheet of paper. I realize now that I actually barely looked at *you* on those photos. My gaze always went to the listeners. Only now do I see that you (mostly) do hold a piece of paper, but that you never look at it.

I myself was never there, in those meeting rooms, but I can well imagine that you looked at the listeners one by one during your speech, no longer angry, but fragile.

I did experience your LFEO at the time in the Beursschouwburg, in the middle of an already 'converted public' (your terms).

It's interesting that you should use such a religious term. I remember that I was impressed by your presence, your courage. I found it a pity, in a sense, that you were performing this text also as a performance in an arts venue, because its power and originality, in my view, lay precisely in the fact that you yourself went with that text into meeting rooms outside the art world. So I kind of felt that you yourself had destroyed it by presenting it to us like that. At the same time I was moved by your text, and also irritated. I remember that I was overwhelmed by an old sort of resentment or discomfort, something that catapulted me against my will into the catechism classes of yesterday. At the time we all needed—a handful of 12-year-olds around a large table—to bring in an object which we were attached to and then tell each other why it was so important to us. I remember well how I was overcome at the time by disgust, and I still don't know precisely why. The strange thing is that I can still sharply recall all those objects in my mind's eye, and the stories that went with them. I think I was bothered by the forced nature of the whole enterprise. I didn't know those other children, I felt that the woman at the top of the table had adopted a morally superior attitude (I didn't know those words then, naturally, but I felt that I was irritated by it and that feeling never actually left me). And at the same time I was absorbed by the stories, perhaps a single communal head really did emerge at the time for a moment, I don't know.

To conclude with something religious myself. I once came across the saying below on a church in Friesland, a famous Remonstrant saying, I later learned. These words came to me spontaneously when I first read your LFEO a few days ago for the first time—six (?) years after having heard it in the Beursschouwburg. The resistance I felt at the time in the Beursschouwburg had in the meantime vanished. I saw that little woman before me while she enumerated the human rights in the train as if they made up a rosary and I wondered whether *I* had changed so much in those few years—or whether it was the world. That brings me to your remark about the art world, that you were naive at the time and that you now have a very different view of the art world. What exactly do you mean by that?

I hope that when I'm a little old woman I'll murmur the following on the train, when a young woman sits down opposite me:

Eenheid in 't nodige
Vrijheid in 't mogelijke
In alles de liefde
(Unity in what is necessary
Freedom in what is possible
In everything, love)

Sarah Vanagt

Hi Sarah, 11.10.2019

Yes, the O is important to me. The O of the oval table but also the O of the empty centre. When ten years ago or so I made *The Miraculous Life of Claire C*—and for that reason myself became in part Claire C—a journalist described Claire as a doughnut, an O, an empty centre. It's no coincidence that you didn't look at me in the photo. I try to disappear, to make myself not so important. It's about the words I say and how they resonate in the space. When I perform, I often feel as though I am made of glass, or a mirror. I adapt myself to the people in the space, perhaps in part intuitively, in part empathically, in part performatively. Like clowns do too. So yes, I am rather fragile. Sometimes I feel that my presence there is almost too much, then I'm very careful with my gaze, careful not to stare at any one person. But sometimes I have to so as to let no one escape. But also: to be taken seriously. That's not always simple.

No, I didn't at all feel like a missionary in my outfit that tried to appear as ordinary as possible. On some days I also found it difficult to get into it, to once more enter somewhere uninvited. No one likes being forced to listen to something, me neither, I was aware of that. And also of the fact that I could always be thrown out—or interrupted at any moment, which happened often.

I often told myself the story of that woman who did that: who went to all those meetings and interrupted them with a lecture for every one. That there was nothing grandiose about that, it was simply what she did, voicing uncomfortable truths. I found that a nice story. And that way I could again become that woman in that story.

I often feel—on other occasions too—that I'm speaking almost in spite of myself. I can't help myself.

It's not so much the missionary or the priest that I feel close to, but to the *parrhesiastes*. The *parrhesiastes* is the one who 'speaks freely' and *parrhesia* was central to the practice of the cynics. Foucault had this to say about them in 'Fearless Speech':

'The *parrhesiastes* is someone who says everything he has in mind: he does not hide anything, but opens his head and mind completely to other people through his discourse. In *parrhesia,* the speaker is supposed to give a complete and exact account of what he has in mind so that the audience is able to comprehend exactly what the speaker thinks…. The speaker or confessor is in a position of inferiority with respect to the interlocutor. The *parrhesiastes* is always less powerful than the One with whom he speaks. The *parrhesia* comes from "below", as it were, and is directed towards "above."… However, the *parrhesiastes* risks his privilege to speak freely when he discloses a truth which threatens the majority… The speaker uses his freedom and chooses frankness instead of persuasion, truth instead of falsehood or silence, the risk of death instead of life and security, criticism instead of flattery, and moral duty instead of self-interest and moral apathy.'

Instead of powerful, I felt vulnerable as I stood there. You're always the potential laughing stock.

Certainly as a woman, as a young woman, it's better to be pretty and silent than loud and weird.

Fortunately things have changed in recent years. 'Your silence will not protect you' (Audre Lorde) has finally begun to resonate, and fewer and fewer women are ready to keep their mouths shut, even though this can sometimes be dangerous for them. Today's *parrhesiastes* is a woman.

It's sometimes also said that Jesus was in fact inspired by the cynics, the first *parrhesiastes.* Which brings us back to religion.

How annoying that religion is so interwoven with the institute of the Church. There is a lot to be learned from the first early-Christian communities, for instance, and the figure of Paul.

When he was in prison, Oscar Wilde wrote how he would love to be part of an order of non-believers. He says: 'whether it be faith or agnosticism, it must be nothing external to me. Its symbols must be of my own creating'. And his artistic example is Christ: 'He is just like a work of art. He does not really teach one anything, but by being brought into his presence one becomes something' (qtd in S.Critchley, *Faith of the Faithless,* p.6). Simon Critchley deduces a political question from this: 'how such a faith of the faithless might be able to bind together a confraternity, a consorority or, to use Rousseau's key term, an *association.*' So, how people who do not believe can nevertheless be connected with one another.

I think I feel an unconditional loyalty with regard to people's need to feel a real connection. Ultimately, I've never met a person who doesn't have that longing somewhere, or has had it.

I hope that this is all sufficiently far removed from the musty memory of your catechesis classes.

Regarding your question about the art world: I think that it bothers me less in fact. When I made LFEO, maybe I needed to relate more to what I did there in that art world—which I considered at the time more as one closed-off whole. Today I think there are so many different sorts of artists and practices, so many 'art worlds', which do not have to be specifically elitist or highbrow or cynical.

Have we both become more tolerant towards what in the past we would have called 'moralistic'? Perhaps today we are surrounded by so much hard language, so much hate speech and fake news, that we are more open to what may possibly connect people? And that we know we won't make it by being silent?!

Love,
Sarah Vanhee

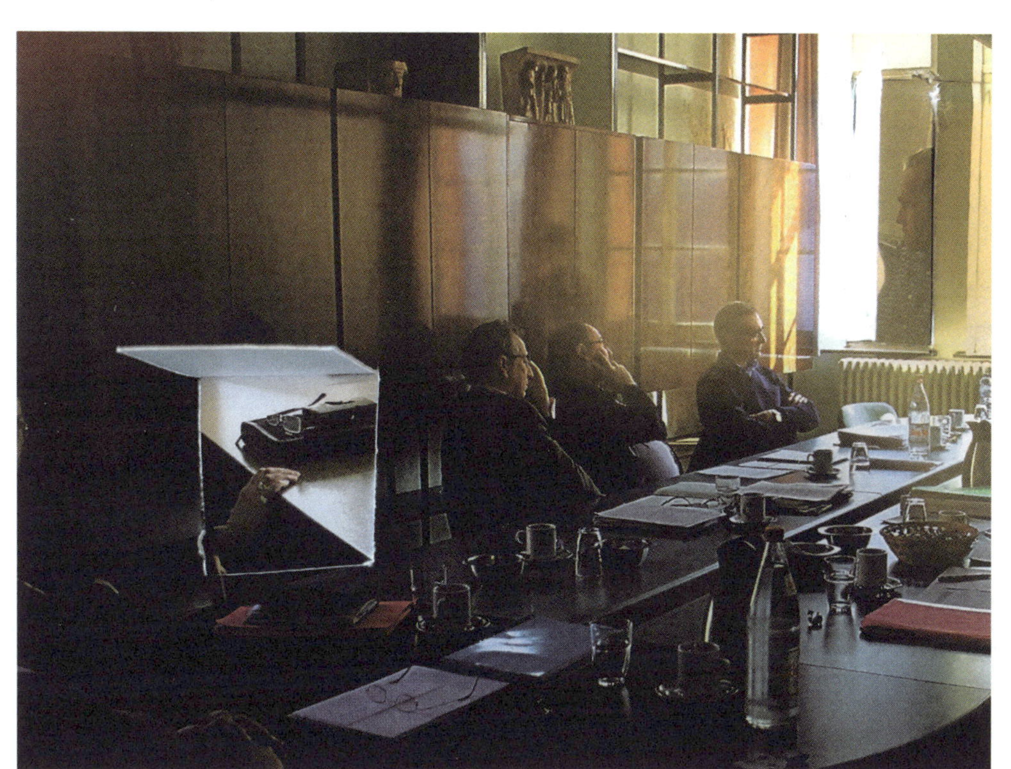

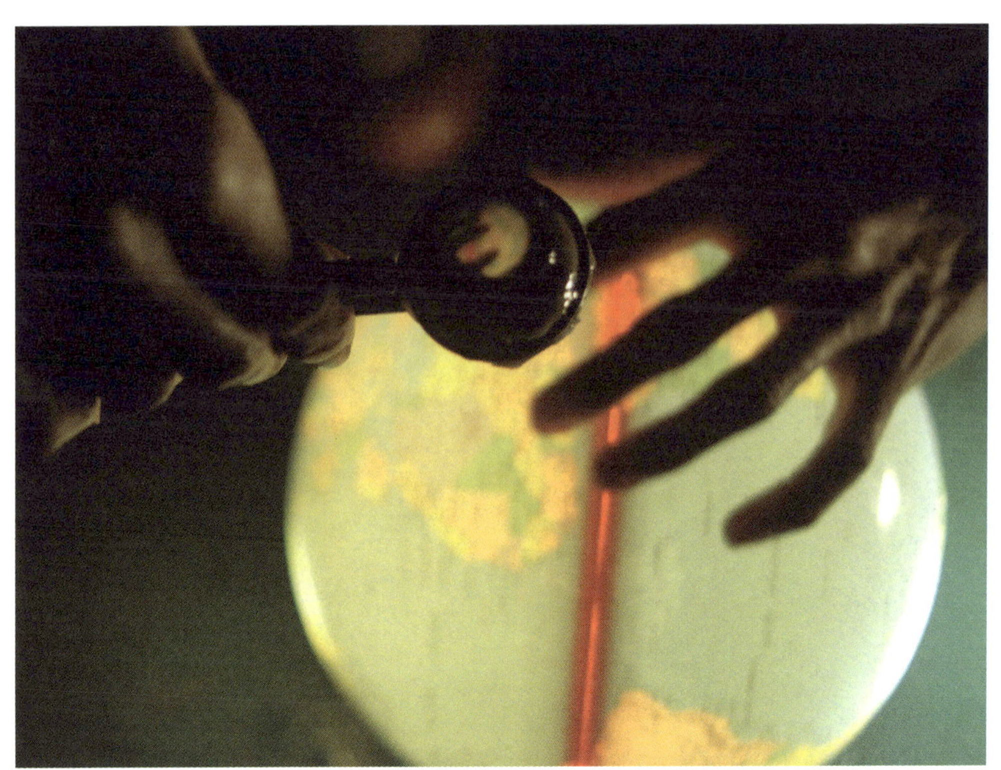

Hi Sarah, 17.10.2019

Indeed, you disappear in that unremarkable outfit without any grand gestures, or rather, you dissolve in the environment. I wonder in fact what name you gave the LFEO, how it was described in the brochures. As a performance? And were you and the other women who delivered the text then performers? 'Performance' immediately makes me think (maybe wrongly) that the physical aspect is very important, predominates even in fact. Whereas the LFEO is in fact a very different type of performance: sound waves in the air, pulses that are caused by the speaking of the text.

A few years ago, together with my cousin Katrien Vanagt, I reconstructed a seventeenth-century optical experiment for the film *In Waking Hours*. Following the Dutch physician Plempius, a friend of Descartes, we cut open the eye of a freshly slaughtered cow and tried to see in the eye how 'seeing' works precisely. After death, the eye continues to work for a few hours. Suddenly there appeared on the retina of the cow eye a miniature film, upside down, in colours reminiscent of super-8, on a natural screen that was no larger than a thumb nail. I had indeed already seen the iconic drawing of the cross section of a human eye: the eye looks at a tree and that tree is drawn in miniature and upside down on the inside of the eye, with two dotted lines intersecting at the level of the lens in the eye. Do you see that drawing in front of you? No matter how often I had already seen that schematic drawing, I only got a new insight when I saw the live images in the eye. Everything we see—the sea, a milk can, our children, a donkey—literally appears on the inside of our body as an image. I'm not talking about a mental image here, but very literally about a physical projection of light rays on a thin membrane on the inside of the eye. So it's not a construction of the brain that interprets light rays, no—there's a film playing non-stop in our body during our waking hours, or rather *two* films. That may sound obvious, but if you think about it, it's really dumbfounding, no?

That something as vast as the sea, with its waves and seagulls, appears in miniature on the inside of our eye. That we carry the sea at that moment (upside down) in our body with us?

I suddenly had to think of that when I wrote to you about the voice's sound waves. Those unseen waves float through the space and bring about physical and easily measurable vibrations in the ear of every listener, vibrations that are moreover also present in the bone (the skull) right behind the ear. So, in the heads of people around all those oval tables you visited, skulls were vibrating in a similar manner, synchronously.

You write that, in preparation of your LFEO, you thought about yourself as if it concerned another woman, as if it was about a story. I recognize that very well. When I made prints (frottages) in the Yugoslavia tribunal in The Hague, I first had to conquer my fear, or rather the tremendous doubt that comes over you when you realize that you are about to do something very 'strange'. I remember imagining that it was a scene from an (unreleased, weird!) feature film about a documentary maker who made frottages in an international criminal court. Another kind of vanishing trick, you could say…

'You must have the courage of your own convictions', an old teacher often used to call out in the classroom. He had a thunderous voice (so many vibrations in my skull!) that suited the message of his motto well. When I saw LFEO at the time, I immediately found it very courageous. That is in fact the main 'feeling' I retain from it: the courage it must have demanded from you. There's also an inherent paradox: having the courage to be fragile. ('You must have the courage of your own vulnerability'…)

You ask me whether we (you and me) have become less silent over the years, perhaps because we've gradually perceived that these are not times in which to be silent, that we're not going to make it with our silence.

I don't know. There's so much screaming and roaring going on. I don't in fact think that there is currently a lack of people 'with the courage of their convictions', but I do think that there is less time to arrive in complete silence at a decently founded conviction that is worth fighting for.

Sarah Vanagt

Hi Sarah, 23.10.2019

Today is 23 October. In the last five weeks I've talked to a lot of people—again—about LFEO. People who have experienced it, contact persons, performers, collaborators, producers... New fictions are being created, a new empty centre. I love the word *omschrijven* (circum-scribe), as if you were circling around something, around that which you can never really *be-schrijven* (de-scribe). There in that empty centre lies the reality for me, i.e. life.

As an artist I'm not at all visually disposed. Pictures actually frighten me. Because they give us the illusion that we *be-grijpen* (comprehend) the reality. Like the picture of the picture of the world you sent me. I'm frightened that it creates a false sense of power: that humanity has power over things because he or she can *be-vatten* (contain), *be-grijpen* (grasp) them in their head in a single image. As in the expression *beelden vast-leggen* (to capture pictures), it always involves *fixeren* (capture), when it comes to pictures. Perhaps that's also why in my film *The Making of 'Justice'* all the images were blurred.

But that *vast-leggen,* that *ver-harden* (to harden) is something you can also say of language, of words. What strikes me now, after all these conversations, is that people remember very little of the exact text, but they do remember the feeling, the experience. What does that say about our memory, that it is affective? Perhaps the words are only there to *om-schrijven* (circum-scribe) the unutterable, to circle around what always eludes us in any case.

I once wrote a short story that was called 'TT', it was a commission. I remember that I decided at the time to take language seriously for once, to use the words to give meaning and to confirm something, instead of only conjuring up more questions, transformation, transgression. I also wanted to do that because I myself get so much out of stories. Fiction is my secret source of life, I can't live without fiction. I'm very grateful to people who dare to choose characters, events, a course. It strikes me also that—when people do remember something from the lecture—it's often the two stories. You can easily remember them as meaning units. I love stories, to me they're absolutely vital, I just don't know whether I'm the one who should write them. That's why the text of the lecture has become such a patchwork, which you can move around in as a listener but never rest in, because you never know where it's going to lead.

When I performed the lecture, in the beginning I had the feeling that we were all stepping into a boat together and setting off on the waves, but that we really didn't know where it was leading us. The only thing we could be sure of was the boat, and each other. It's not a text that is going somewhere, more a text that drifts. Me too, I kind of drift.

Love,
Sarah Vanhee

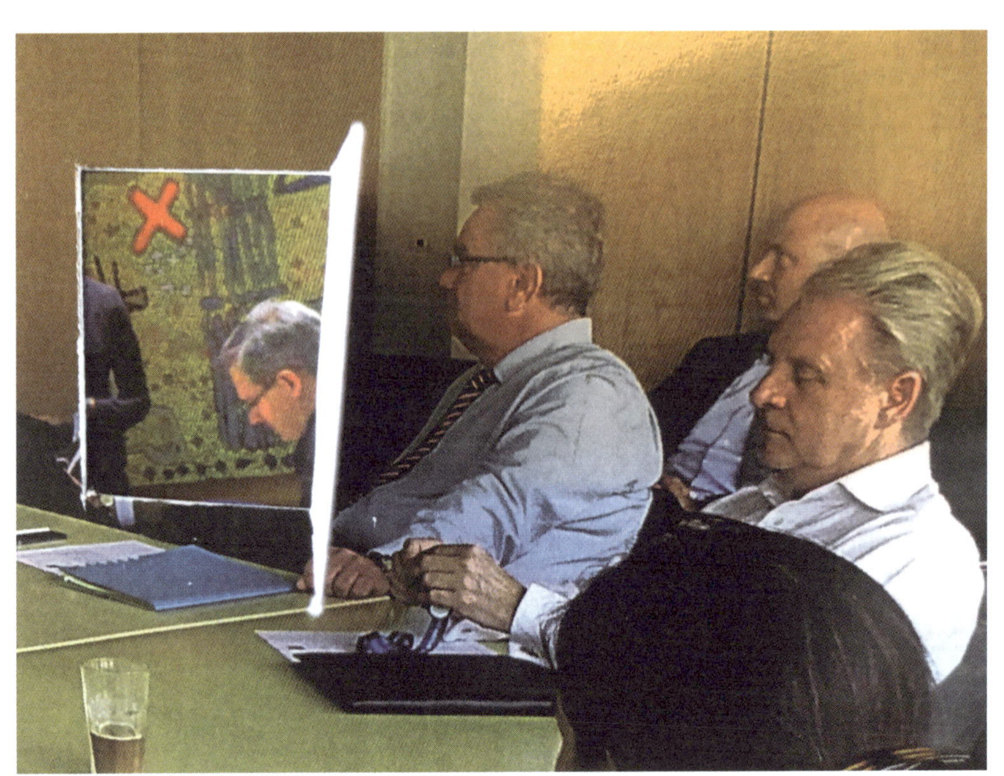

Hi Sarah, 07.11.2019

Last week for the first time in many years I saw the film-maker Laura Waddington again. She moved from Brussels to Lisbon six years ago and was working all that time on a graphic novel about the torture that an Iraqi man underwent during his imprisonment under Saddam Hussein. I read the book *Are You a River?—M's Story* in her armchair. It was still light in the room when I started it and dark when I finished. Dark in all respects. An unforgettable experience, shocking, but without being paralysing.

In the introduction to her book, Laura uses a quote from Nadezhda Mandelstam, a quote that reminded me of you, perhaps most strongly of your latest screaming project, but also of our correspondence, and more specifically of your remark that these are not times in which to be silent (even though silence-loving times never exist of course, or only for very brief periods, on a very small scale).

> 'Later I often wondered whether one should howl when one is beaten and trampled upon. Would it not be better to harden in devilish pride and answer the torturers by contemptuous silence? And I came to the conclusion that one must howl. In this pitiful howling [which one sometimes hears even in the near-soundproof cells, coming from God knows where] are condensed the last vestiges of human dignity and of faith in life. By all this a man leaves a trace on this earth and informs people how he has lived and died. By howling he defends his right to live, sends a message to the free world, demands help and resistance. If there is nothing else left, one must howl. Silence is a real crime against humanity.'
>
> — Nadejda Mandelstam, *Hope Against Hope*
> (trans. Max Hayward)

It's interesting what you write about pictures 'frightening' you. To me, a (good) picture has never been something that tried to capture things the way you feel that—on the contrary. Every picture is—to put it in childish terms—a portal into another world. One of those little windows, a little flap under which another image lies hidden. And behind that lies another vision, and behind that... The still I sent you of the projection on the retina of a cow's eye is to me precisely about the *endless* watching. And that endlessness is movable precisely. During our waking hours, constantly changing images are being projected onto our retina, and it is impossible to record this.

A picture—a photo, a painting, a scan, an MRI, even something as monumental and static as a sculpture...—is, to my eyes, never more than a snapshot. Pictures are like thoughts and dreams, fleeting. Simply rays of colour and light. So simple and so endlessly miraculous.

What you say about stories is something I recognize well. I can't get enough of stories either, and certainly not of small, isolated little stories, fragments, splinters. To me, your mini story about the old woman on the train reciting the Declaration of Human Rights as if it were a prayer is one such fragment. And at the same time it has become an *image* that I carry with me and that records absolutely nothing, perhaps because it's such a comforting image. Comforting is by nature mobile (immobile comforting seems impossible to me). And in that comforting movement lies, I think, the care you talk about in your LFEO. In Catherine de Zegher's book *Women's Work Is Never Done,* I read that the word 'prayer' has the same root as 'precarious'. I didn't know that, but since then *praying* for me has taken on a very different dimension, and I can see its value more than before.

Milica Nikolic, a critic and essayist from Belgrade, died recently. I met her a few years ago in her flat, together with some close friends. She was well into her nineties already.

She told us about a poet she had known well. He always had a pillowcase with him, which he carried over his shoulder, one corner of the pillowcase in his hand. He collected isolated sentences in this material bag, sentences from conversations he had or which he overheard in the street.

I'd like to end our correspondence with that *image:* a man in Belgrade during the inter-war period—not the world wars, but the Yugoslav Wars—a bit shabby and yet dressed very stylishly, that's how I imagine him, with a white pillowcase hanging loosely over his right shoulder.

Sarah Vanagt

Conversations with organizers

Kristof Blom & Matthieu Goeury

Silvia Bottiroli

Christophe Slagmuylder

Adinda Van Geystelen

-5

A conversation with Kristof Blom and Matthieu Goeury

Behind that little door

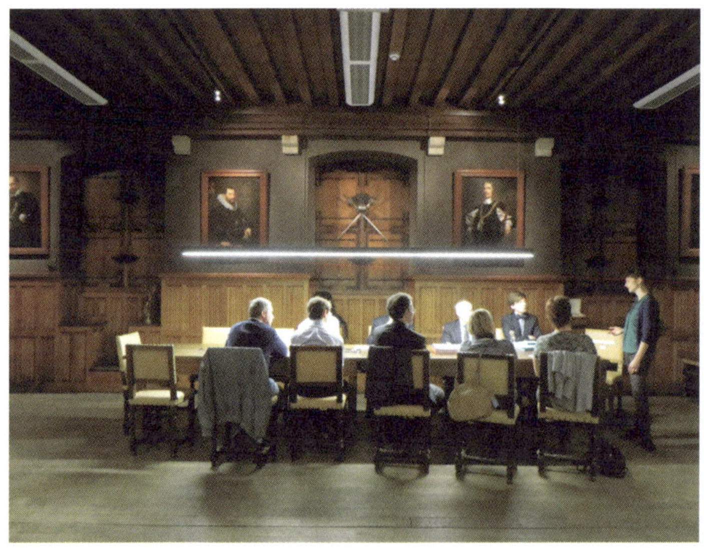

Kristof Blom is the artistic director of CAMPO. CAMPO produced LFEO in 2013 and has been distributing it since then. Matthieu Goeury is the artistic coordinator of the Vooruit. In 2013 CAMPO and the Vooruit co-organized a series of 20 interventions in Ghent.

The following text is the result of a conversation between Kristof Blom, Matthieu Goeury and Sarah Vanhee that took place in Brussels on 2 October 2019.

S

Kristof, do you remember the first time we spoke about the project, eight or nine years ago? What were your thoughts at the time?

K

I think it was mentioned for the first time in a broader discussion about a long-term future. You were one of the key artists with who we were doing research and development on the production and presentation of work. That meeting was really about what we could do together, and I remember LFEO being the first concrete proposal. It was immediately clear that this was going to be a remarkable project—a whole set of rules in the performing arts turned upside down. I found it really interesting and very different from all the social-artistic work that would later be categorized under the later-to-be-defined term 'participation'. This felt like a different proposal with regard to active involvement, an active discussion with people that you yourself decided to perform for. Of course, this came with different challenges as to how to get the work out there and perform it while being invisible to a regular audience and not being able to sell tickets. But in the end it all worked out.

M

The timing was quite unique. In the arts we had come back a lot to the theatre and the public space, but rather in order to use it as a location and not so much to engage with the audience in a disruptive way or in a way that almost approaches civil disobedience. When Kristof proposed the project for the festival, we found it really interesting. In 2013 we celebrated the centenary of the Vooruit, so it was a big year and I wanted to end the festival and the year with an opening towards the future. It was the time of the Arab Spring and of other remarkable social and political movements. The festival was quite activist and there was this romantic idea about revolutions. To me, LFEO contained this idea of bringing about change by entering different communities. I remember the project being quite key in the festival, which in the end was a good festival but which happened very much indoors. We had workshops with John Jordan, for instance, and a lot of other activist practices, but they concerned communities that were already involved in social questions. So your project was a way of reaching out to more than our usual audience.

S

Kristof, you came to one of the lectures at an annual board meeting of St Michael's Guild in Ghent?

K

I felt very alienated because of the location. I'm 100 per cent from Ghent. You think you know your city and then you end up in that very central place, in the Belfry, a little room that I've walked by thousands of times without noticing that little door. And behind that door is that small but very aristocratic club. Just going there was a very strange thing to me. And then witnessing your intervention... The people around the table were confused. I remember regretting having to leave the room with you. Because I think the end is the start of the most interesting part of the project. It's not only you saying your text, but seeing what it generates, like a catalyst. What kind of topics does it raise? You could feel a ripple of excitement going around the table. You brought topics to the table that are never discussed in there—never. And you can feel that the impact is quite big.

M

I think that's what's great about the project. Many programmers are beginning to realize that we think we know society, what's going on in the city. But in fact, as soon as you step out and enter another kind of community, you realize there's a life out there and it's very organized and as networked as the arts field. They don't think they know everything; we have this pretension in the arts to think that we know what's going on. That was one of the beautiful things about the project, and a learning process for the Vooruit. Even in our team, we actually don't know what happens in some meetings. You're not invited or you only spend a few minutes there. It has its own life, its own dynamic, but you can't access it because you're not an active participant.

S

I performed LFEO during a meeting of the Vooruit's bar team. I remember it. I felt that people were quite naked. It was very emotional. There was something tense. I felt people were tired. Do you remember any comments afterwards?

M

This happened at a time when the Vooruit was going through a full-blown crisis. We had just celebrated the centenary of the Vooruit but actually it was like a house of cards falling down. Everyone was tired and very emotional, and there was a lot of crying. I don't remember particular exchanges about it but I know it helped to open up discussions that were very important in the following years.

K

I remember the one in Ikea. I wasn't there but the contact person, Betty, is a good friend. And she often returns to the topic of the lecture in Ikea. It started a long-term discussion over there. Even in the year after the project, people were still referring to that one moment. It had a huge impact. Betty is very thankful. It helped her a lot to work with her team, that one moment that brought values to the table and the discussion it caused.

M

I was wondering whether you ever felt like it was not working and had to stop?

S

I actually never had any predefined idea as to what it should provoke. I was open for it to resonate in the way it did. Obviously, I felt in every meeting that there was always at least one person in the room who just hated me for being there. One of the worst situations was when Mylène had to perform in the municipal council of Molenbeek, and Christine in Evergem. Municipal councils were always the worst. It was shocking to me that in a place where politicians come together to speak about living together, there was no listening. They couldn't listen to someone talk for 15 minutes. If you get people who are moved or who feel attacked, that's fine. But if there's no listening at all… At one point we decided to skip municipal councils—I didn't want to expose the performers to that attitude anymore.

M

It's interesting. In the municipal councils, you could say that there are a lot of lectures for no one. They don't listen. Instead they're already preparing their next intervention.

S

Exactly, or else it's for anyone. It doesn't matter. No one or anyone.

M

Yes, it's all scripted. You could go and speak for five minutes, but it doesn't change anything—the vote has already been decided in advance.

S

That's exactly what's being demonstrated. You could argue that—about this protocol and these scriptures—with regard to a lot of situations. But in a small Portuguese village, for instance, in Minde, there was a professional football training of quite a high level. You could also say that it's all scripted but there they really opened up to the text. So for me the shocking thing is that politicians —okay, politics is full of protocol, but so are other places—are completely hermetic to anything that could potentially challenge them.

S

A lot of money and time go into a work that largely remains invisible. Was it difficult for you to defend that for yourselves, your organizations or for potential subsidies?

K, M

No, not at all.

K

At CAMPO there is total artistic freedom, including in terms of responding to the government. It's totally fine.

M

In terms of visibility, we've done worse. Sometimes artists really don't want to communicate anything.

K

As executive producer in particular, a project like LFEO, which has been touring for many years, has quite an impact on the organization. As a team, you devote a lot of time and attention that are hard to communicate. That's not an easy thing.

S

To what extent does it require an organization to work differently? How so?

K

The project made me think a lot about the role of an art centre or institution in society—the role you can play that is not by definition what you put onstage. Working with people that haven't chosen you. It's a very good example of how you can work in a performing-arts context responding to how our society today is constructed—especially, since we, as CAMPO, were coming from the traditional model involving 'making a show and touring it around the world'. This is a good alternative to an old-school touring mode.

Many partners were already following your work. First it was more about 'Sarah's new project', but then it was about LFEO specifically. It raised a lot of discussions with organizations and festivals and art centres that were only used to ship in a show, perform it and get it back out again. They got this 20- or 30-page rider about how to look for places, what to do… You were clearly asking for a serious commitment. And that commitment wasn't always there, you have to admit. Some organizations were not at all prepared to host a project like this, not realizing what sort of work it would require.

There were also older institutions that clearly said no to working with us—no to other ways of thinking, no to engaging in a different relationship with your audience, no to looking for a different way to communicate with people in your city.

S

It's like an interruption in society, but in a sense it also interrupts the organization in its usual routines?

K

Yes, and the people working there—especially the people working in communication. What do you do if you can't announce it?

S

As a publicly funded art institution, do you believe that art should be for everyone? And therefore that your programme should be for everyone?

M

Our motto was coined by Roise Goan: 'Something for everyone, nothing for everybody'. The danger with 'for everyone' is that you end up doing something that has no edge, something that is so easily accessible that everyone can access it but that is in fact only going to address very few people. So we don't have an artistic vision because from the moment you have an artistic vision you're going to exclude more than include. We're not producers so we can allow ourselves to do a lot more. We don't have to have an artistic vision because we have nothing to sell. We're buying and contextualizing all the time. What we try to do is not only to have diversity in the programme but also to have a diversity of voices who programme.

S

Was it true and is it still true today that I can allow myself to do this kind of intervention because I'm an artist?

M

Well, you have the privilege of emotions. The one thing I remember very well about the project was that it brings a lot of emotions in a very short time and in a very direct way. I remember also from the public presentation that the audience was quite affected emotionally, and in a way I think that this is the privilege of the artist. You enter these places in a certain way without an activist agenda. But it touches upon activism when you raise this topic in a very emotional way that provokes people. Activism is about making people change, making people active, in their own community, or in their own personal lives. I think the emotions that you bring in these 15 minutes are quite strong and intense. I think that's where the importance of the project lies. It's very rare actually. Today emotions are skipped over all the time. If it comes from the male it's seen as fragility, and if it comes from the female it's seen as eccentricity. We skip over emotions in the workplace a lot. So the strength of this project is that it moves people in all kinds of ways. I'm sure that something shifted inside all those who heard the lecture. Unless you're a monster, you have to be moved by these 15 minutes—it goes straight to your heart.

K

Absolutely, I totally agree. One of the roles that art has to play is to make you stand still and think about the things you take for granted. The context we live in today is so much more complicated and more complex than five years ago… So this work has an even bigger raison d'être than a while ago—it's of huge importance.

S

It was a long time ago, I know, but do you remember specific moments of the text?

K

The taxi driver.

M

I don't remember exactly, but there is one figure that I remember, and that was a repetition in the text, you repeat the same phrase.

S

'We are before.'

M

'We are before.' I remember this repetition. To me it was important, something like a waking dream.

A conversation with Silvia Bottiroli
Like a dead end

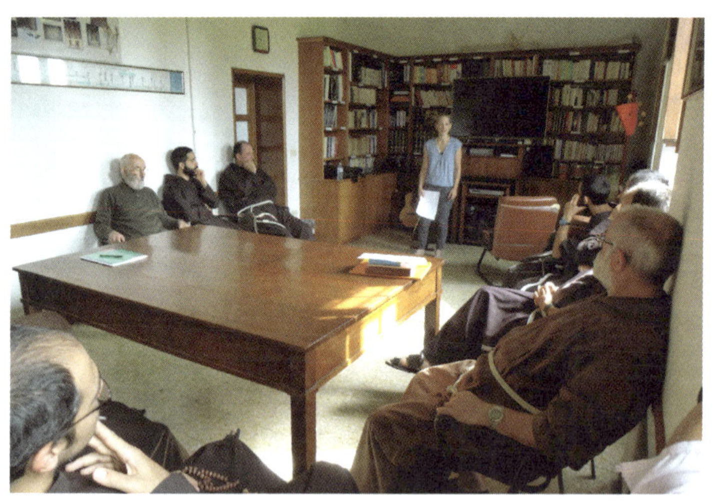

Silvia Bottiroli is the artistic director of DAS Theatre in Amsterdam. She was the artistic director of the Santarcangelo Festival from 2012 to 2016. In 2014 the Santarcangelo Festival organized a series of 12 interventions.

The following text is the result of a conversation between Silvia Bottiroli and Sarah Vanhee that took place in Amsterdam on 19 September 2019.

Sa

Why did you commit to bringing LFEO to Santarcangelo?

Si

I saw the theatre version of LFEO in Brussels in 2013 and I knew your work a bit from before—I had seen *Untitled*. The way the project is organized was also extremely interesting to us in Santarcangelo because of the overall effort we were making at the time to work on the proximity between the festival and the artists, between civic society and the collective life of people. We had decided not to work too much ourselves as mediators, but to really use artistic projects as ways of being close to people living there. So the form of the lecture taking place where people are already gathering for other purposes was very promising. Your project was not about participation; it was all about creating a space where the fact of being present in front of someone and delivering a lecture would be very meaningful.

I sense a certain hesitation with respect to artistic projects that explicitly present themselves as socially engaged. This hesitation mostly comes from the fact that I don't believe that art should replace other kinds of practices. Art has a very specific way of entering the social fabric and this special take of art is also tied to the fact that it is useless. We didn't want to feed the narrative that a festival is useful to a community or respond to needs that the community is able to formulate already. What we were trying to do at the time was to see how some artistic projects could respond to some needs that were actually unspoken, or that were perhaps not conscious but that were present in that collectivity. It might sound a bit arrogant, in a way: not trying to respond to what the people in Santarcangelo were asking from the festival, but trying to give to that community what we believed could speak to them.

I think your project also creates a way of experiencing—for some people, maybe for the first time—the fact of being part of an audience as a meaningful act or a meaningful way of spending your time. And of course we were aware that this kind of project could reach people who would not come to see shows at the festival. Even though the festival takes place in a lot of public places, and even though there are lots of events that are free —and in that sense, the threshold is maybe lower than in other places— still there are people who would never show up because they would never feel invited by something which is part of the programme. We found that was very sad. I started to think that this has a lot to do with politics actually. If people don't feel entitled or confident enough... they had the right to come in and say whether it means something to them or not, whether it resonates or not. And they don't have to be an art critic to do that. Because there will always be masterpieces that don't speak to me either—even if I'm very well trained in reading them formally. And it doesn't make such a difference if you're not that well trained, as you have the right to encounter objects and works of art that can speak to you. In this local context, I thought people should feel that they can come and see stuff and demand that it makes sense for them, but also accept if it doesn't. It's not about an abstract idea of the universality of art, it's about specific works. The works the artist creates can be an encounter or a place of aesthetic experience sometimes.

I like to think in terms of proximity. Your work was not about educating an audience, and not even about developing an audience, but about trusting the potential of being close to each other, of sharing space and time.

Sa

With this project, it's the artist who, together with the festival, decides that the people will *have* to listen, including the people who didn't choose to. What does that mean?

Si

I like very much how you were speaking about being an uninvited guest and I think that's a good definition of art in general—or a potential good definition of some art. Because it's very ambivalent. You can say we are imposing on people or obliging them to listen to something. Even more, we are taking the risk of obliging people to listen to something and they don't even know what it will be about. But that's also an extremely vulnerable position for the artist. I never felt it as an imposition. Also because of how the project is produced and cared for, how the relationship is built up and then the follow-up… There is a lot of care but also a lot of vulnerability in exposing oneself as an artist and the text to those situations.

I experienced one session in the monastery in Santarcangelo and I have a very vivid memory of it. I think there was this mutual vulnerability, which is something very precious, very powerful. That place, that monastery is the very centre of Santarcangelo. It's a place we had been using as a location for the festival. But of course, it's not a building that you would normally enter. And it's a male community obviously. My memory is really of a certain kind of thickness or density to the space, and that small room. They were seated already, we were standing, Sara was speaking; the words had a different weight than at the theatre. It wasn't violent or brutal in any respect.

Sa

What does this project require from an organization that is different from other projects?

Si

It challenges the narrative about the festival as a place where one person takes the decisions and others carry them out, which is in fact never the case. I remember having several meetings about what could be possible gatherings, organizations, contexts for this project. We really had to map out reality in a very different way. This was important for us as a learning process about how people were living in different constellations in the city. Also, the production itself took a long time. At the start especially it's a bit tricky having to involve people who can't know the text of the lecture beforehand. How do you convince somebody to receive the lecture if they don't know what it's about and they don't know the artist. So all this trust, the need to build trust was an interesting process. This project and a couple of others in the end really shaped the way the festival worked. We learned that production could have very different reasons; all of a sudden it wasn't about a certain number of projects, but about a certain intensity too. For Monica [the woman who produced LFEO in Santarcangelo], this was an important learning moment: to know that her work of producing a festival is also about being out in a city or a village and talking with people who are part of that society in very different ways. And looking at it not from an artistic perspective, not from an audience perspective but really from a perspective of where the social or communal life is happening.

For me it gave a kind of three-dimensionality to how we looked at the people living there. Of course, we weren't completely blind before but then we had never really thought about the complexity, in a good sense, of the social lives of people. We like to think that theatre is important because people come together, but that's not the only place where this occurs. And in that sense it was important for us to learn to be less naive and to not only think in terms of this polarization: these poles between the audience as a collective entity, and individual spectators as individual entities; but precisely that there are many things in-between, and actually there are a lot of constellations of people already.

Sa

What is this text as a performative object?

Si

The first thing was this 'We are before' that really stuck with me. When we invited the project to Santarcangelo we also wanted its theatre version to be in the public space on the very first day of the festival, so in a way, dramaturgically, it could totally be taken as an invitation to approach the festival: 'We are before'. There is another part of the text that has stayed with me, for no particular reason, and that was the carpet story. Perhaps it has to do with the particular quality of the whole text. This text is an object which contains other objects. Like that carpet story, it just stays there, it doesn't necessarily build on it. It's a text that is built up in a certain way, but that also makes room for other gems, like a mineral. Maybe that stayed with me more like a mystery: maybe that's why I'm so attached to that part of the text; it's a small universe within this lecture. It draws your attention to something and then continues in a way.

For me the text is very connected to the mineral world. It's like climbing a mountain and finding different stones, different minerals within it. Those mountains where you can distinguish different geological eras, and not necessarily in a certain order, and which are dense. This idea of gems that are more or less hidden within, and are part of it, and this walk.

To me, the text is also a dead end. And I don't mean this negatively. Different lectures take place in different places and they are kind of dead ends in the sense that they don't build on each other. Each of them will produce things that we will not necessarily be aware of.

For me this has to do with trust. It entails a form of trust in things that we won't be able to see or witness but that will happen—a project not necessarily in a sense that each effort that you make has to lead to another one, but that each of them is parallel. The lecture before the monks or the group of women in the house or the municipal council is different and autonomous. It works in a very autonomous way with each group or context, but it's still part of one thing.

The theatre version is not the sum of its parts either.

Sa

You mention a lot the notion of care, which also occurs in the lecture. Where is it, the care? It's not sentimental, it's really in the work, I'd say. What is the work of care?

Si

Yes. What do we care for? If I go back to Santarcangelo, I'd say that I am aware that we, as a team, very often did not take too much care of ourselves in the sense of protecting ourselves, our time. But there was a certain agreement that we would care together for what we could make happen together. In a way this was rewarding enough for us. And that was also a form of self-care. But this fundamental kind of agreement, which was not even spoken, at some point became very problematic for me. Because it was not fair in the end and I was no longer able in this context to demand different conditions for us. This was one of the reasons why I decided to leave the festival. Because in a way I allowed this to happen—we were working too much for too little money.

When it comes to working with artists, or especially with people who are not artists, then care becomes more important, and accountability, but also the continuity of a relationship—how to take care of the relationships that we initiate with some people. Especially because the projects they are involved with can have an impact on their lives. For us, working in this field, what being part of an artistic project means tends to be very clear—there's sometimes even a narrow understanding of it. But for other people it can be a life-changing experience—not necessary dramatically.

Sa

To what extent is this expertise that you have built up, in care and self-care, now also part of the curriculum of DAS Theatre?

Si

A constant subject of discussion with the students is about setting the conditions you need, which by the way we also learned a lot from how artists like you set conditions for themselves. It was important to work with artists who were very clear about what their project required. We have been quite brutal with many projects because of the rush and pressure—you tend to think, 'Maybe I can do it in less time'. So it was very important to work with artists who were clear about what the standards would be for them to make sure things happened the right way. This was definitely the case with LFEO.

In the first place it's the artist's responsibility to decide what conditions are really needed and unnegotiable. How do you as an artist feel entitled to ask for certain conditions? Very often young artists think they don't have the space or the possibility or the agency to decide what conditions they need, so the curators always decide. But in my experience, whenever I have worked with artists who knew exactly what is not negotiable, I would accept that—while of course, whenever there would be room for negotiation I would negotiate. In a sense, the change starts when institutions who need the artists and their artistic projects are obliged to acknowledge certain conditions as needed. That's how they learn more about how artists work or how certain projects work.

Sa

Do you think it's arrogant to assume it's possible to speak to every one?

Si

I'd like to answer by quoting Gofreddo Fofi, an extraordinary figure in the Italian cultural and political context, now over 80, who always worked in very marginalized situations, communities, starting with *Operaismo,* the workerism movement. I had the chance to meet him in Santarcangelo in the early 2000s, and then to collaborate with him in various ways on the experience of the magazine *Lo Straniero* and the award connected to it. Once we were sitting in a *caffè* in the main square of Santarcangelo, together with other artists, among them Italian film-maker Alice Rohrwacher, who was having her film distributed internationally. She was speaking about those moments of doubt when you start making a new project, wondering whether it would be relevant for someone else. Goffredo suddenly interrupted her and said, 'Come on, you're not so special. If it's important to you it will be important to others as well!' I think that's a good take on this—this trust that if something matters to us individually it probably also matters to others. It's an interesting reversal: you're actually very arrogant if you raise this question, because you're not so special. It's never so abstract with this 'every one', it starts from you, from the people around you, from what you think matters. At the same time, I do trust in art for every one, in the sense that these works can resonate and speak to each of us in different ways. That's also an important political work to do, to claim this space.

Sa

I feel I can allow myself to do that, to just appear and give a lecture for every one because I'm an artist. And I couldn't do that in another public role, as a politician or a priest or a lawyer. Do you think it's true that artists have a special position there?

Si

Yes, I think that's true. And problematic of course, in some respects. This may be a Trojan Horse, the potential that art has to open up certain possibilities or spaces because it comes as art. Which means it can't be harmful or not serious—it's 'just' art or fiction or… At the same time, it is problematic. At some point we had to face the situation where we would claim that certain things, certain actions were possible because they were not 'for real', but were artistic actions. On the one hand it's great that art can create the premise for a shift in the understanding of what is legal and what is not. On the other hand, what do we do with this privilege, that as artists or as art institutions we can do things that are not possible for others? How can I claim that Frank can piss in the square and other people cannot?[1] I find it ambivalent and for me this is tied to the relationship between the norm and the exception. So yes, art can be a place of exception but then do exceptions just confirm the norm or can a norm shift because of those exceptions? So yes, artists do have a special position, and this comes with responsibilities.

[1] This refers to the choreography '(untitled) (2000)' by Tino Sehgal, performed in Santarcangelo by Boris Charmatz in the Lavatoio Theatre and by Frank Willens in the public space, where, quoting Jérôme Bel quoting Marcel Duchamp, the performer urinates on stage.

A conversation with Christophe Slagmuylder
What is a space for art and what not?

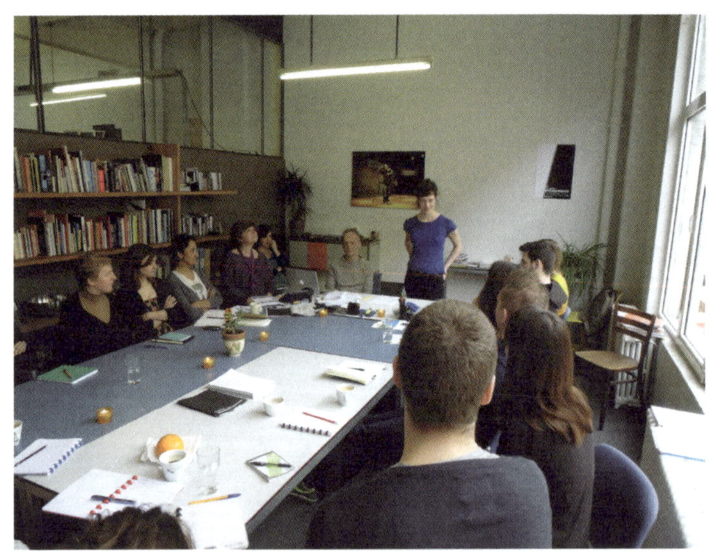

Christophe Slagmuylder has been the general and artistic director of the Wiener Festwochen since 2019. He was the artistic director of the Kunstenfestivaldesarts (KFDA) from 2006 to 2018. In 2013 the KFDA co-produced LFEO and organized a series of 40 interventions in Brussels.

The following text is based on a conversation between Christophe Slagmuylder and Sarah Vanhee that took place in Brussels on 12 October 2019.

S

The KFDA was the first festival where we performed LFEO. Do you remember why you decided to invite it?

C

The project answered incredibly well a lot of questions I had as a festival director in a city like Brussels. For instance, how can you reach very different groups of people in the same city? How can you be nomadic inside the city? How can a festival test different kinds of formats beyond the theatre? In itself, this was nothing new, but with this project, it was no longer about entering public spaces, but about entering semi-public or private spaces. So there was this intrusive dimension as a way to reach different people.

S

But when you approved the project, you didn't know what the text was going to be.

C

That's true, but the concept was a powerful one: what words can you use to address very different groups of people in the same city? What words, but what content too, of course.

S

I hadn't even written the text yet!

C

That's right, the text was not yet written. When was the first time I heard it? Did you come to the office?

S

Yes, there was a team meeting, one or two weeks before the festival started. What do you remember about that experience or the text?

C

It's a long time ago… I think I expected it to be about notions of solidarity. But in a sense, the content was also the project. The project was about bringing the content, and this question was at the centre of the text: what can create a social bond between very different kinds of people? The text was a way of extending these questions, and of making them more tangible and understandable for different kinds of people. Maybe what I remember most was the rhythm, the silences, the pauses. Not only the words, but also the space between the words. These were as important to me as the words themselves. And probably also the situation of listening. And the way you left the room, that was probably the most… not shocking, but… that was a very weird situation for me. You'd probably explained it to me in advance, but that was something that made the experience very different for me. Like, 'Wow, she's delivered something, but then she leaves the room and we're left on our own with this'. Yes, that really was a dimension that only the experience could bring.

S

I have the feeling that we are both concerned with the issue of how to find language, or work, that is potentially accessible to everyone. But saying something like that is also dangerous in these times because it almost sounds populistic. So what's the difference? What prevents this from being a populistic language or project?

C

I think it has to do with not simplifying something that's complex. But also showing that we don't have to complexify things that can be said in a very straightforward way. You're not looking for the way slogans and formulas work. It's not a question of falling into this populistic way of addressing people, but of how to keep or contain complexity without reducing it, instead actually condensing it into words, into a tone, a way of constructing or introducing a speech. How you position yourself in the room, how you place your voice. It's not only the words, but the performance, and how you deliver the lecture in the room.

S

When LFEO was introduced, it was clear to people that it was a project that came from the KFDA. Were there people who addressed you about it afterwards?

C

The weird thing about this project was that it reached a lot of people, although nobody knew exactly when! *(laughs)* Where to go, and when? There were no tickets, and you couldn't meet people who had attended it. I found this complicated, of course, but it was part of the concept. No, I was never really confronted, in a way. That was frustrating to me, but you were also very clear—and I found it also good—that we couldn't come as spectators, because we would disrupt those situations.

S

How do you situate LFEO within the discourse on audience, inclusion, participation?

C

To me it remains a very important project in my career as a curator, because I found it very experimental. It doesn't happen that often that I get such a proposal from an artist. I had the feeling that I could try something that was always on my mind but without knowing how to do that. There's always this utopia of a festival 'for everybody in the city', the idea that we should diversify the audience, etc. OK, we are doing this little by little, and we have different tools for that. But this was very different: going to places with people who have nothing to do with the KFDA. It wasn't about the festival, it was about trying to enter with an artistic project into spaces where you are not supposed to go. Nobody expects you there, but you don't ask, you just go!

S

That sounds like a very impolite project!

C

Yes, I think it has this dimension. I still believe it's an extremely unique way of trying to bring an artistic creation or discourse beyond a space that is always a very safe space for the arts. It's important that we create these safe spaces. But how can we also get outside them? It's a form of activism.

S

Usually you offer something, and people can come if they want. But here you're saying, 'Now you're going to listen'. How do you feel about 'imposing' something?

C

I think this is my role anyway. I would be happy for it to happen more often. I'm supposed to follow what an artist wants to realize. And to make sure that my institution, the one I'm heading, is flexible enough to follow certain rules. It's not, 'This is my space, these are the rules of the space, and you as an artist, just have to find your place within it'. But instead, 'How could this space be transformed by an artistic proposal?' So it's never easy, and I would say it happened several times with you and your work. That's also why it's very valuable work for me. Like the title of the project, which is really a way of raising the question of participation, and asking the question as to what is a space for art and what is not? And how you constantly try to break, displace, move these borders. So yes, it's a question of responsibility, but I think this was clear from the beginning. When you explained the project to me, I didn't feel like I was being abused in any way. From the moment I accepted and said, 'Yes, I want to do the project', it was all part of the game. I was responsible for a sort of intrusion, and a gesture of forcing people. I really wasn't against that in any way.

S

Would you say then that, in the same way that I intrude in these spaces outside the arts sector, the lecture is also intruding in what the festival usually is and how it is run?

C

Yes, absolutely. And it's actually also about the artist taking responsibility for her- or himself, saying, 'I'm not only being programmed in your space, I'm also imposing', although I don't like the word… It's about how the work is presented, shared. All the conditions to get access to the work are part of the work. It's also about redefining the role of the artist, and the dependence between the artist and the institution, and how it works, and its role. It's challenging, and that makes it very interesting and important for me.

S

Did you ever feel that you had to defend, with regard to third parties or the authorities, a work that you supported generously within the festival, but that largely remained invisible?

C

Honestly, in Brussels and in a festival like the KFDA, we could allow such invisibility for this kind of project. I never really had to justify or defend it. That's a great chance I had. The context we created allowed these kinds of projects to exist. So fortunately, no, I didn't have to 'defend' it. But otherwise I would have. Three people or three thousand people, it's the same thing. The impact of a project is not only measured by the number of people it reaches. And the festival space is much more than the presentation of pieces onstage—it's a space for all kinds of exchanges and translations. And this project was a very interesting way to provoke unimaginable, unexpected encounters.

S

With which other phenomenon in the arts or elsewhere would you compare LFEO?

C

I can't think of many examples where one and the same thing can be so nomadic and enter so many different contexts. I don't think that in the reality we live in there is something like that… I'm sometimes invited to share my experience with people who are doing the same job or who work in the same field, but I'm never confronted with people who work in fields that are very different from mine. I should really provoke that, because it just doesn't happen spontaneously. This is a very unique project: you enter extremely different contexts but confront them with the same face. People are organized by 'milieu', which is important because that's how it works. But you also sense that it creates a lot of misunderstandings. There are not that many spaces where we are really confronted with the other, and I mean this in a very positive sense, in the sense that we can enrich ourselves.

A conversation with Adinda Van Geystelen

It's not as if you'd ever perform in an operating theatre

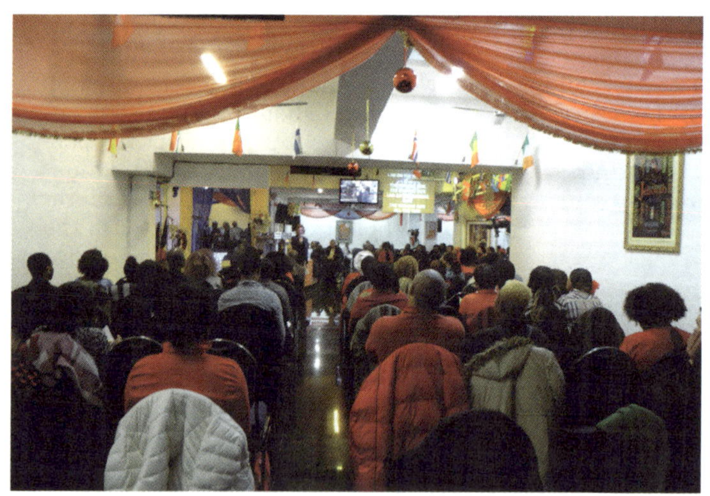

Adinda Van Geystelen is the general director of Kunsthal Extra City in Antwerp. In December 2017 Extra City organized a series of seven LFEO interventions in Antwerp.

The following text is the result of a conversation between Adinda Van Geystelen and Sarah Vanhee that took place on 30 September 2019 in Brussels.

S

Could you briefly describe Extra City as an institute?

A

We are a *kunsthal*, an exhibition space that presents contemporary art but that, unlike a museum, does not have a collection of its own. Three years ago we repositioned ourselves and decided to choose a thematic focus and to show exhibitions that have links with the contemporary city.

S

What did LFEO mean to you when we performed it at Extra City in late 2017?

A

At the time we had an exhibition with visual art on the theme of 'citizenship'. Michiel Vandevelde put together an off programme in that context, in which he suggested to include your lecture. We receive subsidies as an exhibition space for visual art, so the subsidizing authorities expect us in the first place to show visual art to the public. Any remaining means with which we can organize peripheral activities are very limited. But to demonstrate that those themes, which we approach through art, are embedded in a contemporary societal discourse about a society in transition, we believe the off programme is very important. Your project was a wonderful occasion to look beyond the walls of the *kunsthal* and to show how someone as an artist assumes her civil responsibility. Moreover, the lecture also addresses people directly as to what citizenship could mean.

S

How do you, as the director of an art institute, defend or justify a work that is largely invisible?

A

We show the public what it means to be an artist today in relation to society. So it would be a terrible missed opportunity not to show such projects. I myself have a great affinity for the performing arts, which often move me more easily than the visual arts. To me the performance was an opportunity to broaden the visual arts programme. In budgetary terms it wasn't obvious. It was an expensive project within the context of our programme. So you could easily be inclined to question the relevance of the project: 'Does it make any sense to do something invisible when you have so few means?' That is not an easy choice. In an ideal world, there is sufficient budget to make such projects possible. So that, simultaneously to the exhibition within the institution, it would be possible to also have artists work in the public space, in schools and all sorts of different contexts. Such projects in the visual-arts sector have long been relegated as 'social-artistic work' and as a result they have often been looked down on artistically.
I'm happy to observe that things are slowly changing in that regard and that these social-artistic projects have also been receiving more acknowledgement in artistic circles in recent years.

Within the context of the visual arts, I have often been confronted with this situation: the art market is an important indicator of the artistic valuation. What falls outside the market is quickly seen as of little value. But who gets to judge artistic quality?

I don't see Lecture For Every One as a social-artistic project, nor as a participatory or art-educational project, but as an artistic project. The moment the meeting or gathering takes place, it becomes the context of the artistic project. And everyone becomes a part of it: there is not 'the audience' on one side and 'the performer' on the other. That's a very interesting field of tension.

S

You came along to the Lecture For Every One in the Redeemed Church of Christ. Can you describe that experience?

A

It was a memorable morning in several respects. Behind the façade of a former shop in the Statiestraat in Berchem, two to three hundred faithful of the African Pentecostal community come together every weekend. The preparation of the lecture had not gone smoothly. Pastor Mike would only authorize the lecture if he obtained the text beforehand. That wasn't the intention in fact, but we found the context interesting and that is why we agreed exceptionally to his condition. I attended the service that Sunday, together with you and Marika, and suddenly we found ourselves among hundreds of praying, singing and dancing Africans. The context was absolutely fascinating, but to us also fairly uncomfortable.

When you were delivering the lecture, I had the feeling that a lot of those present were listening carefully, although the intervention was undoubtedly strange and surprising for them. But after the lecture, Pastor Mike refused to follow the agreed protocol. He demanded that you do not disappear in silence, but that you answer a question he had. He had prepared well and integrated the lecture in his sermon. He took control and invited the faithful to seek the answer to the questions that Sarah had raised in God. All three of us were rather bothered by the situation and left with a strange feeling: shocked, frustrated, surprised, angry, fascinated… Was the intervention a failure? You weren't the only performer in this prayer service. Pastor Mike is a natural, a performer who uses his rhetorical talent to convey a personal or religious message to the public. His 'action' bothered us but was also, from another perspective, very clever. I found that quite fascinating. How does the Western performance artist relate to the African performance-preacher? Should we have stuck to our guns and not provided the text in advance? When do we consider the lecture as 'successful'? In any case, I won't forget that morning any time soon.

S

For Extra City you were also the person who sought out the venues. How did that search go?

A

I enjoyed doing that a lot, because I believe in the project. It is a very interesting opportunity to explain the project to the most diverse people and to discover the reactions to such a question by an artist. Kunsthal Extra City absolutely reached another public with this project than with an exhibition. The city's green department, the African Pentecostal community, etc.

S

Do you believe that a public art institution should be 'for every one'? If so, how do you go about creating access 'for every one'?

A

I'm convinced that it is possible theoretically, that you are there 'for every one', but a lot of people need the appropriate accompaniment and in practice that's unfeasible. One of the things I often have trouble with is that we in the arts sector have increasingly tended to focus on specific target groups because we can then ask for extra subsidies. As a result, we sometimes forget to broaden the existing audience as much as possible. It could also be meaningful to enquire as to who doesn't in fact dare come in but would actually like to? How can we enlarge that circle? I know a lot of people who take part in culture but who say, 'Unfortunately I don't understand a thing about contemporary visual art!' Reaching that group of people too seems to me to be an important first step. The unpapered Polish builders in the Statiestraat in Berchem have other priorities than getting acquainted with art in our *kunsthal* and that's alright too.

With your project you show that there are also projects with which you could potentially address everyone. Nothing is too difficult as art. There is only the question of having the right tools and setting to work with them.

S

What does it means if the art institute decides, together with the artist, that the people should listen, even if the people did not make the decision themselves?

A

You know that part of the audience will be annoyed or even irate, but hopefully also stimulated positively or enthusiastic in part. When you know how much time is lost in unproductive meetings, then I believe that a quarter of an hour is something they can afford to lose on such a project. After all, it's not as if you'd ever perform in an operating theatre.

I deal in words, they deal in doors and car gates

Memories of LFEO performers

-4

BERLIN

04.10.2014
6:30 P.M.

St Mary's Church.
Evening service.

Mariel Supka performed LFEO in German

I was a little nervous before the lecture in St Mary's Church. Not because I thought that I mightn't be able to reach any of the listeners. I was worried that the text, delivered during a mass, would sound like a sermon and that it wouldn't be perceived as an intervention coming from outside.

The atmosphere in the church was unexpectedly ceremonial by Protestant standards. The ministers involved—all men, as I recall—were dressed festively and crossed the high nave in a procession. They were swinging censers about with burning incense, and loud organ music was playing. After the bishop and then the pastor had spoken, I was invited to step up to the slightly raised choir area, from where, speaking quietly through a microphone, I directed the text at the people in attendance.

My fear that the text and my performance would blend into the characteristic style of the church service proved to be unfounded, at least judging by the reactions of the church officials. They showed their disapproval while talking to each other noisily and shooting bored glances my way in the apse.

By contrast, the (albeit few) parishioners in attendance remained attentive and well-disposed towards me. When a man in a wheelchair approached me at the end and told me, 'That was the best sermon I've heard in a long time', to my surprise I was delighted.

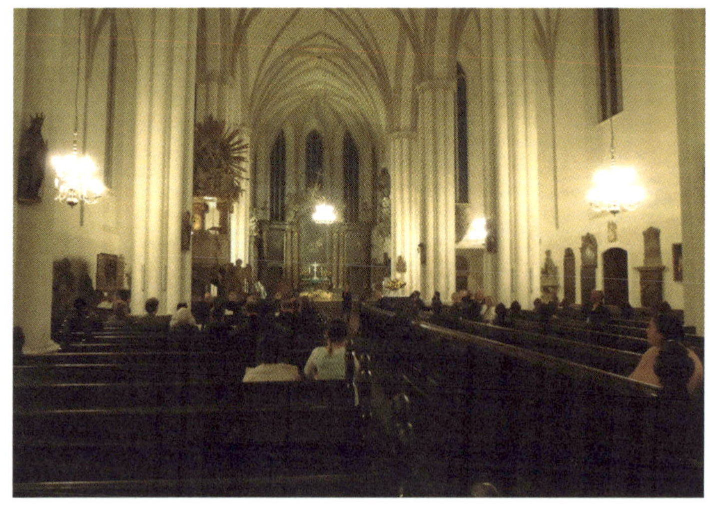

STOCKHOLM

11.06.2015
8:15 A.M.

Karolinska University Hospital. Meeting of the doctors specializing in gynaecology and childbirth.

Salka Ardal Rosengren

performed LFEO in Swedish

I remember walking into a room at the Karolinska Hospital at 8:00 a.m. Women and men dressed in white doctor's coats, all with a weight on their face—tired, but focused. I felt that they were all bracing themselves for a successful work day. I started to speak and some faces got curious about what this young, seemingly formal woman was doing, lecturing them at 8:00 a.m. on a Monday morning. Others zoomed out. The faces that did open up towards me seemed relieved to be addressed with this other attention, so different from what the hectic day at the hospital normally provides. The 15-minute lecture became a reminder of another imaginary realm, maybe even a comforting pause that enabled minds to travel before dealing with all that life and death.

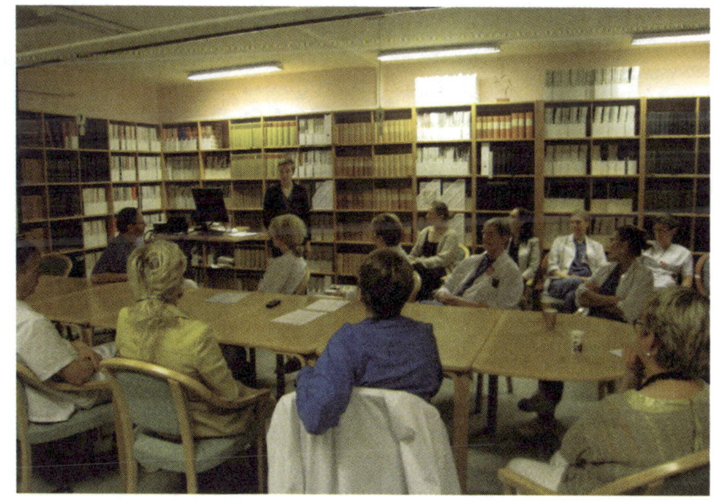

BORDEAUX

11.06.2015
10:30 A.M.

Many Vigier Équipements, regional company specializing in the adaptation of utility vehicles. Planning meeting.

Lara Barsacq performed LFEO in French

Lecture For Every One was a very strong experience for me as a performer. If I think about why, it's the text of course—the silences that are a bit too long and that push the listener to let go. But I had an adrenaline rush mainly because the situations were unfamiliar and there might be unexpected reactions… I remember being overwhelmed by the whole idea of delivering the text in these improbable places, entering with electronic badges in spaces that were not designed to have an intruder trespassing with a poetic message.

I remember one particularly strong lecture. It was performed in a regional company specializing in the adaptation of utility vehicles.

The company director was a 30+ woman with impeccable red lipstick who welcomed Linda and me on her 10 cm red stilettos. She was sharp and talked quickly. She immediately warned us that it might be complicated to perform the text because we would have to deal with a crowd of about 25 men who normally tend to be loud and say what they think, adding that they would probably laugh at me. So I should be prepared. I felt that she was nervous and scared of their reaction. She wanted to know what the text was about and we had to convince her to wait and trust us.

As we entered the huge space filled with utility vehicles, my heart was pounding in my ears. I was thinking I might end up in one of the ambulances.

We entered in front of a large crowd of men. They were expecting their Monday meeting and she introduced me as a performer who would perform Lecture For Every One by Sarah Vanhee instead of the meeting.

I started the text and slowly, as we were inside the first moments of the text when I talked about faces and bodies and watched them, I could see that they were listening and attentive.

No one spoke, no one laughed, some even nodded at times, agreeing with the text as I talked of care.

»

BORDEAUX

11.06.2015
10:30 A.M.

»

The silences of the text were not awkward, as they sometimes had been when I had delivered the text in other contexts.

They were present and agreed with the lecture. As I neared the end, I saw the company director crying on the side.

We left and I felt full of energy. It was touching. This crowd was present.

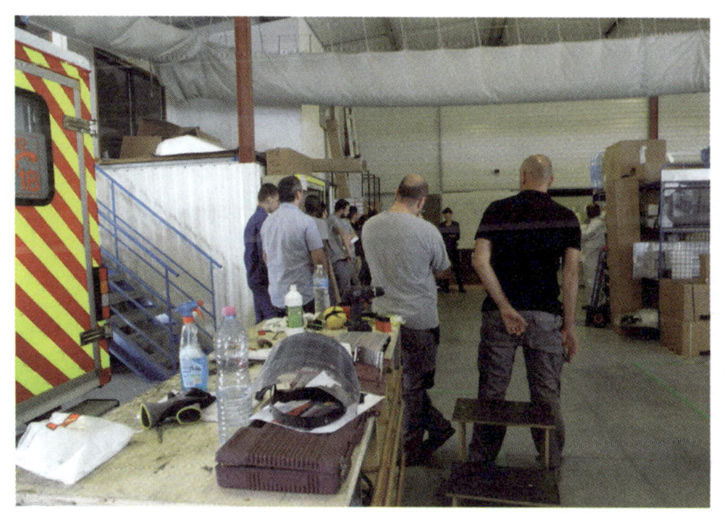

HELSINKI

07.08.2013
1:00 P.M.

Ministry of Social
Affairs and Health.
PR Department meeting.

Elina Pirinen performed LFEO in Finnish

During 25 minutes my skull explodes in millions of pieces in front of them, and the tiny breeze of the room's air conditioning makes the bony pieces spin in the air, landing in their faces, making wounds from where sweat, blood and tears run onto the table, overwriting the language of the room, and the sun shines outside and my body walks through the sun without the skull and takes tram 4 to a new room where during another 25 minutes my lungs explode in millions of pieces in front of a new them and the interstitial fluids blend into the lunch soups of the room, creating a flood, and the pressure detaches their skulls from their bodies and our torsos surf out together to the August dust of Helsinki, gradually seeping into the bottom of the East Sea.

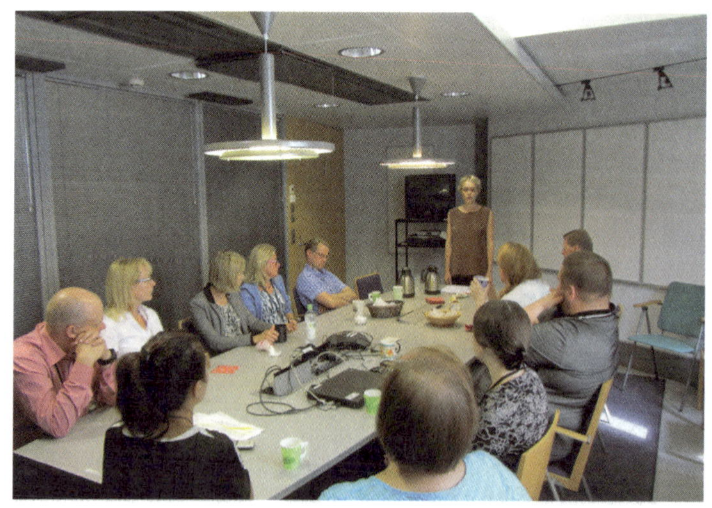

BERN

17.09.2014
8:00 A.M.

Berner Kantonalbank.
Board meeting of different departments.

Carola Bärtschiger

performed LFEO in Swiss German

I expected resistance in this room, but instead I spoke to attentive listeners, who looked at me warmly and openly. I was confronted with my own prejudices about bankers on this early morning in the autumn of 2014.

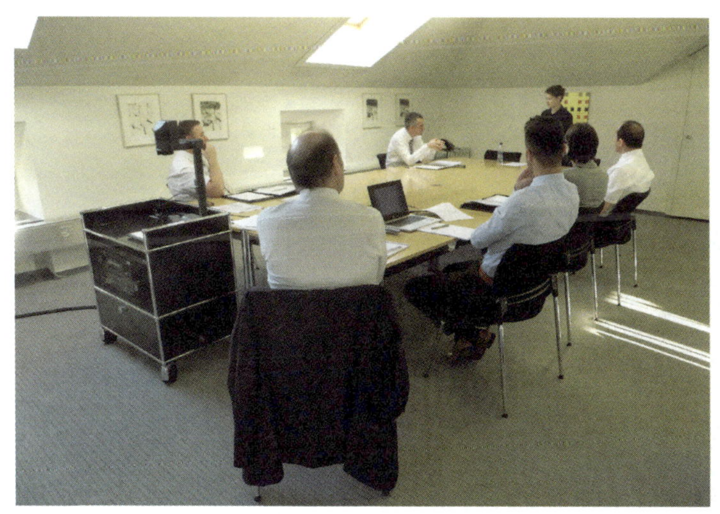

VIENNA

20.03.2014
2:00 P.M.

Josefstadt Prison. Informal meeting of the prison board.

Deborah Hazler

performed LFEO in Austrian German

Participating in this project made me more aware that I can't accurately read facial expressions. In this *Justizanstalt* the faces seemed grim and bored, but the feedback was that the people were touched and the lecture made them question things. To this day I try not to get stuck interpreting facial expressions as true facts.

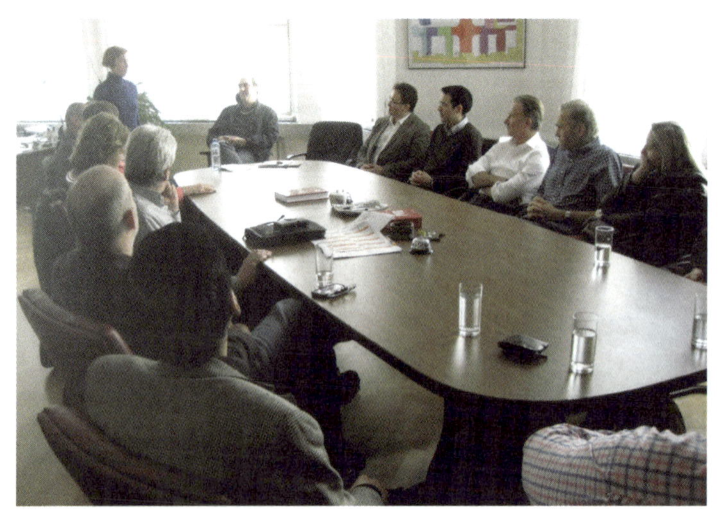

MINDE

20.09.2016
7:30 P.M.

Atlético Clube Alcanenense, 3rd division football club. Daily team practice.

Anabela Almeida

performed LFEO in Portuguese

It was the first time I was doing Lecture For Every One in the open air and in a such big open space: on a football field, to a young football team. I was nervous and they were too. 'What's going on, coach? What's this?'

I was afraid they weren't going to listen to me, that they'd look at the football field next to them or all over the place… The beginning was frightening, a lot of answers to the questions being asked and, soon after, the silence, the looks, and the attention with which they listened to the words.

From that, we went on together, a team of which I was a part, and suddenly the enormous field became intimate and cosy. It was so moving and great!

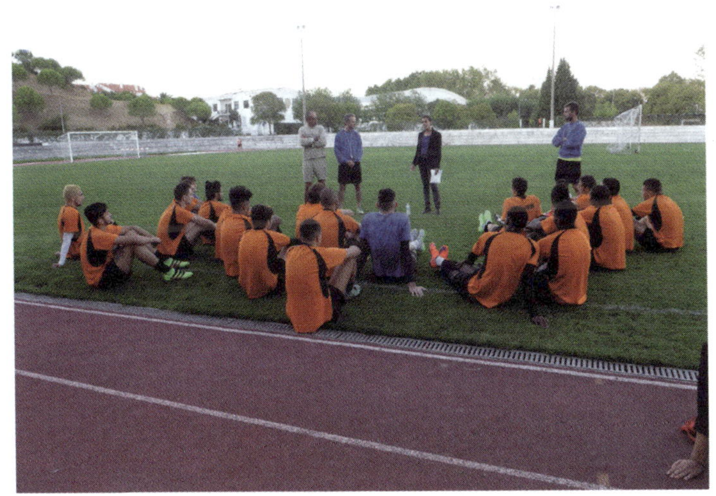

EVERGEM

20.04.2015
9:00 A.M.

Maldex, a family company that makes doors and (car)ports. Weekly meeting of the sales team.

Christine de Smedt

performed LFEO in Flemish

It is a sunny Monday morning, 9:00 a.m., in a residential neighbourhood. The garage door opens. A group of young entrepreneurs are sitting and standing around a table with fresh energy and in a good mood. It is the start of their weekly meeting and planning.

I deal in words, words written by Sarah Vanhee.

They deal in doors and car gates.

I am introduced to the entrepreneurs. Two potential buyers arrive and join us.

Every one listens carefully. Confusion arises when the questions come. Here and there someone writes down a word—maybe an answer, maybe a note to remember for the meeting. We listen together. For me, this encounter through these words is *a gift* in which we feel uncomfortable together. This encounter only happens once in a lifetime. This disturbance connects us through these words. It is my first Lecture For Every One and I sense the impact of the intervention, the impact of this unique situation, created for them and for me. These ideas, concerns, shared in and out of context, like an unidentified object, so close and yet distant, make you question what life is, what living is.

Maldex is a family business. Their banner says, 'Maldex, a gate for life'. Leaving through the gate is abrupt. I cannot explain or listen to their questions and answers because this is neither a conversation nor an inquiry. This is an extraordinary art piece that opens a door to look through. Kindly invited to keep looking. They go on living and working once I leave. Maybe with a difference in opening and closing the doors they sell.

PS: the two potential buyers apparently bought a car gate that morning!

EVERGEM

Christine de Smedt

performed LFEO
in Flemish

20.04.2015
9:00 A.M.

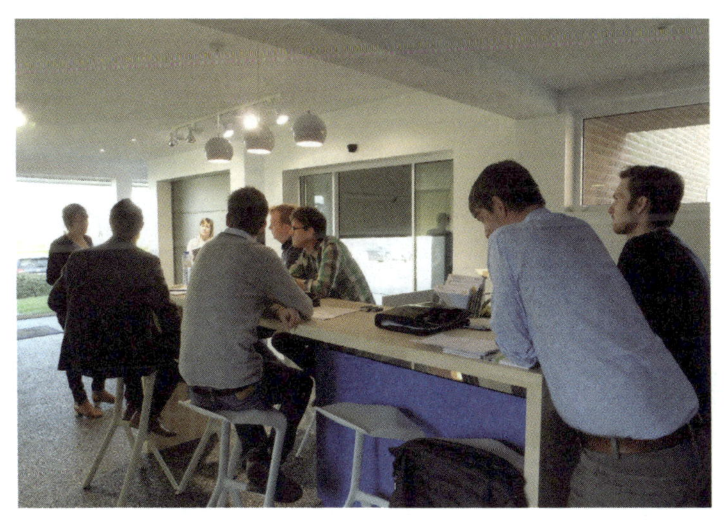

TALLIN

27.08.2014
10:00 A.M.

Estonian Parliament. Meeting of the Social Democratic Party's ministers and chancellors.

Iiris Viirpalu performed LFEO in Estonian

The lecture I delivered at the Estonian Parliament for the ten ministers from the local Social Democratic Party had a strong effect on me. The mere fact that I, then a 22-year-old girl, just a student, had the time and attention of decision-makers to make them think and feel about things that we all share as human beings, is a sign of democracy and possibilities. From the lecture series held in my home country, this one definitely emerges as the one where I actually felt even more responsibility and presence than I thought I would when jumping into this project. Thinking back, the format of this lecture held so much more in it than just provoking people to think. Caring, loving, noticing our deeds and actions towards those surrounding us and forming the ties of society—I feel that the lecture gave all the participants and the lecturers the time to reflect on their responsibilities and their values, getting the sense that everything you do has an effect on someone. How you live your life shapes the lives of others and you can either give and be human or shut yourself down in your own bubble. I definitely stepped out of mine. Maybe everything we do leaves traces...

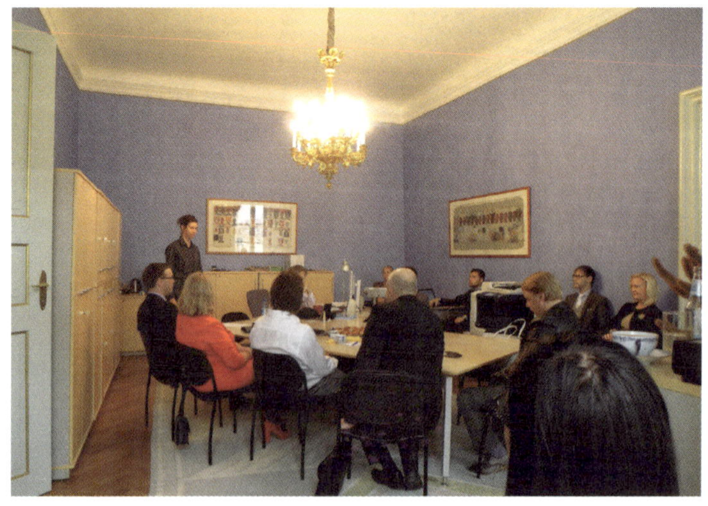

That big invisible part of the project

A conversation with LFEO production managers

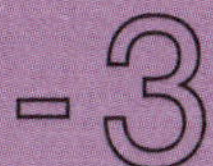

Kristien Van den Brande was a freelance production manager and dramaturge for LFEO in 2012–2013.

Marika Ingels was the artistic collaborator working on LFEO for CAMPO (executive producer) and a production manager for LFEO in 2013–2018.

Edith Goddeeris was a freelance production manager for LFEO in 2013–2017.

Linda Sepp was a freelance production manager for LFEO in 2013–2019.

All four worked closely with the art institutions, the contact persons and the performers. With each lecture, one of them joined the performer in the meeting and took a picture for the LFEO website.

The following text is the result of a live conversation that took place in Brussels on 21 October 2019 with Linda on Skype from Berlin.

S

Kristien, in terms of organization, you were the one who set up the entire project in Brussels in 2013, for the first series of 40 interventions. Your work became the template we used for all other cities. Do you remember the first steps?

K

I remember the first three meetings we went to together. With sociologist Eric Corijn, for instance. It was important for me to hear you, Sarah, speak about the project not just with me, but also with other people. I learned a lot from you, how you were doing research beforehand. To see, for instance, what the context was around such a place, the anchors, the buttons you might have to push. To notice how, even though LFEO was the same text for everyone, what you said to people changed slightly. There was kind of a cold reading also of where we could find the connecting points.

This is where it started, with the question of how to convince people of something they know nothing about yet. At the time, the text didn't exist. On a personal level, you need a kind of performativity: to be self-convinced even though you don't know what you're talking about.

S

Eric Corijn is someone who's extremely networked. We didn't go to him to ask if we could intrude in his context but basically to open up his address book and share his contacts.

We realized we didn't have a huge network. Or the places we wanted to go to weren't the places that were in our address book.

Perhaps that was one of the very first realizations: we want to go to different places, so how do we get in there?

K

Yes, that performativity of the network is also super important. Like, 'I'm here because that person advised me'. So how do you build up a trust network around, again, something you know nothing about and for which they also have to take responsibility. I found that very beautiful and challenging—to observe how that developed.

S

Back then, did you also try to get in touch with places where we didn't have any contacts, like out of the blue?

K

No, it was always through a network.

L

I remember that in the beginning, when we were touring, like in Helsinki, we tried to contact some places where we didn't have any personal contacts, but it never worked.

So later on we decided to go for personal networks. Even if they weren't well known to us or close, it was still much more efficient and realistic.

S

In the very beginning we drew up a list and divided society into different groups, places where people met. The list mentioned social gatherings, professional gatherings, etc. We had this idea of wanting, each time we went to a new city, to be able to speak to everyone, which is of course an illusion, but it implies different kinds of groups in terms of age, background, profession, etc.

M

We used that list a lot. When we were in talks with other organizations inviting LFEO, we used this list as an example of who we had to cover in a city.

K

I think this also came from the experience of collaborating with the Kunstenfestivaldesarts (KFDA).

They made contact with their immediate network, but then I saw it moving in one direction, and I'd sometimes radically have to pull it the other way.

S

What was the direction the KFDA was steering you in?

K

Social organizations.

M

Or sociocultural ones.

K

Even socio-artistic ones, with existing participatory set-ups within their frame of audience participation.

E

We really didn't want LFEO to go to those places to start with. That was the challenge.

K

I remember a preparatory meeting we had with the director of the KFDA. We discussed the places they were thinking of and I could feel that he wasn't on board: 'You can't go there'. He invited the project but wasn't completely ready to stand behind it, to give us his own contacts, out of fear. That was striking.

S

What about the rest of you? Were people from institutions ready to give you access to their address book/personal contacts?

L

Yes, the list really helped to get to this point. The first impulse was indeed always to activate the artistic and social partners. They thought they were the only contacts they had, but then looking at the list they realized that they actually knew people working in other places too. People were really open to sharing their personal networks.

S

Including the artistic and general directors?

L

(laughs) I'm talking about team members because they're the people I worked with. I wasn't there, in person, when they spoke to their artistic directors to ask for their contacts. But I remember some in leading positions who also helped, maybe not in a very personal manner, but by sharing their contacts.

M

I remember that for Ghent, we had a meeting with some people from CAMPO and the Vooruit and we wrote down their contacts. It was a very lively and nice meeting, and everyone was sharing contacts.

E

Yes, Marika called her ex for a building company, Kristof contacted a friend working for Ikea, etc.

S

You've all been in the situation where you had to look for places yourselves. How did you do that? Kristien talked earlier about performativity or about adapting the narrative to the person you were talking to, do you recognize that?

E

I really recognize what you said, Kristien. Although the text already existed, we couldn't share it with anyone beforehand. You really tried to convince someone and you needed that person to have an open mind. For instance, I remember calling the manager of InSites Consulting, and he asked, 'What's the promise? What's the use?' I found it sometimes difficult to find a way when people were purpose-minded.

M

It was a question that came back often: 'What's in it for us?'

E

And people find it so difficult when they can't pay for something. It didn't cost them anything, not even too much time. It seems like this made it even more difficult.

S

So because it was free, they mistrusted it?

E

I think so.
(general laughter)

M

I remember that when people asked, 'What's in it for us?', I said that it was like a gift you receive—a gift we offered to a lot of different people in society.

K

In Brussels, in 2013, there was no material yet, no website. So I was playing much less on the idea of the gift and much more on the element of surprise. Were they willing to take the risk with us, were they ready for the challenge? To gain trust, but… the narrative had a bit of terror in it. Much less the idea of a gift.

M

But once we'd done it, we could say, 'We've been to the European Parliament and to Nestlé and other', and it made a huge difference. People seemed to think, 'If you've been there, it must be OK'. It must have been totally different for you, Kristien.

S

For you it was more, 'Do you dare?'—daring people to take a risk.

K

Yes, and to let them come also. It's like what we talked about a lot in the beginning, the act of *parrhesia:* I need to get you to take the risk of saying 'yes'.

S

In a way, it's taking people very seriously.

K

Exactly.

S

How could you speak about the project in a way that was truthful to you? Or maybe not?

K

I think I was quite truthful in taking things that I found important. And there is a way, even with more right-wing people—because it's about common human values. Together as a group they might be very critical, but you can pick out things that you know will resonate with this or that person.

S

When they asked you what the text was about, what did you say?

E

I talked about the notion of 'living together'.

M

I also said it was a mix of different kinds of texts: anecdotes, poetry, reflections… But the 'living together' argument was also something I would start with.

L

I found it very helpful once we had collected some feedback from the contact persons. Some descriptions were repeated very often, and I used those keywords, like 'It's thought-provoking', 'It gives time for reflection', 'It was an interesting and special moment for the team or the group', 'Something out of the ordinary that kept inspiring thoughts later on', etc. It showed that it had a clear shape, that it was an organized project and not something chaotic, not artistic in the clichéd sense. It showed that it was very sharp in its form but that the content had elements of surprise—what you can't describe, what you're ready to invite and give a little room to. And that's just thought-provoking and inspiring.

K

I would also phrase it as a question: that we weren't sure either whether it was always possible to speak the same words in every context. That it was also a kind of research for us, that it wasn't just a given product. Yes, in the sense that it was always the same, but it wasn't stable—it was a research.

S

Marika, when people asked you this very concrete question, 'What's in it for us?', did you try to give an answer?

M

I said there was nothing really in it for them except for the experience and the risk-taking. And that it's a gift.

S

The answer is probably multiple, but why did people say yes then, do you think? Why did they finally accept?

E

Curiosity, maybe.

M

Also, people were happy to have art come to them. Or people thought of themselves as thinking outside the box by taking it on.

E

Yes, to show that they were open-minded. Sometimes they would also propose to add one or other subject.

K

Through this question of living together, I sometimes got the idea that organizations were also in trouble. For instance, with the RVA, I could see all these leaflets about *'pesten op het werk'*, bullying at work—so there was also a certain hope for something 'group-building', for the cohesion of a group. For instance, when we went to Volvo, I had to speak with five quite highly ranked people—while usually it was more of a one-to-one type of meeting. It was challenging because I then had to adapt to five people. I had to dispel some fear here, some fear there… They took a huge risk by bringing the project to their biggest meeting with so many different people working for that organization, from very low to very high. How to bring them together? Even though it was maybe not our best one, they still took a huge risk in scheduling it. And with a lot of hope, which was nice to see.

S

This question is more for Edith, Marika and Linda, who took over after the 'model LFEO series' was created by Kristien: how did you manage to help the art institutions who invited the project to their city since they had never realized a project like LFEO before? I remember it wasn't always easy, for different reasons. Could you talk about the challenges and about how you operated in the end? Eventually, we had protocols for everything but only after a long process of trial and error.

L

After a while and through experience, we had quite good guidelines. For instance, the idea that we should start looking for places three months before the presentation. That was a realistic period—counting on what I call the two 'waves of frustration'. You would have to contact a lot of places and be ready for a first wave of frustration coming from people saying, 'It's an interesting project but actually, no'. In the beginning many people were open and interested but then realized they couldn't do it. Either because they couldn't make it happen or because they became too impressed or afraid. About 20 per cent of the people we contacted in the beginning would finally say 'yes' and make it happen. Then you would have to contact another round of people and have again quite a few of them say 'no'. It took a lot of time to follow up the contacts. So anticipating these steps was very helpful and then having regular Skype or phone calls with the local team to see what kind of selection had been made already and to shape the local selection of places according to the list you mentioned earlier. We would select only one sociocultural place, and then head for the more complicated places like industries or what you call the hard sector—heading for those more intensively.

The hard sector is where economics and market logics are very present. For instance, the multinationals that you find in bigger cities, or smaller ones also.

S

I remember that it was easier with some institutions and organizations than with others?

E

What often happened was that they gave the task to a young intern. That made things difficult because you need people with a mature position to be able to break into this hard sector. Cultural differences were also a challenge. In Lisbon, for instance, three months in advance didn't work. Even when we were there, things were changing all the time: the planning, the hour, the way we would get there, etc. So that made it difficult too sometimes. In Kortrijk it went well because Kristof Jonckheere had taken the lead in finding places and he had a quite high position.

L

In Tallinn we had a very nice team. The person that worked with us, Eneli Järs had enough time and a lot of experience. She was really inspired by the project and personally dedicated. She even said she herself was becoming 'something of a performer'. She said she chose her dress depending on who she was going to meet to present LFEO. She had a similar experience to the one we had, adapting a bit to the place. She was translating the project more than selling it.

S

While you were 'selling' the LFEO project, did you ever feel like you were taking on a role or a persona?

M

As Kristien said, I had to be more self-convinced than usual. Sometimes, I needed courage to call contacts, I had to get over something. Emailing was easier than calling. It didn't feel like performing, but still it wasn't my normal self that would call some people up.

E

I also had a LFEO dress to make me look more mature and serious.

K

Me too.

E

I still have it and it feels like a costume.

M

In Antwerp, the head of Extra City contacted the places herself. The first talk with her was really inspiring and she had so many good ideas but the organization was so small that she ultimately didn't find the time to do it. In general, everybody underestimated how much work it was. You could repeat a thousand times that it would take a lot of energy and time, and still people would always underestimate it.

S

It's not only about the concrete time but also about the mental space. You have to become that other person, and then do the follow-up. You can't just say that you'll work on it later.

E

No, it's all the time.
(general laughter)

K

Also, if you take it seriously, you get into this guerrilla mode. 'I wanna go everywhere.'

E

I had my own objectives in Ghent. It became very important.

K

I can't remember if we received that many 'no's' from Brussels. I really had the time to take it super-seriously, and I met everybody personally, even several times. People had a lot of confidence in the project because they saw how serious it was in terms of organization. It wasn't sloppy. Sometimes they have this idea that artists are never on time, etc. To me it was really like going for a job application.

M

I don't remember meeting a lot of people beforehand. I called a lot, but I didn't meet so many people.

S

I think you all had your own personal style in doing this.

E

I had the feeling that when I could go to them, then I could get a 'yes'. Because then you can talk face to face, it gets much more personal, you have a connection, we have a project together. It's more complicated to say 'no' there than during a phone call.

S

Someone once said that LFEO is 'deceptively simple'. It appears very simple in the fiction or in the narrative: there's this person who drops in on a meeting, says this text and then disappears again. But you were doing most of the work behind the scenes: the first contact, the coordination, the planning, the logistics, the feedback calls, etc. How do you frame that big invisible part of the project?

K

You want to name that role?

S

For me, it's almost intrinsic that something that appears so simple—well, it's like a magic trick—behind the trick… it's never simple. All the work happens under the table, in the pockets, behind the back, etc. in order for it to appear that simple. For the performers it was very important that you were there as was the care you gave them. So the performer only had to perform. All the other work was done by you in terms of how do we get there, where do we wait, when do we enter, what sentence will be said by the contact person, which position in the meeting does the contact person have, etc. You prepared all that so they could emerge like the white rabbit pulled out of the magician's hat…

K

I think you're right, the lecture doesn't begin when you start to speak. It's not only those 15 minutes, but the whole thing…

M

But for most people in the meetings, this is only the thing, it's only these 15 minutes. Most people don't know anything about everything that goes on before or after.

E

I felt really together with the performers. Whether it was Mylène, Anabela or you. I felt like we were doing it together.

K

It's a bit like the role of a mediator. By then I also felt very close to the contact person inside the meeting and had a lot of respect for the risk they were taking. I wanted to protect them sometimes. You could hear the text anew through their ears.

E

I agree. That was the other part. You also felt the energy as the lecture was going on. You really felt with your contact person, 'Oh, perhaps it will be difficult…'

L

I think that some people—with the part where you say, 'Yesterday I was there, tomorrow I will go there, and today I'm here with you…'—realized that it was part of a bigger project, a network. It was even presented in different countries, so some people then maybe also realized what kind of work was behind it. I don't want to say they had respect for the work we did in the planning process, but just a feeling that it was really about living together and that you meant it—realizing, 'She really goes to different places, and I'm part of this experiment right now'.

On a more personal note it was great to be able to learn how to bring together different worlds with different values, necessities, etc. For instance, the performer often needed to concentrate and have some privacy. The contact person needed some support during this stressful moment of sneaking us into the building. The group we were visiting needed to be reassured: this is a surprise, but you're safe, we will be gone in 17 minutes. It was really great to do the managing and the mediating between different actors that met in that very specific moment. Maybe the process of preparing added to the question of how to live together, because they could see how long it took to prepare the performance and the effort that was needed to visit another 'milieu' in this society, a place where you are an intruder.

I often thought about how we live in a world of different, separate and sometimes interconnected groups. It's interesting to see the difficulties but also the creativity that sometimes happens when you try to bring the groups together that are usually rather separate.

M

I've always felt privileged to be able to sneak into all these different worlds, where I would normally never go.

E

I completely agree.

S

Do you think that the project had an impact? If so, what kind of impact?

L

It's very tempting to answer with my own projection. I would say the impact is this and that, but then I realize this is my vision, or this is the impact it has on me. And the impact on the people was, at least from what

I heard, so different. For some people it was very personal. They reflected on their own life and situations. Others took it on a more conceptual level—the level of their teams or the company they were working for. Still others took it on the level of society. And then you don't know if it had an impact right then, or whether the impact lasted, whether it impacted them later on. I can imagine all these impacts happened—the whole panorama of impacts, but it's hard to say to who or when.

K

I agree. It's the same text but you know people will pull it to them, so it's not the same anymore. It goes to the individual, the group, the organization, etc. They all pull it to them, which is fine. For me, where it most addresses a collective is the idea of 'the impossible is possible'. That did radiate somewhere: somebody had this idea, and through art…—that kind of courage: if you want, you can organize yourself to make things better. Or at least to produce another discourse where you make things possible. You shift the way you speak about collectivity, about being human, about relating, etc. It's a big mountain to climb, but it's possible.

M

Do you mean that's the impact it had on you or the people?

K

On me, as facilitator, but you know you're not the only facilitator —there was also the contact person. You're doing the same kind of job. Mediating between two registers of speech. I'm also projecting, of course. So it's not just the impact on me, but the hope, what I would have liked to see, what I project to have seen—the idea that the impossible is possible, if you organize yourself around it. It's the creating of a collective, not just through words but by aligning the energy on that side.

S

You've all heard me or another performer say the text many times. Were there instances in the text or in the performance, the appearance, that would always touch you, or did it very much depend on each place?

K

It depended very much on the place. Sometimes it was very surprising. Sometimes it felt like I was hearing something for the first time.

M

I agree. I remember certain places where the word 'power' really fell on the table. It depended a lot on where we were.

L

Each time, I felt like I was listening anew. You listen to the text, but you also observe and feel the resonance the text has on the group. So each time the listening experience is very different. I remember the part in the beginning of the text, where you say that you don't want to sell them or teach them anything, where you cut away all the thoughts people might have like 'What's this now?', 'What's she doing here?' These options—not teaching, not selling, not convincing, etc.—fall away more and more, and you end up with 'She's just here, just to say something'. That was a great moment each time, because people were really blank at that moment as they realized it was just about sitting together and letting things happen. Someone is speaking to us without any underlying intention. The only intention was to share the moment. It was always great to arrive at that atmosphere, how people would sit together, while before there was always suspicion.

S

Do you think a certain kind of person or personality is needed to give LFEO, both on the side of the performer and on your side, the collaborators? There are also only women behind it—not a coincidence. What skill, personality, attitude do you need to be behind this project?

E

You need to be courageous.

M

You need to be very open and at the same time you need a kind of—I don't know if this is the right word—softness.

E

You need the quality to be together, to connect. To adapt to people, in such a way that it's possible to connect—even though it's always the same words, even though it's the same strategy.

L

I think the person presenting the text has to be able to reflect the projection people might have on them and handle it—which is quite a big task, one I couldn't do. In this respect, we don't have a very varied experience because all the performers were women, all were white and most were young. As a performer, you have to handle the kind of vibes people send out to you or what they might think of you when you enter—as a white, young, slim woman. It would be different if you're not slim, for instance. The person would have to handle that in the very moment, while also presenting the text, which is totally challenging. I don't know what kind of experiences we would have had if we had had other performers… I know I'm speaking about stereotypes, but you can't deny that it makes a difference when entering a group. This is something one must be aware of and must also be able to handle.

E

You can't be too theatrical. You have to be there as a person who makes the connection.

K

You have to be like an 'empathetic alien'.

S

That's like the icon of LFEO.

K

Yes. And I agree with Linda —we shouldn't be naive—it's not the total alien that comes in, it's actually somebody who is very close to them. It's recognizable but then it adopts a position, like 'I'm not one of you'.

S

I also put this question to the contact persons and they came up with completely different things. One person said it wouldn't have mattered at all if I'd been a 60-year-old man, but another said that the fact that I was young could have undermined the whole thing, in the sense of not having been taken seriously. A consideration along the way for me became very much this slim-bodied whiteness, which was very difficult to negotiate because of the risk of tokenizing and maybe exposing people in the other direction: what does it mean, who does this, and then also depending on the context. For instance, I went as a white person to Wi Masanga, a Surinamese meeting place in Rotterdam, where it suddenly became all about being white.

In the beginning with Kristien I talked a lot about trying to be just anyone, but that's just not possible, just by your sheer looks. I thought we had worked very well on the costume, that we would blend in everywhere, whereas the guy from IBM told me how he knew directly I was an artist just by the way I was dressed. And I thought I had done my best.

K

They still recognized you as an alien.

S

Yes, no matter how much you disguise yourself.

K

Which bodies do we let speak in the public space? On the one hand, privileged bodies indeed, but on the other hand, and you can see this now in the climate discussions, bodies are read and judged according to whether or not they are consistent. For instance, very concretely: you can't say anything about the climate if you fly too much, or if you wear Nikes, etc. There is a purging that is happening that is really problematic: nobody can say or think anything anymore publicly if you first have to be 100 per cent consistent, if we reject bodies on the grounds of inconsistency. How does the LFEO body relate to that? A body that is difficult to read: it cannot be written off as inconsistent because we know nothing about it, and also a body that uses its privilege to enter public space.

S

How do you look at the project in hindsight? How do you reflect on it, personally, artistically, politically, professionally?

M

It has brought me to places where I would otherwise never have been. It feels as if I have 'seen the world' a bit. I've always found LFEO to be a very challenging project. For you, but also for me personally—it was a challenge to help find all those places and to go there—sometimes very exciting. But it was also a project that gave a lot back—by going to all those places, hearing your text again and again in all those different contexts, hearing and seeing all those reactions, etc. There were definitely negative reactions, but I remember especially a lot of warmth.

E

I learned intrusiveness from it. I do that in my work now, I visit companies all the time. I go and perform plays about communication on different topics. It takes one hour and a half and then we're gone.

L

It helped me to understand that things are more complex than I had thought. I became aware that I had a lot of prejudices about what kind of people work in what environment. I realized how everything is mixed up and complex. The negotiations of your own personal values are complex. How do you become an individual in a work context? It strengthened my desire to really listen to people and to get rid of my prejudices. I realized how it separates me from people when I stick to my own bubble, values, social field. Workwise, it helped to sharpen the questions about where I want to work and put my energy in. And what has an impact really? Before LFEO, I naively thought that so-called political artistic projects have an impact. But then I realized that it wasn't always the case—even less so if they happen in a black box, like a theatre. It helped me to reflect on the impact of the work I'm involved in. Maybe I got a more realistic and engaged vision of those questions.

E

It made me want to learn more about connecting and communicating. So afterwards I started a postgraduate course in coaching. The theory is simple but exploring, really going through with your question and trying to visualise what the other wants to say is tough.

K

Making the impossible possible: to see, also for myself, that you have a capacity to do things and organize yourself around it. So that's both on a personally emancipatory level and in my relation to society.

S

This talk's been very interesting for me because it speaks precisely from the perspective of organizing and its importance. Maybe it has even more weight than the performance itself. The capacity to organize and connect through a project. And to translate ideas into strategies and tools that are transferable to a next organization or institution.

From public maintenance department to union meeting

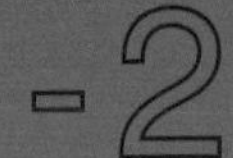

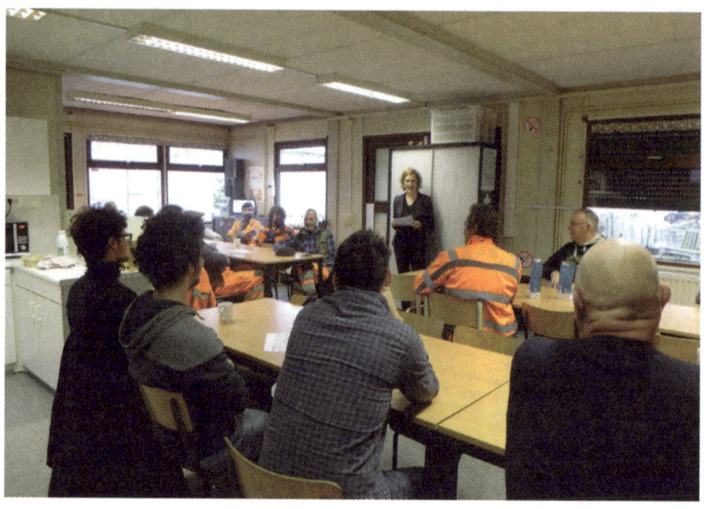

'Normally they're not quiet so easily. The fact that they sat and listened so attentively means a lot. In their group, the item "living together" comes up a lot, the multicultural aspect is very present and they talk about it often. When Sarah talks about "different faces, different bodies...", it's a very recognizable situation for them.

After that they talked for a while about "power", the word that Sarah gives them at the end. They mainly talked about power in the negative sense: abuse of power, powerlessness, greed for power. Many found it very clever how Sarah performed the text before a group that was totally unknown to her. They felt personally addressed, with her looking directly at them and making eye contact. It was also uncomfortable, but still fun. Someone thought he'd seen Sarah on TV before. The story of the taxi driver had stuck with many—there are a lot of young dads in the group, so they felt it spoke to them directly. One of the men fled Afghanistan himself (and had to leave his wife and children there) and for him that story was very recognizable.

Thinking about a catastrophe wasn't difficult either: many thought about something bad that could happen to their children'.

PROGRESS Lawyers Network Antwerp, law office. Weekly team meeting.

Some feedback

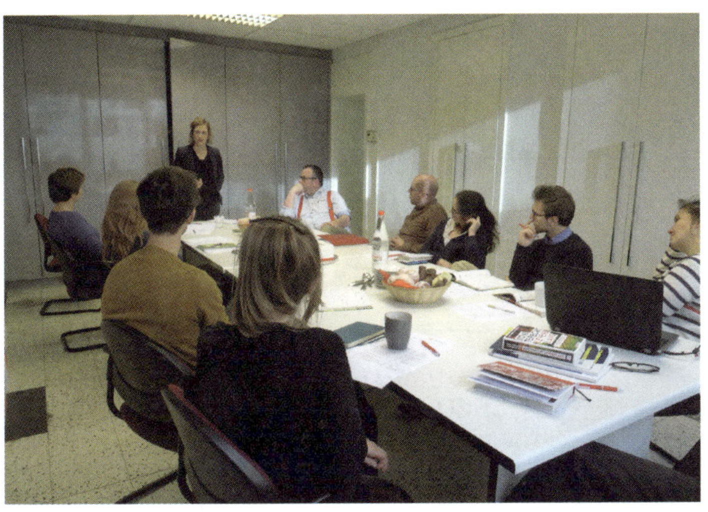

'It's good to hear extracts from the Universal Declaration of Human Rights. That's the ABC of what we do. We should read it more often and tell each other.'

Anonymous. Weekly meeting.

Conversation between Linda (LFEO collaborator) and our contact person

'What was LFEO like for you and your team?

LFEO was a pleasure, they enjoyed it. It meant stepping out of the normal daily routine and thinking about things. The guys are not used to this kind of thing, they usually don't hang around with performing artists.

LFEO was unusual—both the content and the action of interrupting a meeting. We usually don't do that in the office. The guys usually don't think about meanings. They only think about money.

Do you include yourself when you say 'the guys'?

No, I think about meanings all the time.

Maybe it's necessary for them to think only about money? Maybe it's part of the system mentioned in the text?

If they stopped thinking about money, they'd find that their life is meaningless and they'd leave the company. The company would fall apart.

And that's something you don't want.

Of course not.

But maybe it's possible to work without having a completely meaningless life?

Yes, meaningfulness is important, but we don't want too much of that. Otherwise everyone would just walk around barefoot and have spiritual revelations. Capitalism as we know it would have no meaning anymore, wouldn't work anymore.

And do we want to avoid that?

Yes. Well, we could do a revolution, but first we should earn a lot of money. And when we have that, we can do the revolution.

Maybe there's something in-between total meaninglessness and walking around barefoot.

Everything in moderation.'

ATHENS	01.12.2014	7:15 P.M.
Greek in the Agora, association for newcomers, run by volunteers. Greek class.	Some feedback from our contact person	

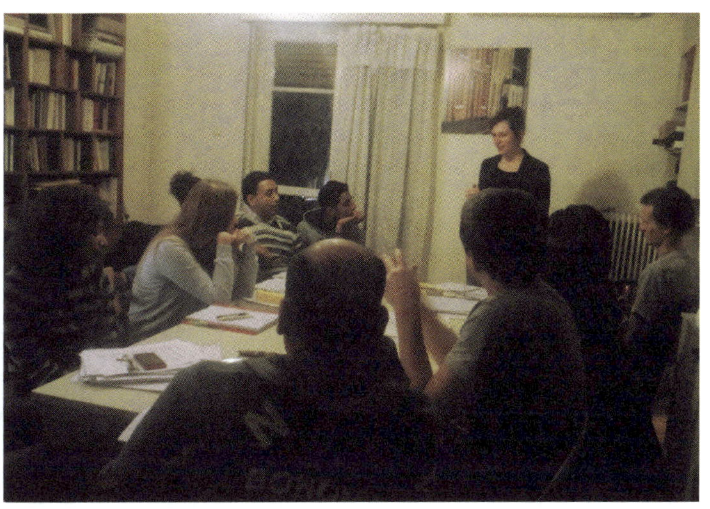

'The class thought that the text was about thoughts they all have. The part that touched everyone the most was the part about the catastrophe since everyone in the class has faced different ones.

The performance lifted everyone's spirits.

I think that Sarah was very sweet, charming and sensitive. Even her appearance, her way of speaking and moving around was a piece of art itself. I admired her for her courage to invade a group and talk about so many personal thoughts in such a sensitive way.

I didn't think of the Greek situation in the part about the catastrophe. I thought about an immigrant from Syria that the group shelters in the house where the class takes place, or two of the students from Ukraine who don't know if they'll ever be able to go back home.

I think the part about the catastrophe doesn't apply to Greece because in order to define what's happening here you need a word that describes a slow death.

For me the project was art. Descriptions such as "social experiment" or "political art" would give the project a very strict and aggressive description which wouldn't be true.

I was very happy to have it presented to my class, but before the lecture I felt scared and insecure.'

ATHENS

National and Kapodistrian University of Athens. Postgraduate class of the Communication and Mass Media department.

02.12.2014 | 8:45 P.M.

Some feedback from our contact person

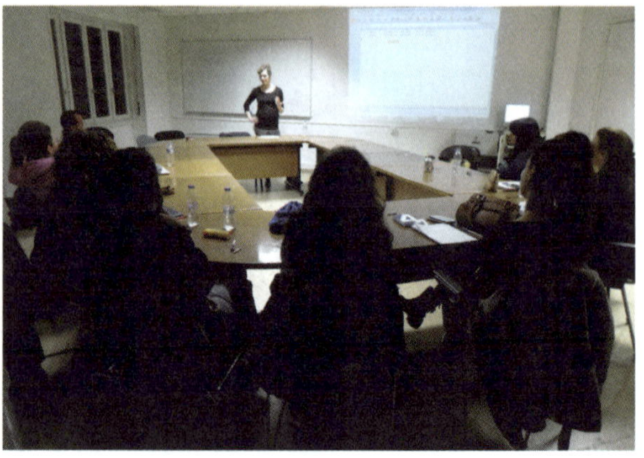

'Several people were astonished by the notions, words and ideas.

One girl said she was shocked by the content of LFEO: by the questions, by the thoughts about how we interact with people, about daily life.

It was different, it was beyond the university lectures the group is used to hearing.

I think that LFEO posed questions to investigate our psychological minds and show our faces. Sarah read what's on our minds through our faces.

LFEO was useful. It put the students outside the academic procedure and into life's procedure.

Within 15 minutes, people got really engaged through their interaction with Sarah, the text and their own thoughts.

(During LFEO, police sirens could be heard down the street.) Over the past four years this has been our daily life. The police is in front of the university, whether or not demonstrations like yesterday are going on. It's a district with a lot of banks and the police is there to guard them. This is a common spectacle for us. That's how power interferes with our daily life. As individuals we are part of political, financial and social systems. Personal daily life interacts with the social context of this big city, Athens, and the current state of Greece.

We are individual creatures and social creatures at the same time, in a political context. LFEO makes us reflect on our behaviour. Things like commercialization and freedom don't have to do only with each of us as individuals, but also with the systems we are part of. Both dimensions—the system and the individual being—co-existed in the lecture.

LFEO has elements from the fields of philosophy, art and politics. The artistic element is probably the way in which Sarah addresses the audience and captures the attention, the way things are said.'

betterplace.org, donation platform.
Organizational meeting.

Some feedback from our contact person

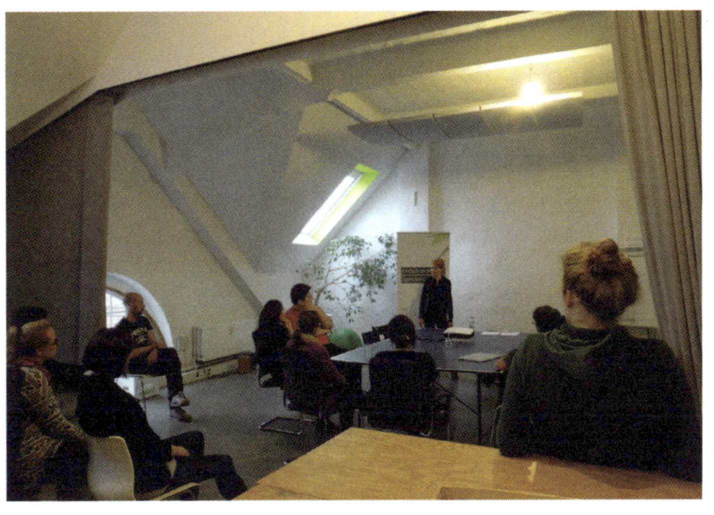

'After you left, everyone was smiling a bit. Everyone was lost in their thoughts… The atmosphere after LFEO was different than usual: it was silent.

People gathered in small groups to talk about LFEO, or left to go home, or went back to work.

It was interesting to hear something completely different from what we usually deal with.

Of course words like "care" are familiar to us. But we work outwards, we help to realize projects. In the case of LFEO, "care" was related to us personally and to us as a team—that was unusual. You normally don't connect those notions to yourself. Also, the text used vocabulary that was different to what we use.

No specific part of the text was more meaningful than others to me, but I was astonished by the calm that came up at some point, I can't remember at which part of the text. After the questions there was complete silence. And the whole presentation created a particularly calm atmosphere, which is unusual.'

taz, daily newspaper. Daily editorial meeting of the department heads.

06.10.2014 | 9:30 A.M.

Some feedback from our contact person

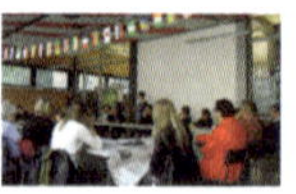

'LFEO created a very special atmosphere. There was an unusual, concentrated silence. They weren't even playing with their phones!

After LFEO, the meeting went on straight away, which was a bit odd—it was as if the lecture hadn't taken place as the performer disappeared so quickly. Many people discussed it informally afterwards and some people posted things on Facebook.

Some said that they didn't dare to look too enthusiastic or positive, so on Facebook they messaged each other saying they "caught" someone smiling. It's very typical of this work environment not to be too positive about things, one should always be critical first and not find something too good. So maybe their facial expressions conveyed their attempt to remain distanced.

It might be a journalists' disease: they probably couldn't listen to the text as an audience, couldn't think of themselves simply as listeners, but immediately perceived it the way a reporter would, analysing it, thinking about the context and the reasons for doing such a project. This is a problem with journalists—they never stop being journalists.

The seriousness and the presence of the performer were very impressive. It is unusual to hear such serious words in the morning.

It's a mixture of strong sentences, words, anecdotes and then more serious points that bring you back to reality. Many people found "We are before" very strong words.

In the text there is nothing you could criticize or take issue with—people can relate to the text more or less but it is difficult to criticize it, it's banal in that sense. They are all things that you can easily hear. The situation is what causes an irritation, the fact of not knowing what's going to happen, then listening to such an intense, serious text, especially so early in the morning.

Some people thought it wasn't enough of a surprise. They disliked the fact that I, the contact person, knew about it beforehand, they thought it should be a real surprise for everyone, someone just turning up.

I wanted to invite LFEO because I wanted to be given a lecture, a lesson. I was a bit scared beforehand but I think bringing culture to other places is a good thing and I'm proud that I contributed to making it happen.

Some people, one editor in particular, thought that this shows that theatre has lost its relevance: because no one wants to go to the theatre anymore, now theatre has to go out and seek its audience itself.

Some people thought it was like a morning prayer.'

Saint Elmo's, communication and marketing agency. Weekly team meeting.

An email from an employee / Some feedback from our contact person

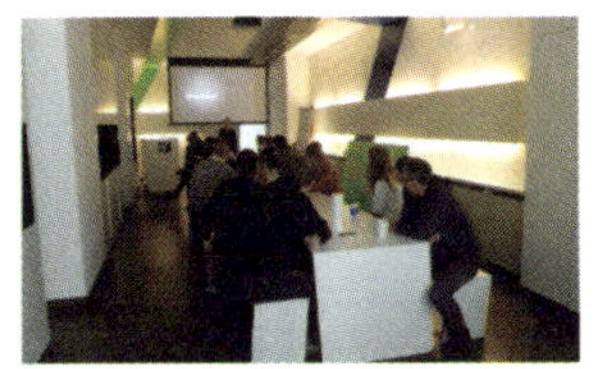

An email from an employee:

'I found the presentation very pleasant. Interesting questions were asked—they were not really "new" but still we speak and reflect too little about them, especially in the direct working environment. Most of all I remember the question about whether we think we have more or less money than her, the performer. That's totally irrelevant, because "enough" money is a totally individual impression, and having "more or less" than the other shouldn't matter.

I found it amusing how obviously unpleasant some of the questions were for some of the colleagues. They started to giggle because these are important questions but, obviously, they don't think about it, or think about it rarely.

All in all, a great action!'

Some feedback from our contact person:

'The thoughts represented in LFEO have a deepness that concerns us because we work precisely in the field of quick communication, superficial online social networking, advertising. One can say that we, Saint Elmo's, are in part guilty of all of that.

I felt provoked, but in a good way. These are inputs you don't necessarily want to hear.

I agreed to invite LFEO because you don't move forward when always only speaking to people with the same opinions. I could just as well talk to myself.

People working in culture and the arts are people who reflect on the world and have something to say about it. That's a precious input I wanted to bring to the company.

I especially liked the beginning of LFEO, where Mariel, the performer, says she wants to reach the people directly (not on Facebook, etc). I think it's clear that this "old school communication", personal live contact between people, still works best.

It's clever to do it as a surprise. If you were to announce it, people would have expectations. People are used to googling everything, reading comments about everything, before they personally experience things. And people are bored so easily. Spontaneity gives them a punch, and an authentic moment. I think that's the idea of LFEO, to do something real.'

BERLIN

LKJ, state umbrella association for cultural youth education. Monthly team meeting.

07.10.2014 | 1:00 P.M.

Some feedback from our contact person

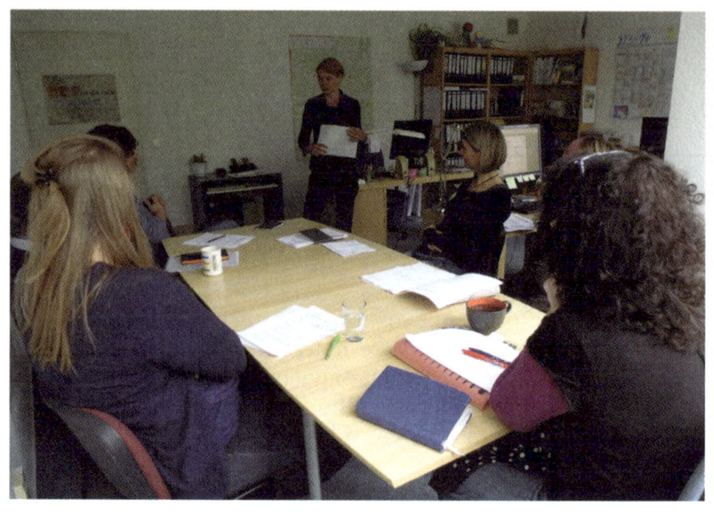

'LFEO works like a brake, therefore it has the effect of deceleration. It gave us the chance to meet each other in a different way than usually. After LFEO, people actually wanted to have a break, go out for a walk. But we didn't have the time.'

Otis Elevator Company.
Development centre meeting.

Some feedback from our contact person

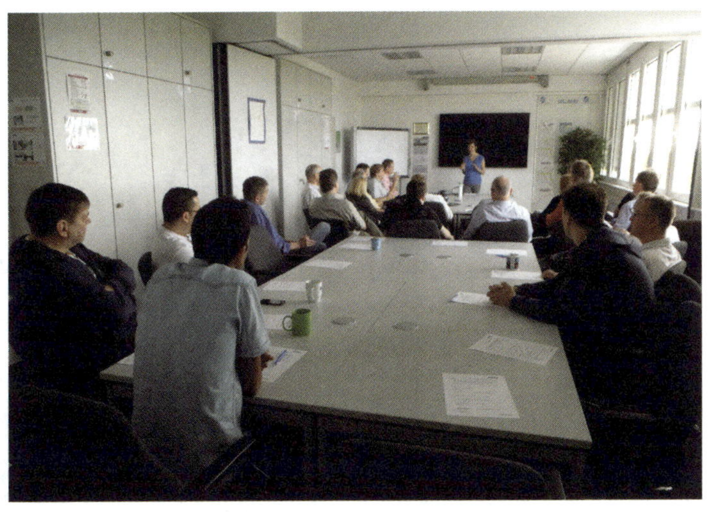

'Ninety per cent of the people had only positive reactions to LFEO, except for one man who found it absolutely horrible. Everybody was impressed by the boss: we appreciated that he had taken the risk to accept and invite LFEO. The boss himself also liked it a lot—both the text and the art performance.

All the people in the meeting are engineers, so people are most probably not interested in the arts. They're sort of the opposite of artists. They think technically, less emotionally. But alright, maybe that's my personal prejudice...

Speaking in an emotional way is unusual for our work context. I would describe LFEO in the following way: We live in a system, wake up and realize that. Sarah is somehow saying: Take some time with me, have a break, think about human things. Are you caring? Are you loving? And then there's the word "power". It's like a call, saying: If you don't agree, then do something, you have the power.

One person said that in the words part, he had expected "hope" to be one of the words.'

BERLIN

Café Wippe, Berlin support for gay men.
Weekly open meeting point and café.

10.10.2014 | 3:00 P.M.

Some feedback from our contact person

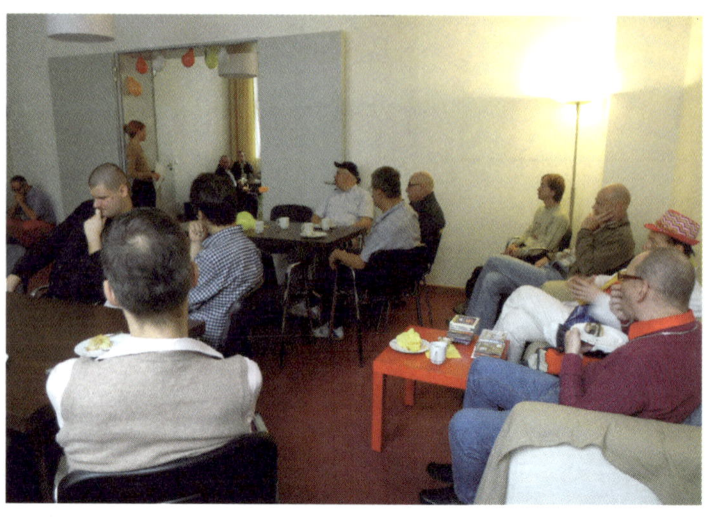

'There were only positive reactions to LFEO.

The people at the gay meeting point are men with psychological problems. It's unusual to have this concentrated atmosphere here for 15 minutes. But Mariel has a wonderful voice that makes you want to listen to her. That's strange because people didn't even know her, her appearance was a surprise, but still all of them wanted to listen to her.

For the people at the café, "We are before" meant that they were really living this moment together, it was good to become more attentive to that.

Our people are very often alone. LFEO shows that we are together, here.

It was good to have LFEO as a surprise because you can also speak too much about things in advance, you can "out-talk" things when you already know about something beforehand.

The people at the café are not "brainy". They stand in the fringes of society. For our people, the café is something special. And then having a surprise there is even more special. It was meaningful that they were addressed personally, that they were asked for their opinion, that the text called them "you". Also, the invitation to the public talk was meaningful. The invitation meant, "You are invited, you are important".'

BERLIN

LFS Financial Systems GmbH, consulting and management company. Argumentation training for international junior managers.

13.10.2014 | 9:00 A.M.

Some feedback from our contact person

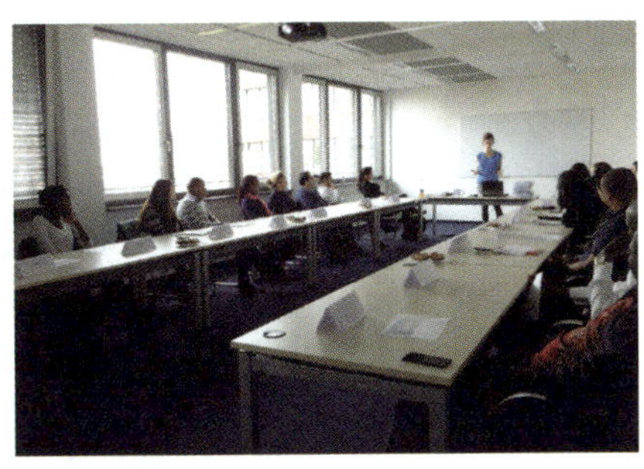

'It was a pleasant experience. The group usually has trouble concentrating on things whereas during the lecture they were very focused. The laughter seemed to be due to nervosity and insecurity, uncertainty as to what was coming and how to deal with it.

I think they sometimes felt criticized, they reacted very defensively, especially when the idea of a catastrophe was mentioned and they replied that they were not a catastrophe. Being defensive or making something look ridiculous can be a way of not letting the message get to yourself, so maybe that's why they reacted like that.

During my break I caught myself thinking about some of the questions the lecture raised. I found it an emotional text. The moment when the text mentions the world we are part of, the people we communicate and live with, and how we communicate using digital networks touched me particularly.

I was happy with the lecture, but because I felt responsible for it, I was always a bit on edge. I was worried that the part about the carpet might make the group uncomfortable or shock them, as sexuality is a taboo in some of their cultures, so I was relieved when that part was over. That was the only bit I thought might be difficult or critical, the rest was fine.

The people are quite used to criticism of the system. However, in some of their cultures it's not usual to think about yourself, about what you want or feel so I thought this might be a bit of a shock to the group. In the countries they are from, they focus on performance, on numbers, reaching their financial targets at the end of the month. Therefore taking the time, even just 10 minutes to think about yourself, is a big thing to do, so the lecture was quite foreign to them.

I particularly enjoyed the part with the four words (care, freedom, love and power)—this was the most powerful moment to me. The fact that the performer said "power" but didn't expand on it, unlike with the other words, struck me. It also seemed very interesting and very fitting because the next modules on the same day focused on what it means to be a leader, whether you should exploit your power and whether hierarchies are natural.'

BERLIN

NHU, neighbourhood centre Urbanstrasse. Project meeting with long-term unemployed people.

13.10.2014 | 11:30 A.M.

Some feedback from our contact person

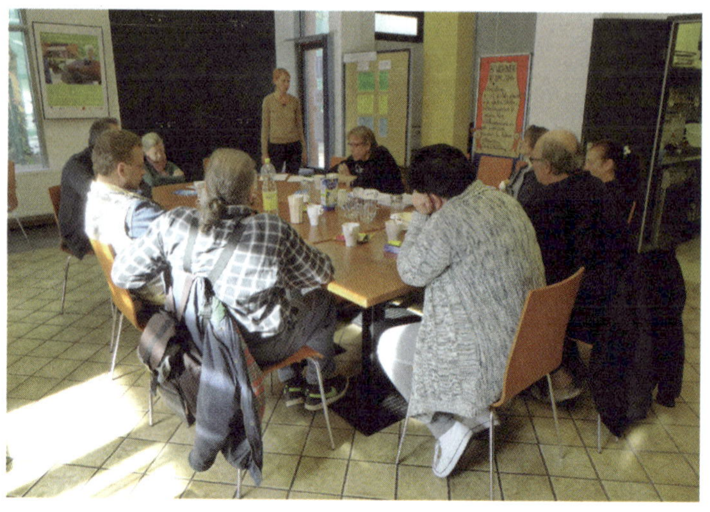

'For one woman, LFEO was somehow a trigger to open up. After you had left, she started to speak a lot, told the group some private things, things she didn't even talk about during individual talks. The group is not meant to be a therapy group, but I think this brought the group further.'

Eitner Security, security service / protection of property, watchkeeping, construction site guards. Team meeting.

Some feedback from our contact person

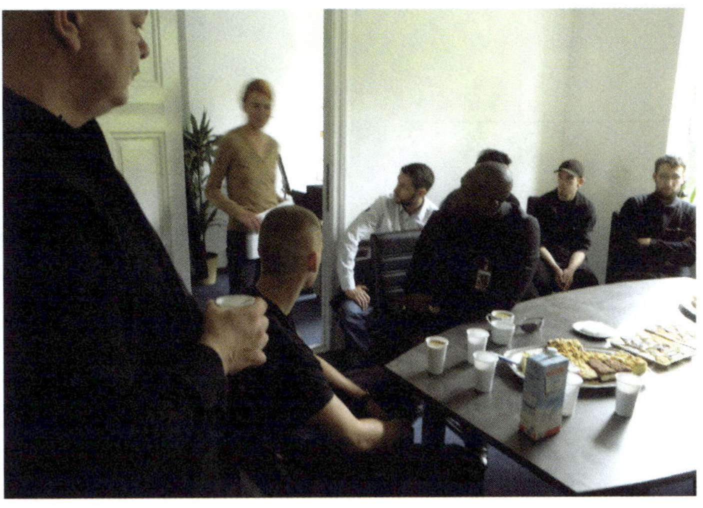

‘We had a lively discussion among colleagues. Some of our colleagues come from Cuba, the Dominican Republic, etc. They have a bigger horizon, because of their culture. They believe in God and go to church, so they’re more used to such words and texts. Others were born in Marzan Berlin, in a “Plattenbau”. They’re also good people, of course, but these people didn’t identify with LFEO.’

BERN

Society Club. Weekly lunch meeting.

15.09.2014 | 1:00 P.M.

Some feedback from our contact person

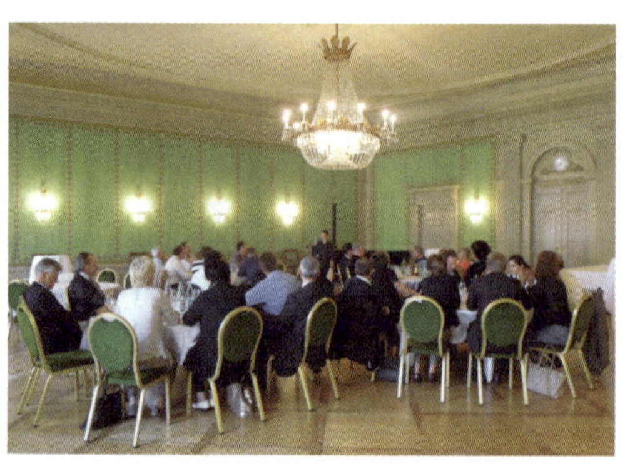

'People had very different opinions about LFEO, from very positive to very negative. Later that day it came to a big discussion.

Positive reactions:
LFEO was interesting because it uses a vocabulary we're used to from advertising, etc. (the freedom part), but it invites you to think further about what the words really mean. It was courageous of Carola to invite herself to the meeting. Someone is "interfering" in a context that is unknown to her, she is simply speaking to us about her thoughts. The "message" of LFEO were things that should matter to us as human beings.

One person said that at some point she found the text problematic and she would have liked to argue against it, but then the text made a turn and in the end it made sense to her. LFEO is an inspiring text that you have to open up to and listen to until the end.

I even received a phone call and an email from people thanking me for having invited LFEO.

Negative reactions:
One man said: "If something like this happens again, I'll never come back". Some people were really scandalized by LFEO, but they didn't speak about the text as such, they were just offended by the fact that a stranger had appeared and spoken uninvited. The ones that did not appreciate LFEO just shut down right from the start and didn't listen to the text at all. If the problem was about not understanding LFEO, they could have asked, and not just close up. Then we probably would have had an interesting discussion. If you don't like LFEO, then you have to explain why, talk about the content of the thing—not only about the action of interrupting an official meeting.

LFEO provoked a lively discussion and very contradictory opinions, which was interesting. This is a provocation that is pleasant, that is wanted.'

Aquitanis. Public office for accommodation in Bordeaux. Meeting on the site of BTP Archi.

Some feedback from our contact person

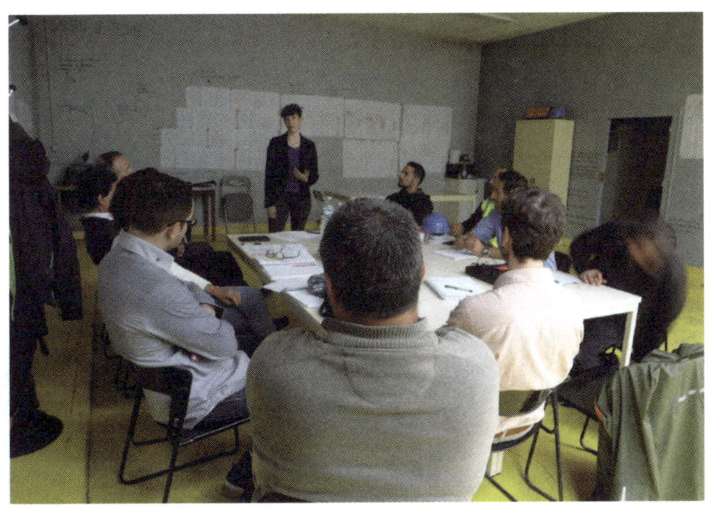

'After Lara had left, there was a long moment of silence, a moment of peace and astonishment. Smiles everywhere. It wasn't an easy meeting, so everyone was very gentle. Finally someone said, "So, shall we start?", and the others laughed, knowing that this was a technical meeting to begin with—not easy after LFEO.

It's a meeting of people who are not actual friends. These are people who have contracts, who are mostly asked to make money. It's about technical and economic issues, and the atmosphere can be tense between people.

The most striking thing for me was "the moment", but also the other moments of silence in the text. And also words like "care". My job, as the person responsible for the renovation of the former secondary school, is closely tied to the notion of living together. But this term is found everywhere today. LFEO puts forward other sensitivities in relation to this term.

LFEO introduced a change of rhythm. People are used to being very active in meetings, but there, everything was slow.

One woman said she was touched by the way Lara looked at people. She directed her gaze at them. It was touching.

I work a lot with Roma. In LFEO I recognized some of the experiences I've had with these people: words are less important than being there. In meetings with them, it's less about contextual things and more about emotions and sensations. It's about small gestures. And it's the small gestures that make us human. Like Lara's gaze directed at each person, not just at the whole group. And the way she stood.'

BORDEAUX	10.06.2015	2:35 P.M.
Constructor, social landlord and developer. Budget meeting.	Some feedback from our contact person	

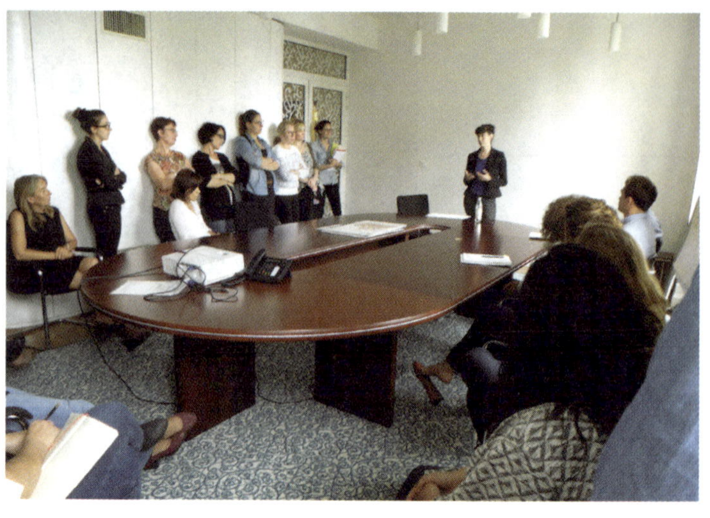

'There were opposing views: LFEO is sad vs not sad at all, theoretical vs very concrete. Or we could say that LFEO is just realistic, talks about the world we live in. But the phrase "We are before", for example, indicates that we can influence this situation, we have the choice to live differently.

There was a lot of discussion about whether LFEO is dark or not. The director allowed time for discussion. Everyone stayed, no one left.

About a third of the group spoke about LFEO—it was remarkable that these were also people who usually don't say much, don't see anything.

The group was very disconcerted by the silences. Silences have an important role in LFEO, they're unsettling. We're not used to them. Usually the group is fighting over the right to speak. We don't know whether the silence is questioning us or not.

LFEO really shook me up. And it still does. After LFEO, I wanted to send everyone out for a walk. LFEO makes us distance ourselves from the agenda, makes us think, "In the end, nothing is all that important".'

European School of Podology, Brussels.
English course.

Some feedback from our contact person

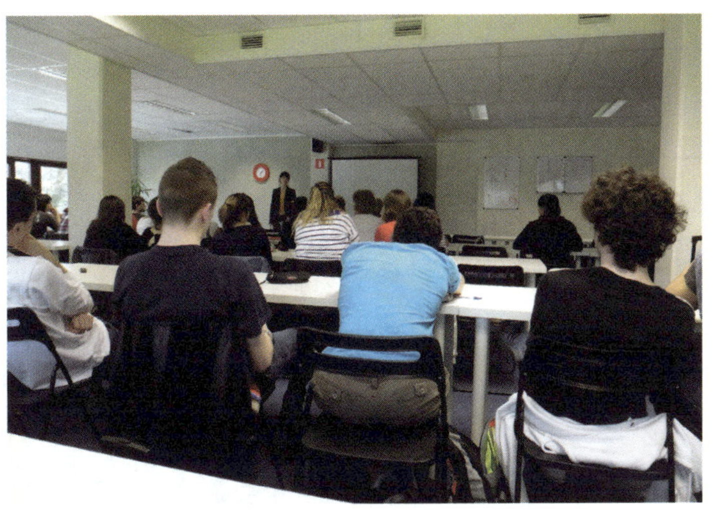

'I didn't teach afterwards, we continued talking about LFEO. Everybody was deeply moved—me, the director and the students, even the "bad boys" in the back. After class they came to me and said they were really impressed. It was a gift, and a political act. It made everybody think about what we're doing here. Some felt like dropping out of school and travelling; others wanted to be better humans, taking care of other people; some felt like making art, being more creative.'

BRUSSELS

BECI, Brussels Enterprises Commerce and Industry. Executive committee.

15.05.2013 | 7:00 P.M.

Some feedback from our contact person

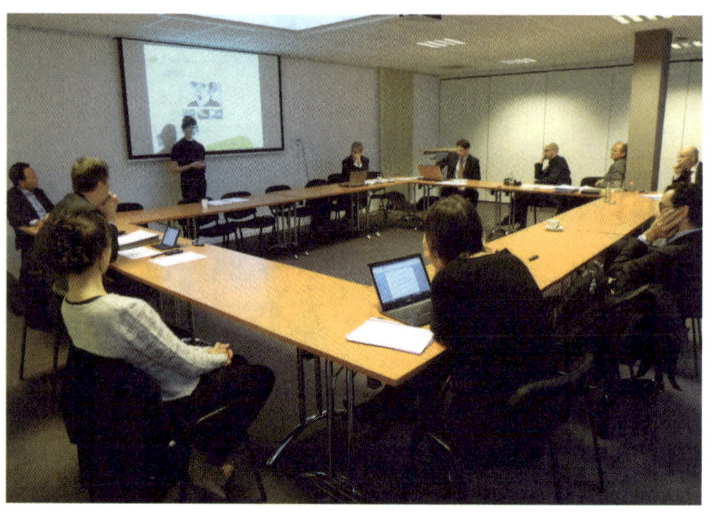

'I only heard very positive feedback, people were touched, including people I didn't expect it from.

The text didn't really speak to me as someone of the organization of BECI, but rather as an individual.

But you do answer questions differently when you think of yourself as a father, man, woman, family head or entrepreneur.'

BRUSSELS

Natagora, a nature protection organization.
Meeting Communication department.

15.05.2013 | 10:00 A.M.

Some feedback from our contact person

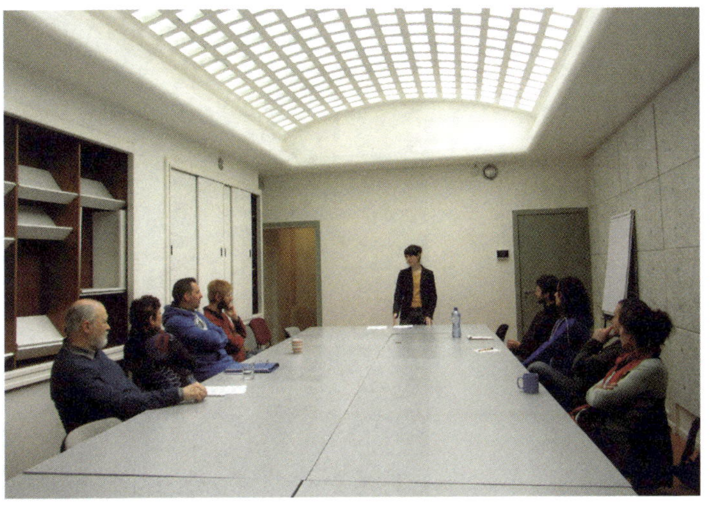

'LFEO happened on a special day: the meeting took place because two weeks ago someone had been fired and for the first time the team was meeting to discuss this. Everyone was tense. I was afraid it was a very bad day to bring LFEO—as the person responsible I was afraid of how my colleagues would react. But actually it was the best day to bring LFEO to Natagora: it had a concrete result, the meeting became human instead of being aggressive as everybody expected, which was appreciated by everybody.

At first the text makes you feel very uncomfortable, but then with the taxi story you can relax and enjoy the discourse. I also observed a physical reaction in my colleagues, from tense to relaxed.

The text is all about humanity for me, I didn't perceive it in a political way. One girl expected a more political discourse, a text more about enterprises and our professional world. But it was more about personal issues, and that's another way of being political.'

BRUSSELS

Belgian company. Factory meeting within the ICT department.

13.05.2013 | 3:00 P.M.

Some feedback from our contact person

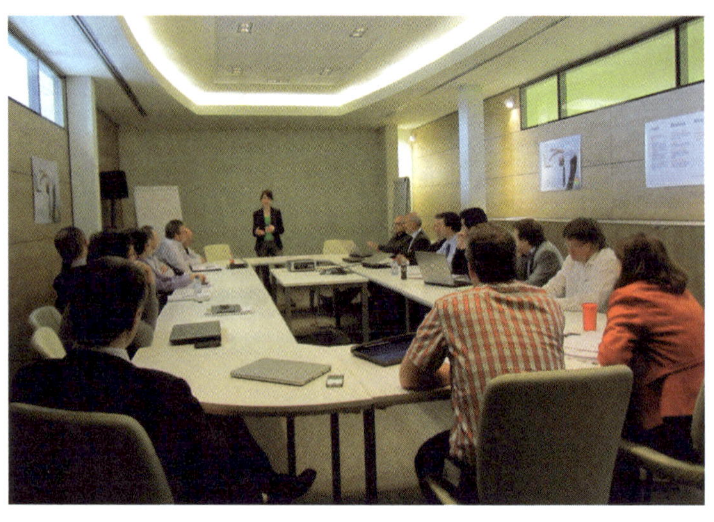

'The most common reactions within my team were: "quite confrontational", "very engaging", "quite heavy", "this is going to stay with us",...

The person who, after looking at the photograph taken, says himself that he does not seem to be very attentive, formulated it as follows:

"Jeez... I'm one of the only ones in the picture who doesn't seem to be paying attention. Yet I swear it captivated me and it was a totally surreal and unforgettable moment. Quite special, it's true..."'

BRUSSELS

BNP Paribas, a bank. Conversation table in the HR department.

21.05.2013 | 1:30 P.M.

Some feedback from our contact person

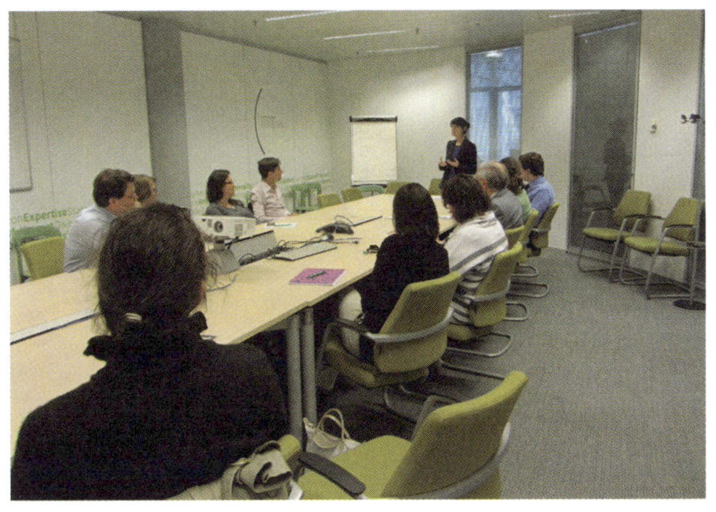

'The most important thought for me during LFEO was the question as to how different your lives (as artists) must be compared to mine. I go from meeting to meeting all day long. I think you're driven by a sort of idealism. That makes you do what you do. Entering groups that will probably be critical of your projects, but you go there anyway. You have courage.'

BRUSSELS

Multinational corporation.
European Affairs meeting.

17.05.2013 | 9:00 A.M.

Some feedback from our contact person

'The meeting lasted four hours, and only after, during lunch, did we start speaking about it. It's strange to bring something to the table and then not have much time to discuss it.

It was remarkable: never before was there so much silence at this table. It's a notorious table because normally they never stop speaking

The rhetoric of companies is always about being positive. You don't think in terms of problems, but in terms of challenges. You focus on what is strong, on winning. The discourse of LFEO is about being weak, about softness, love. It worked like a piranha at a pool party, but still I find it valuable.

I appreciated the personal aspect of it more than the political.

LFEO is critical towards society, but I see this as an attitude, as a different point of departure. I prefer to look at life positively, not from the perspective of what is vulnerable or fragile, and to start from what is feasible and desirable.'

Café Marché, an orchestra. Rehearsal.

Some feedback from our contact person

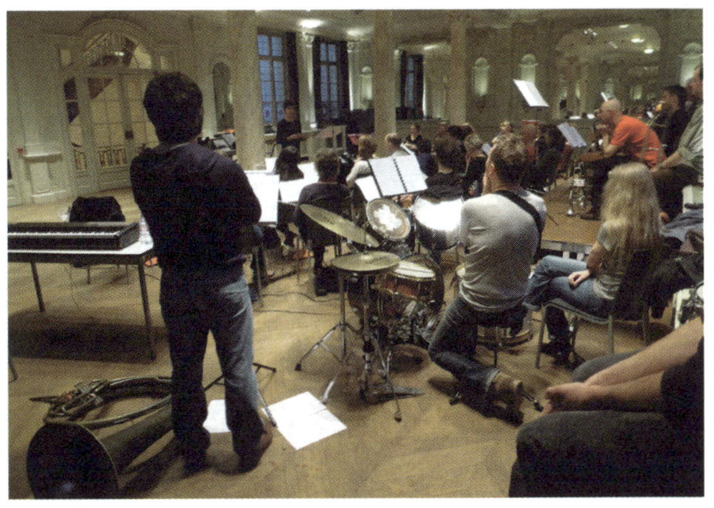

'LFEO was surprising and nice, we were impressed. Some of us had read about the project in the Kunstenfestivaldesarts programme or in the press and then it's extra weird when it enters your own meeting. It's very nice that you thought about us.

We were impressed by how the text was performed, with so much power, and how she looks at you! We didn't know whether we should answer the questions or not. One woman said afterwards, "We were so lazy, look at us, we didn't even dare to answer."

We were rehearsing for a show, and the conductors were afraid we wouldn't have time for this, but afterwards they said: "Time is very relative. Look at us: highly educated, Flemish, intellectual—and then we don't want to give up our time for this."'

European School of Administration.
Interinstitutional newcomers' training course.

Some feedback from our contact person

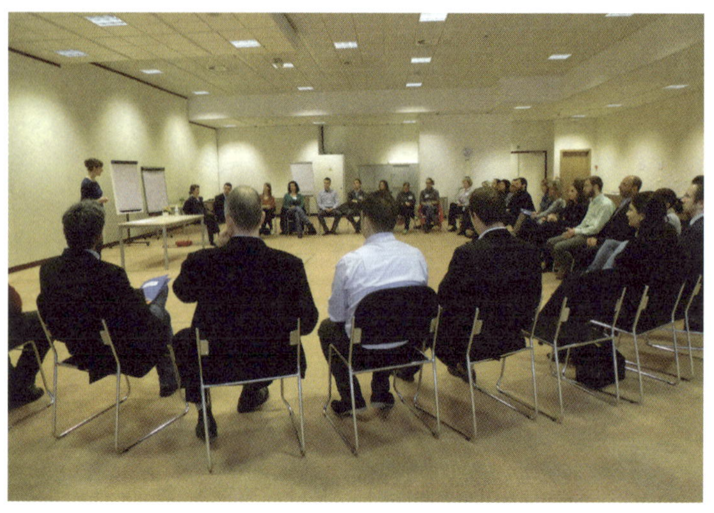

'LFEO is closely related to the subject of the course: how to deal with the system you don't understand as a newcomer, how to be a person and not just a civil servant, feelings of isolation, and building networks between people who might feel the same.

We are all individuals in two directions: when we speak about "the Commission", we forget that it's people like us; and the other way around: "the citizens" who are not happy about the European Union become abstractions.

In this environment, talking about emotions is a taboo. Europe is very high level, very powerful, hierarchical: you ignore emotions. LFEO pronounces these words in a politically incorrect way. I appreciated having Sarah there as an artist, independently.'

DARMSTADT	28.07.2014	7:15 P.M.
Concert choir. Last rehearsal before the upcoming Stockhausen concert.	One choir member posted the following comment on Facebook	

'I experienced the visit of the actress, who presented this standardized text here in Darmstadt during an extremely tiring rehearsal, and found this action to be totally misplaced. To me—and others told me the same thing—it was a disrespectful theft of other people's time and concentration. For me, doing such a thing, without presenting oneself and one's request, and without asking the listeners for permission, is simply arrogant. I wish we had been spared this visit!
I can therefore understand all those who don't want anything to do with such an action! The approach underlying the concept might be good—at least I suppose it was thought through?—, but the way in which it was implemented is bad! The concept of a caring, better togetherness—is that the basic idea behind all this?—is incomprehensible in this form, and the implementation isn't an example in itself. It only makes the compelled listeners unhappy and therefore can't work like that. Such actions demonstrate the absurdity of your own ideas. This is in fact a pity, and essentially even grotesque. An opportunity that was seized violently is thus wasted—wasted by you yourself!'

EVERGEM

Municipal Elementary School Belzele. Monthly meeting of the management and teachers of the nursery and primary school.

21.04.2015 | 5:00 P.M.

Some feedback from our contact person

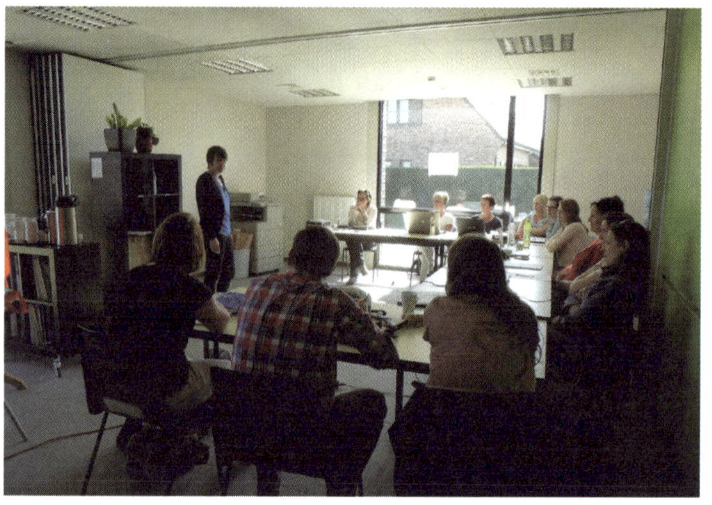

'The teachers liked it, they also liked the fact that someone like that would come, but they thought it was demanding for a meeting: "You have to listen so much already, and then there's that kind of text". The topics are really to be talked about, but you can't do that in a meeting like this, and then you stay with all those thoughts and ideas in your head—too bad. Something more optimistic might have been easier.

Someone said: "In the text, 'systems' are denounced, and then the meeting starts and you have to go back into the system".'

Municipal council Evergem. Public hearing.

Some feedback from our contact person

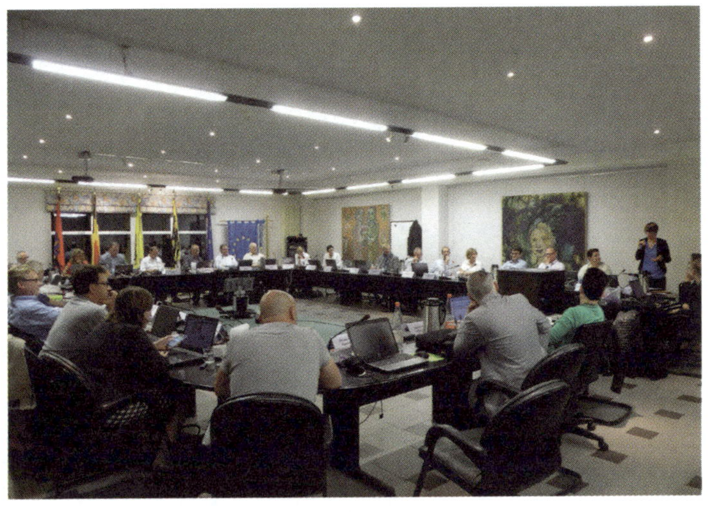

'The forum of a municipal council is not ideal for LFEO. The municipal council is a theatre in itself. The context doesn't lend itself to it, so there was no rhyme or reason to it. This has nothing to do with the content of the text, but only with the event itself. The reactions (after the meeting) were therefore that it was inappropriate.

Someone from Vlaams Belang had immediately reacted, during the meeting, that the municipal council cannot be suspended for something like this.

I, as chairman of the municipal council, understand these reactions—I also thought that it was not appropriate at all. The fact that I saw the public leaving and that many councillors were tapping at their laptops made me very uncomfortable. I have no regrets—I've seen all sorts of things already—but I certainly wouldn't do it a second time, although I found the text in itself (in terms of content) very valuable, but within a different context.'

GENNEVILLIERS

Mosque Ennour. Inter-religious meeting at the mosque's cultural centre.

02.06.2016 | 7:00 P.M.

Some feedback from our contact person

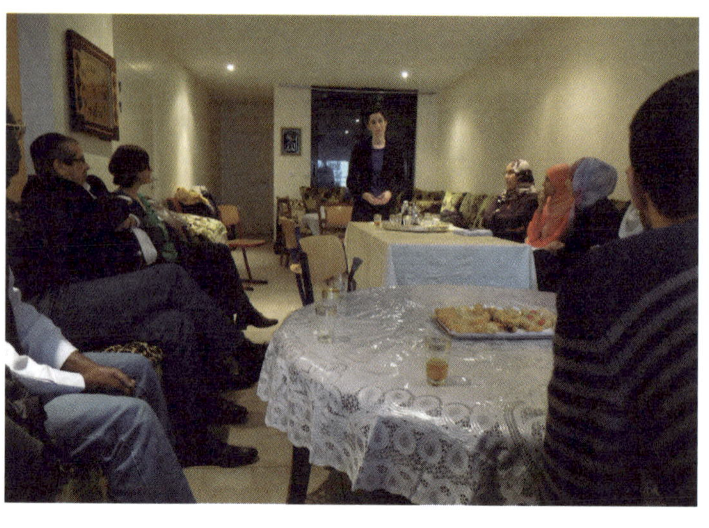

'In the group there were atheists, Muslims, Jews and Christians. Two people were experts in their religion. They were invited specially and for the first time there. It was very exciting. The group was frustrated not to be able to talk with the artist about the context of her project.

Some said, "Religions respond to what is said in the LFEO text". I think that's true, but not every practising believer necessarily asks him- or herself the questions or thoughts mentioned in the text.

We wanted to reread the text, to have it to share it with other people. One person said that we should read the declaration of human rights to high-ranking politicians. One person said that his sofa liked him a lot.

The text is pedagogical, in a positive sense: the way Lara took the time, played with time. The silences, the gaze, the rhythm. Time was taken and imposed, we were obliged to take the time to listen to this text and to reflect. It's not a violent gesture, but a necessary gesture.

LFEO delivers universal messages. For everyone. Whether religious or not, French or foreign.

The text and also Lara's presentation are full of respect for others, for the other. I'm not a great "culture buff" or art fan, but I think that sometimes theatre provides useful tools to reach out to others.

The work of a theatre and the work of an interreligious group are very much linked, it's about reaching out to others. The aim of the interreligious group is to create a space of exchange, where everyone can speak and be listened to. The theme of living together is therefore exactly the same as that of the group.'

GHENT

ABVV East Flanders. Meeting of the judges of the Labour Court.

16.10.2013 | 6:00 P.M.

Some feedback from our contact person

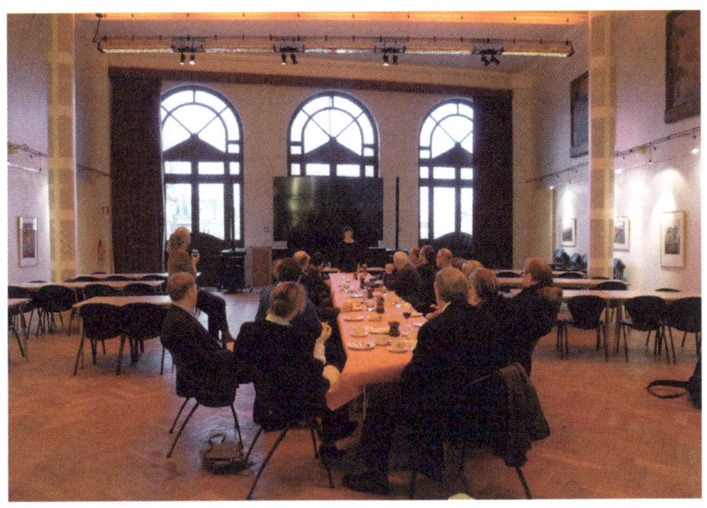

'There were two groups: people who loved it and people who were totally uncomfortable with it and found it irrelevant. One man said, "Women like that scare me a lot".

Afterwards there was a discussion about what freedom is. Someone said that we could always think freely, but that we have only been in a situation for 50 to 60 years where we can also be free and act freely. Sarah/LFEO puts that into perspective: are we really free? Maybe that's a bridge too far now: we have the illusion that we're free, but are we still really free?'

GHENT

ACV, Christian union. Propagandists meeting.

11.10.2013 | 10:30 A.M.

Some feedback from our contact person

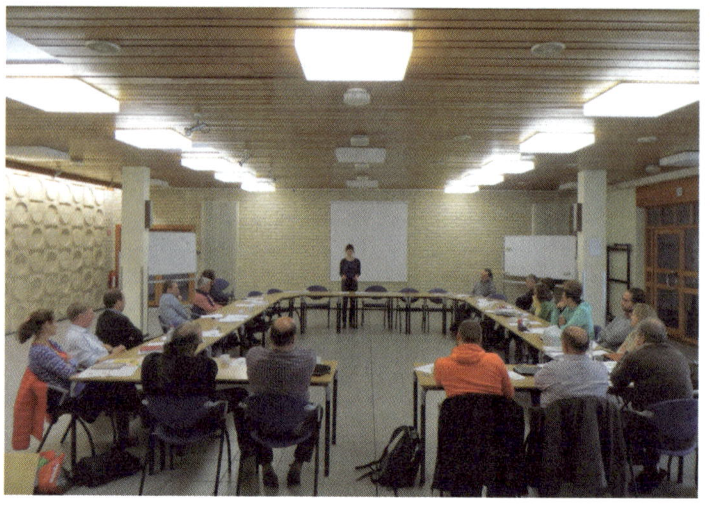

'I was amazed at the attention of those present, it was abnormally quiet—even X, who is always so sceptical, liked it.

The content of LFEO is about themes and a way of approaching them that is not part of our jargon. For me it was about personal considerations, about your connection with life. Yet it wasn't a show that's not directly of interest to us, the story of the taxi driver, for example—this is the kind of people the union is often in contact with—we often hear very poignant stories, reality surpasses the imagination. People who work for the union have to try to disconnect feelings from the facts, e.g. people who are stripped of their unemployment benefits or when lots of jobs are lost. Many flirt with that boundary: how do I engage without becoming too vulnerable?

That's why we felt some friction with "Indifference is for monsters". We agree with that, but it's difficult. We actually know about the misery of others, but we prefer not to be confronted with it too much, out of self-protection.

The things that were said about care and freedom were supported by the group.'

Report of a soft guerilla

Newspaper article by
Evelyne Coussens

-1

Evelyne Coussens is a freelance journalist. She joined Sarah in Brussels at two different LFEO interventions and wrote about it in *De Morgen* of Saturday 25 May 2013.

Saturday 25 May 2013 — *De Morgen*

Theatre-maker Sarah Vanhee enters uninvited into places where people meet. *Lecture for Everyone* is a speech like an ignition mechanism and *the* bomb of the Kunstenfestivaldesarts, which ends today.

6 May, 11 A.M.

A department of the Flemish government, Ellips Building, Brussels

A staff team prepares for the weekly meeting. The civil servants trickle in, get coffee and exchange the latest. None of them, except one person, knows that the first point on their agenda will walk into the meeting room in a moment.

During three weeks, Sarah Vanhee and her French-speaking colleague Mylène Lauzon crisscrossed Brussels with their *Lecture for Every One*. They descended on 40 places: the Belgian Air Force, a meeting of the Lions Club, a course in electricity at Syntra, a Congolese religious service. With the exception of the couple of presentations at the Kunstenfestivaldesarts, all lectures took place in non-cultural contexts. A deliberate choice.

Vanhee: 'If you want to talk about the way in which a society takes shape, it would be really inefficient to do that in theatres only. Social criticism is self-evident in the arts sector. But does that type of speech make sense there? With *Lecture for Every One*, the public doesn't choose to come to me—I choose the public. I am an intruder. I can only allow myself that aggression because I am an artist and not a salesperson, politician or missionary. My status lends me a safe-conduct, while that artistic speaking naturally also conjures up a resistance.'

And yet, Vanhee stresses, it is important to intervene in these extremely streamlined places precisely. Like many of her projects, in this *Lecture for Every One* too she channels 'fiction'—a story, a dream, a utopia—into reality. Today that reality is the agenda of the day, given shape in agenda points. Vanhee enters the meeting room, defies the curious, amused, annoyed gazes of the civil servants, and starts talking. 'Living alone. Living with others. Here we are.' Vanhee looks at the faces around the table, one at a time, makes eye contact. That's important, because *Lecture for Every One* is a speech for everyone but also for every-one —for each person individually.

Vanhee: 'Everywhere we go, the speech is exactly the same. The text is a common ground. I don't address a well-defined "we", I always find such a "we" problematic. You can see that at a meeting table too: I address people individually, but they look at others to assess their reaction. In *Lecture for Every One,* there are no spectators, everyone is a participant. Including myself. I try to speak as a person who also finds herself between the private and the public sphere.'

That morning, that even holds for those who claim that they don't want to participate. Some of the civil servants in attendance are listening carefully and nodding unconsciously, others are staring intensely at the sheet of paper or pen in front of them on the table. How come this lecture—which doesn't contain any moral accusations, any shocking revelations or explicit political messages—also provokes embarrassment or discomfort? Why does it make some people uncomfortable that someone wants to share certain thoughts with them?

Vanhee: 'It's the intrusion in the everyday course of events. You have to imagine that such a meeting is aimed at efficiency and expediency. Self-reflection—a standstill, therefore—arouses uneasiness in a system that always wants to progress. In addition, participants in such a meeting are there in their capacity as employees, while I'm addressing them in the first instance as people. In the role of the employee, it's not done to talk about bodies, for instance, as I do in the beginning of the lecture, although everyone has a body. But awareness of one's own body, and of that of others, causes a shock in such a meeting room.'

There are more words or concepts that resonate in the meeting. 'Care', for instance. Do we care enough for each other? Is it not time for a 'politics of care'? The paradox of the word 'freedom'. A perverted term like 'love'. Vanhee distributes her words—not as reproaches, but as precious little gifts to take home and reflect on. The last word is not a gift—rather, it's a bomb. 'Power.' Vanhee thanks her listeners and leaves the room.

22 May, 10:45 A.M.

Executive committee of a listed company, Brussels

Power. It sticks to every little bit of the company which Vanhee is infiltrating today. To the discreet sign on the front door of the stately Brussels townhouse, to the stern hall, to the bleach blonde secretaries and to the stately board room where the executive committee gathers. A person starts whispering spontaneously. Will it be possible to make an opening here—to bring about a moment of reflection in this world of money and power?

Seven white male executives in middle age look on impassively as Vanhee positions herself at the head of the table. The contrast with the session at the Flemish government is impressive. These men are not used to averting their gaze. Their body language is self-aware but very aloof. It is striking how Vanhee immediately adapts to the vibe. How decisively she walks in, how assured her gaze is, how steady her voice, through the humming of the smartphones. She looks at the men, without averting her gaze—'Living alone. Living with others. Here we are.'

Vanhee: 'I try every time to be a chameleon, to absorb the atmosphere and the sensibilities of the group. The first minutes are crucial. While I go over each face, I can feel an affective dynamic take shape that lets the people melt, makes them "fluid". If that doesn't happen, my words will bounce off.' In the board room this morning, that danger was real, but Vanhee sought and found the tone. 'I immediately thought: I'm not letting them escape.' *(laughs)*.

Now, to be a fly on the wall. To see how the words, after she has left, take on a life of their own, whether and how they linger in the meeting. Upon inquiry, it appears that most people, regardless of the nature of the meeting, are surprised and moved. During a municipal council, the text found not a single listening ear. In one company, someone later claimed to have felt provoked by the text. The ensuing discussion with the other attendees is just as precious to Vanhee. In this committee, one of the executives had immediately asked about 'the objective' of this unexpected point on the agenda. The objective? Vanhee's goal is precisely to disrupt expediency.

In *Lecture for Every One,* a moment is created—a moment of standstill, of reflection, of potency, the moment *before* the action, *before* the change. *Lecture for Every One* is a beginning. 'We' are the possibilities that are really open.

Lecture For Every One

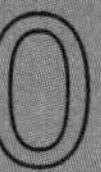

play with papers

real, spontaneous
smile, concentrate
light, energy

LFEO 2018

Good afternoon.
Thank you *(name person who introduced me)* Mr. Kukk
And thank you for giving me the coming 15 minutes to speak to you.

Living
alone
Living with others.

stop

Here we are
Some of us more damaged than others, some of us more troubled, some of us more wounded than others.

include everyone, don't forget anyone

Faces. Faces I've never seen before. Special faces. Curious faces. Tired faces. Funny faces. Suspicious faces. Sad faces. Faces that don't give themselves away.

Bodies. Nervous bodies. Sexy bodies. Weak bodies. Trained bodies. Bodies that have lived. Unreadable bodies.

Three questions:
Do you think you have more or less money than I have?
Do you think you know more or less than I do?
Do you think you are stronger than I am?

Sometimes just speak through
questions for real
I want to say this
hands: choose yes or no

strong & vulnerable
think, comment in the moment
glass

1

I'm going to tell you a story.

Yesterday evening I was going home in a taxi and I started to chat with the driver
and at a certain moment, he asked me about my accent.
So I told him where I was born, where I'd lived, (and) how I'd got the accent I have.
And then I asked him in return where he came from.
He answered that he didn't have a country anymore
his country used to be the most beautiful, he said, like paradise on earth,
but it all got destroyed
from both the inside and outside
he said a lot of promises were made for the future
but he'd never seen any of them realized
He said he only believed in the law of nature now:
"When you have a child
you either raise it or you kill it
soit tu le grandis soit tu l'étouffes
that's nature", he said.
I asked him if he was bitter
"no", he said
I'm a realist."

I didn't agree. But at that moment, I couldn't say anything.

I am here because I want to share some thoughts with you. There is nothing I want to convince you of, I don't want to teach you anything, and I have nothing to sell you. There are just these thoughts that I want to share. I could have also written this down in a book or posted it on facebook, but I really wanted to be here the moment you hear this. My words are not meant for just anyone. They are meant for every single one of you.

So then now
the next word.

Moment.

(long pause)

This was a moment.
We've just created a moment together.
(pause)
This is a moment before
(pause)
There is always a moment before

before you push the button
before the war starts
before you kiss
before you really decide

Like this moment now
This is a moment before.
We are before.
We are before.
WE ARE BEFORE
WE ARE BEFORE (…)

We. People.
But who are 'we'? How can I speak about 'us'?
We are individuals (you and you and you and me her and him) … every one of us.
But we are condemned to live with each other (her and him and you and you and me),… every one. Every-one with his or her pleasure, every-one with his or her pain, every-one with his or her concerns.
Common concerns – different concerns.

One of my concerns is what is left unspoken.
What you don't say. What I don't say.

The taxi-driver
I wanted to ask him for his phone number. But I didn't.

One more story.
Last month I was on a very long train ride – through Germany. A woman was sitting in front of me – very old, she could have been my grandmother. I was gazing a bit out of the window, watching the landscape. Then I heard a very soft mumbling, coming from the old lady. First I thought she was praying and I got worried by the thought of having to spend 5 more hours with her without my headphones. She kept going, it was hard to ignore, so I closed my eyes to hear her better:
All human beings are born free and equal in dignity and rights. They should act towards another in a spirit of brotherhood
Now I could hear her voice very clearly:
No one shall be subjected to arbitrary arrest, detention or exile
Everyone has the right to freedom of thought, conscience and religion
Everyone has the right to freedom of opinion and expression
Everyone has the right to freedom of peaceful assembly and association
This was no prayer – the woman was reciting the entire universal declaration of human rights, by heart.
Everyone, as a member of society, has the right to social security,
everyone has the right to work, to free choice of employment,
Everyone has the right to rest and to leisure
Everyone has the right to education.
I wanted to interrupt her, and ask her why she was doing this. But then the train stopped, and she left.

Something else now.

A catastrophe.
Think about a catastrophe
that could happen to you.
Something really bad.

Try to really imagine it.

Does everyone have his own catastrophe?

The current state of affairs:

Experts tell me I live in a system. I'm born into it and I co-create it, every moment, every day. They tell me I have to maintain the system, together with you. I have to move forward, not look around me, not look back.
Specialists help me to understand what I really need
and what the system needs from me:
insurance, information, holidays, networks, bank-accounts.
It works.

This system has to grow continuously. It never rests.
The damage it causes, is out of our control. The institutions I have to deal with, I cannot talk to.
Some of the laws we are submitted to, we can no longer read.
The products I buy, are programmed to break.
I'm a product myself.

I'm stupid, paranoid and powerless. I'm over-rational and un-reasonable. I'm constantly under surveillance and I feel unsafe. I'm ignorant about how to live with people who are not like me. About the future I'm cynical. I think I am unique and original but I don't dare to stand out from other people. The list of what is called abnormal behaviour is getting longer and longer. I live in fear, a fear that isolates me. Recently I was advised to only trust myself, not to trust anyone else.

We don't need a catastrophe
we are catastrophe.

There would be no system without us
I don't see a system here
I see us

What do you think?

Faces. Bodies. We are before.

Different groups of different people hear these words.

Yesterday I was *(there)*
tomorrow I will be *(there)*
I say exactly the same words everywhere
the exact same words to
every one

This is for you. I know: you create the meaning in the end.

A Lecture For Every One
about living
together.

But these words linked to 'together' scare me. I don't trust those words. They've been abused, exploited, perverted. By the hippies, by the media, by politicians, by advertising, by religion. The words linked to 'together' are empty, they are worn out, they don't fit with the current state of affairs.
But when I decided not to use these words any longer, I ended up missing them. I would like to try them again.

The first word might sound very un-sexy.

CARE

I want to care.

Not caring is so poor.
I'm so tired of the poverty of carelessness.

By "care" I don't mean hair-care, skin-care or car-care, that's not the kind of care I miss, it's not about care as a market or a label.
I'm also not speaking about child-care, health insurance or an old people's home – instutionalized care; that's very important, but it's not what I mean now.

Now, I'm talking about our care.
When you care, you use your attention, your intelligence, your awareness.
No bullshit, no money, no magic, no cowardice.

Caring about each other
means creating a new politics.
The politics of caring
here and now.

Care first.
Care more.
Care again.
How to care better for each other?

What do you think?

The second word, I actually never understood:

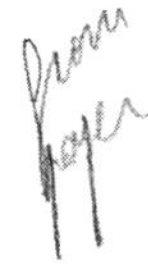

FREEDOM:
my car– my freedom, my credit card – my freedom, my sanitary towel – my freedom, my fitness centre – my freedom, my cigarette – my freedom, my day off – my freedom, my privacy – my freedom, , my drugs – my freedom, my clothes – my freedom, my smart-phone – my freedom

I didn't know that I was un-free until someone sold me freedom.

I don't want to choose from what is being offered to me as freedom
but I would like to be freed of what I don't choose.

my refusal – my freedom
my anger – my freedom
my failure – my freedom
my craziness – my freedom

The third word has nothing to do with Hollywood or red roses:
LOVE

I want to talk about love as something concrete.

Your love.

Is your love a plan? A practice? A concept?
Do you love enough?
Do you love yourself?
Are you forced to love?
Do you love your sofa?
Have you ever felt that your sofa loved you?
Are you open to more love?
Are you open to love more?
Is there a crisis
of love?

Living with others.
Living alone.

Here we are.

This is a moment before. We are before.

One last word.

Power.

This is for you.

Thank you.

take props

leave

10

Note on Lecture For Every One

This is the latest version of the performance script of Lecture For Every One.

With three exceptions, this text differs little from the original text that was written in 2013:

– In 2013 it included a small paragraph which, when spoken, felt rather moralistic. It was deleted in 2014.

– On p. 5 the listeners are asked to imagine a catastrophe. When we performed LFEO in Gennevilliers in June 2016, France was still in shock following a wave of terrorist attacks and it didn't feel right to ask listeners to imagine a catastrophe. The word 'catastrophe' was temporarily replaced by 'monster'.

– In 2016 the original story on p. 4 was replaced by the story of the old woman. Initially there was an anecdote about a man who felt that his (carpet) fetishism was worse than the thought of suicide.

Otherwise the text has always remained the same, sometimes with minor nuances and differences across the many translations.

When the project first took place in 2013, it was far from obvious to me that we would continue doing this for so long. With each new place, I wondered whether the action and the text were still relevant. Together with the performers, I would then check what that text meant today, in a local context. Feedback showed that people continued to experience the text as very topical.

Eyewitness reports

Jan de Zutter

Robin Vanbesien

Anne Thuot

Bojan Djordjev

Lex Bohlmeijer

Now and then an eyewitness was invited to join an LFEO intervention. In return, they were asked to write a spontaneous report, to be published the day after the intervention on the LFEO website.

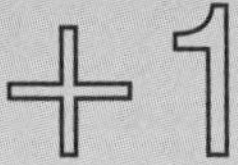

Jan de Zutter

Silence as autumn approaches

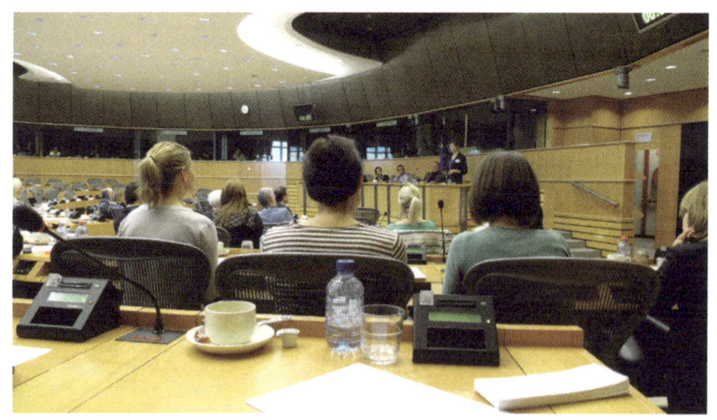

Jan de Zutter is the press officer of the Socialists & Democrats Group at the European Parliament. He was one of our contact persons in the European Parliament and was afterwards asked to write an eyewitness report about LFEO at a meeting of the transport work group on the 4th European Rail Package, 10 October 2013, 4:15 p.m.

They weren't prepared for it, the social-democratic members of the European Parliament. The planned meeting of the workgroup Transport, responsible for the preparation of all major European transport dossiers, had as a second point on the agenda, 'Lecture For Every One'. No further explanation. It also seemed as if no one had noticed this item until president Saïd El Khadraoui (sp.a) asked everyone's attention for a short intervention by an artist, Sarah Vanhee. Being caught out in the moment when you least expect it, by a young woman who just takes the floor, at the pulpit where statistics, legal texts, numbers and ideological statements compete with each other in a phallic measuring contest. I had taken place among the MEPs and carefully gauged their reactions. At the right, some young women listening, captivated, although their look revealed a sort of disbelief. A text about democracy in the House of Democracy. Uncanny. There's something the matter with our democracy. Everyone feels it, like rheumatics feel autumn approaching. Maybe the simple words Vanhee uses sound like gibberish in an environment that in splendid isolation has invented a jargon that has alienated ordinary citizens from the political elite. Not that they should be seen as evil. Contrary to what the crowd thinks, a lot of MEPs work like crazy in the political rat race and they do consider a long-term vision, much more often than national MPs. But they do this within the outlines of 'the system', the very same system that Vanhee questions. What does the system desire from me? Can I talk with the institutions that represent me? A rhetorical question, in the heart of European democracy. 'Are you listening to who I am? To who you are?' 'Let's create a moment together.' A silence follows. A moment of silence. An absence of speech that does not belong in a place where the word impatiently wants to convince. Even words are made subject to doubt by Vanhee. She singles out concepts that are being abused like choir boys by their priests. 'Care.' Not the organized, institutionalized care, but a deep involvement, originating in empathy. What do we still care about? How are we, all these Is in this room, going to live together?

Vanhee disappears as quickly as she came. The guest lecture has taken about 15 minutes. Europe focuses once more on small solutions to big problems. Meanwhile a shutdown of the US government looms, and rejected asylum seeker and plumber Navid Sharifi lands in Moscow, a stopover on his forced return to Afghanistan. Care? Or law?

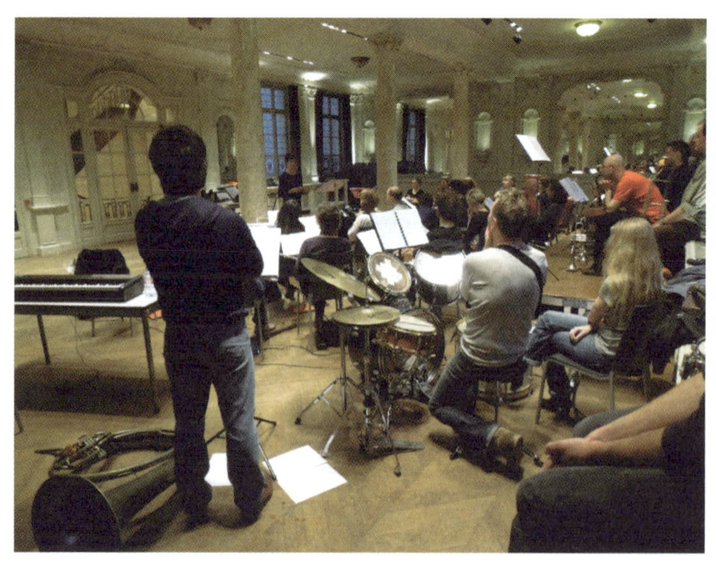

Robin Vanbesien is an artist and writer. He attended LFEO at the weekly rehearsal of the amateur brass band Café Marché in De Markten, Brussels, 16 May 2013, 9:15 p.m.

The location is the Spiegelzaal in De Markten—a ballroom with mirrors, pillars and windows. The occasion is a rehearsal of a brass-band collective. There are about 35 musicians, each playing a different instrument (!), collectively trying to approach the exact shape of a song. Then the rehearsal is interrupted, Sarah takes up the position of the conductor and starts giving a lecture. It is said to be a 'lecture for every one'. The musicians, the conductor, Kristien and me start listening. There is one 'lecture for every one', but it is continuously performed again and again, every time at a different location, interrupting a gathering of one kind or another. Spoken words intersect different situations of accidental and less accidental meetings; they only take 20 minutes. It is a temporary consolidation that enables us, the ad hoc spectators, to exist in movement in a field circumscribed by connotation. The words evoke questions, announcements, statements, confessions, jokes, but are never exactly any of those things, as all orientation remains suspended in the text. Or rather, the orientation of the words is entangled in the individual interpretations and engagements of each one of us. These words apparently embody a rehearsal that asks for common appeals but doesn't ask for collective shapes.

One of the words in the lecture that held my attention is 'care'. A friend once told me, 'Responsibility is freedom', to which I instantly added, 'Because there's no magic about it'. Lecture For Every One is elusive and deceitful about the way it embodies care and empathy. It is for us to act on. Consequently I started fantasizing about how we should continuously be deceitful about the responsibilities we take. We shouldn't tell, we can't expose and we don't care if our responsible attitude is not recognized as such. (At night, when we 'dream', we get up and try to solve all problems, while during the day we keep acting as if all the problems are unresolved and nothing is to be done about it. Secretly, we only live for the night!) The language of Lecture For Every One can appear deceitfully naive, while the affective relations it allows are as many as each one of us. Above all, the continuously suspended shape of the lecture invites clones. Yesterday evening, when sitting in a bar in Paris, I noticed how a boy walked up to the karaoke stage and took the microphone.

Anne Thuot

AAAAAAAAAAAAH

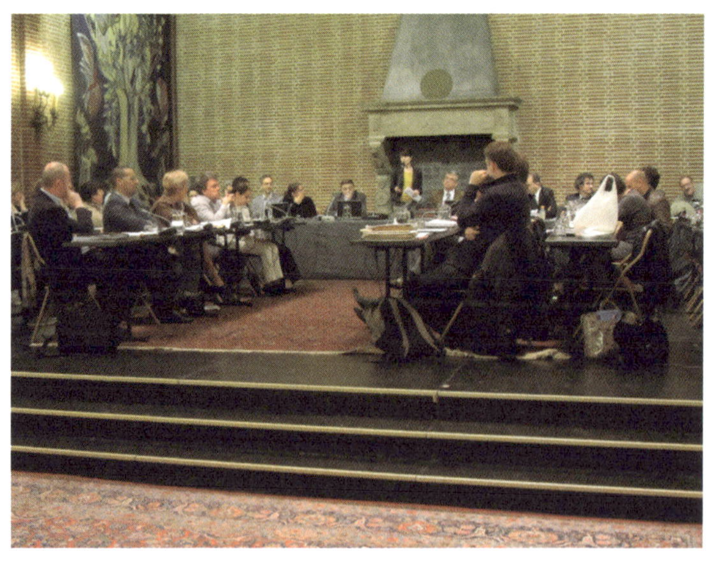

Anne Thuot is a director and performance artist. She wrote an eyewitness report after having experienced the LFEO intervention during the monthly public hearing of the municipal council of Molenbeek, 23 May 2013, 7:30 p.m.

Today is 3 June 2014.

It's been 11 days since I attended Lecture For Every One at the opening of the municipal council of Molenbeek on 23 May 2014 at 19:30.

Since then it's like I have a fishbone stuck in my throat —a bitter taste.

I want to shout

AAAAAAAAAAAAAAAAH

to say

STOP

and to yell

'You, councillor, an elected representative therefore, can't you take your eyes off your computer screen for 15 minutes? And you, other councillor, can't you stop gobbling up your fries and mayonnaise? And you there, who sits there in the middle, can't you stop exchanging polite smiles with your colleagues, as if you were saying: "Don't worry, we'll get them"? All of you gathered here, can you listen? Listen to this young woman reading a text? This young woman in your midst who is speaking, speaking differently, who is proposing an exchange? A meeting? An act of living together for 15 minutes?',

and also to say:

STOP STOP STOP

I'm going to yell, to denounce—your inability to share, yes, you, representatives, hurts me; and Mylène's body, thrown to the lions, exposed, like the trace of the non-communication in which we find ourselves, I'm struggling to catch my breath—:

'Yes, we are the catastrophe, it's not external, it's us—us, the bodies that manage the community; us, in the way in which we abuse the power relations in our various councils where it is no longer possible to listen to a different speech, a speech which addresses a different level of humanity, which brings together. Your only watchword is: "disagree", with the opposite camp, and wanting to win, to prevail. The citizens who have come to make their voices heard also engage in this competition of "who will speak loudest". Mylène stays there, in the middle, she makes progress in her lecture, in her proposal to meet, to listen together. To share a common gaze.

There she is, fragile, reminding us that perhaps we could try to give up, I don't quite know what, perhaps our old enmities, our certainties; aren't we all in the same boat? The playground is behind us, we know that not everything is black or white, that the law of "the strongest" is not necessarily a good thing. That we need to re-invent a way of thinking, of thinking about what comes next, the time to come, and that perhaps we could start by listening to each other. What do we have to lose? Why do we need to make such a show? To stage everything? Just to feel that we are alive?'

And again I want to cry out:

—but at that moment, I run out of breath I can no longer even utter a STOP!—I tell myself as I see what I see: no, it's not possible, she's not going to dare, is she?! And yes, Madam Burgomaster, you dared to do the unthinkable, you sent your assistant to ask Mylène to finish her lecture because the 15 minutes were over. You opened up a chasm, created a rift. And that probably wasn't enough because you asked your assistant to go back a second time, because now we had taken up 17 minutes of your time. How could your assistant accept to play this role—because you must at least realize that it is not 'polite' so then you delegate?

Even today it still leaves me speechless.

I am left speechless by the lack of respect you showed, Madam Burgomaster; by your inability to create a climate in which to listen to the lecture that you had decided to welcome in your municipal council—no doubt you thought that this 'event' would contribute to your level of popularity—;

I am left speechless by the inability of a good many councillors to listen, to open themselves up to what was coming from outside, to this woman reading a text and who was proposing to spend a moment together while also being alone with oneself, one's own thoughts;

I am left speechless by some of the citizens in attendance who, no matter what was being said, since others were speaking, those from the other side—politics is rubbish, nonsense, a mockery!

Aaaaaaaaaaaaaaaaaaaaaaaaah!

That is what I wish to say, 11 days later.

But nothing.

I try again.

Aaaaaaaaaaaaaaaaaaaaaaaaaaaaaaaaaaaaaaaaaaaaaaaaaaaaaaaaaaaaaaaaaaah!

Still nothing.

I could sink into a profound abyss,

Tell myself that the world is nothing but a farce.

Endless power games.

But I refuse to.

I refuse to.

So I shout:

But it's a:

HIIIIIIIIIIIIIIIIIIIIIIIIIIII

The sound is powerful and lugubrious.

It's the sound of laughter.

Yes, Madam Burgomaster, I am laughing.

You are so ridiculous.

And I realize that you are nothing more than a puppet!

Lecture For Every One put its finger on your inability to receive, to welcome, to invite the outside in, that which is different. But humanity, through Mylène's body, her voice, her words, entered into the heart of your arena and has revealed its ridiculousness.

And I'm happy to have witnessed how absurd you look!

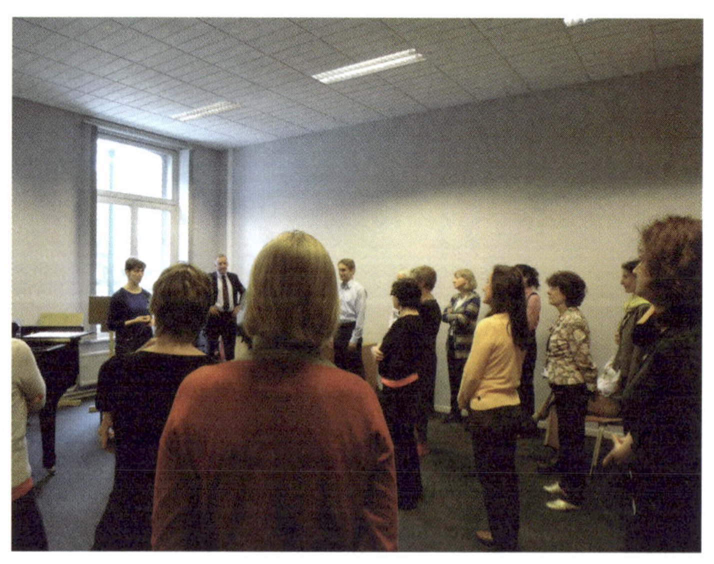

Bojan Djordjev is a theatre director and theorist. He attended the LFEO intervention at RTD Chorale, a choir of people working for various European institutions, at their rehearsal on 16 May 2013, 1:00 p.m.

It's a rainy morning, but the Sablon is very charming even in this weather. Kristien is taking me to the place of today's lecture. While talking about the piece and all the different events that are taking place induced by this simple set-up, I admire Kristien's newly acquired knowledge of the city after arranging all the appointments for Lecture for Every One. Forty meetings covering all spheres of life and classes of society. We meet Sarah at the metro entrance. I ask her if she has a specific policy on me taking notes. I guess I am preparing myself for a lecture, still confused about the format. I have refrained from reading other eyewitness accounts of the lecture. I want to stay as neutral and as close to the 'source' as possible. Then why take notes? Sarah agrees.

We arrive in the European Quarter. The place we are going to is a building with thorough administrative security procedures. After filling out the forms with all our letters and numbers, we are given guest stickers and are admitted. It's empty. Our contact is very enthusiastic. She has prepared herself and wants to give Sarah a proper introduction. Sarah checks out the room. It is pleasant and white with a very nice view onto a patch of green grass—a park, I guess—that is visible through the window. Rain makes it even greener. It is light and very acoustic, there is a baby grand piano, shiny black. The sound a conversation produces in this room makes the entire situation somehow... delightful! We sit in a side room, a kind of improvised salon/cloakroom, waiting for the people to arrive. I ask Sarah details about the performance. I'm exercising my fantasy, letting it loose. We talk about remembering things. How I can remember random facts that are somehow systematized in my head as an autonomous hard drive. People are gathering in the corridor and soon we can hear a choir warm up. Cheerful noises of riffs, glissandos and melismas. These people who work for European institutions come here on their lunch break to sing. It's their precious rehearsal hour, their love for singing that will be chipped off today with a different kind of love.

Our host gets us, we enter quickly. Everyone is standing. Our host introduces Sarah. For her, this performance is about communication between different people. The sentence does not sound neutral, spoken in the capital of the EU and in this context. Sarah stands next to the piano, like at a *Liederabend,* and starts the lecture. The people from the choir are also standing. They have had their warm-up, they are ready to sing, but their conductor has been replaced with a lecture. I am standing at the back, in the last row. What were the people's reactions? I heard laughter at certain places, also direct and intuitive answers to the questions posed by Sarah. But what performance took place on the people's faces? How do they 'sing'? I realized that I was missing a big and important part of the performance. But then again, if I wanted to see it I had to deliver a lecture. Then what kind of a witness am I?

What kind of performers' skills does one develop to be able to deliver a text and at the same time observe what the text is inducing and producing in people's faces and behaviour, because one is so close to one's listeners. It is really a situation where you send the message into the air and see it reflected, and really the only thing one should care about is the effect the speech produces. But that's what we do all the time in life, no? This simple everyday reality of a conversation comes as something unusual in the context of an art piece.

And what kind of 'neutralizing' practice must Sarah have as a performer that is exposed in such a way? How to digest all the faces, all the reactions, the radiation that is reflected back from the lecture? It's a new kind of exhaustion.

I must say, I wasn't thinking of all this during the lecture. I was one of the every one. I also performed. I was listening to the lecture. It slowly led me to the point of my personal explosion. It happened somewhere in the middle of the lecture, so I could vaguely follow the rest. I reconstruct it in my head. I will probably reconstruct it in conversations I will have about the lecture. I am excited to work on its performance virally.

Where did the performance take place? Who are its audience? What kind of public space does it create? With this simple gesture, the fragmented, powerless public sphere of today is literally sewn back together manually by Sarah with each lecture. It's for EVERY ONE, but really an attempt at WE. This WE we were robbed of. Maybe some new WE. It's a brave artistic gesture, at once ambitious and humble.

We leave immediately after the end of the lecture. While trying to find a way out through confusing doors and corridors, we can hear the choir singing some African-sounding song.

Lex Bohlmeijer

The soft crowbar of her imagination

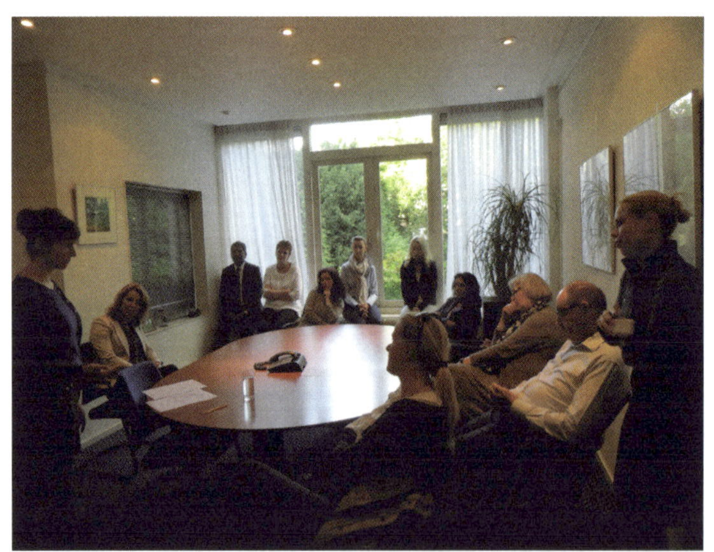

Lex Bohlmeijer is a journalist and writer. He formerly worked as an artistic advisor with Sarah on The C-Project. Lex witnessed LFEO during a daily morning meeting of Kooijman Lambert Notaries, Rotterdam, 19 September 2013, 8:45 a.m.

This text was broadcast on the evening of Friday 20 September 2013 during his radio show 'Amoroso'.

I got an email from Sarah Vanhee. A theatre-maker. As far as I'm concerned, one of the most original and bravest around. She wrote: 'How are you? Long time since we've spoken or seen each other... pity. It's probably due to my disappearing from the Dutch landscape... But I'm coming back, briefly. I'll be in Rotterdam all week with Lecture For Every One: I go to a meeting where I'm not expected, perform my "lecture for every one" and leave immediately afterwards.' Typical Sarah. Disappearing, appearing, the same old game. I agree to meet at 8:45 sharp on the Straatweg in Rotterdam. There is a notary's office there. En route, the autumn is gold-coloured and my eyes and ears are open, and it strikes me all the more how everyone, yes, I say everyone, is locked up in their own world. People stare at small screens, listen to messages from elsewhere, brush past one another. This is what we call society. I reach the notary's office. I have a few minutes—buzzing movement around me. A car stops in front of the door, a man loads a case of beer and a wooden fold-up chair. A party for one. Thank you. How are you? On the façade of the bourgeois house I see the names of Suzanna and Adriana, the women or girls who laid the first stone ages ago. At least they were together. Between them hangs the angel. Borne up by the light. She holds a pile of things in her arms, holds one up triumphantly. What's that? Hey, that's not possible, they look like mobile phones. A moment later I sneak into the morning meeting of the notary's office behind Sarah. I suppose that they are surprised, this is a surprise attack, they don't know, they don't show. Sarah addresses the notaries as faces, as bodies, what lies behind, what lives inside. She has three questions ('Do you think you have more or less money than me? Do you think that you know more than me? Do you think that you are stronger than me?'). She conveys her thoughts on care, freedom, love and power in crystal-clear sentences. The tension rises. People conceal their uneasiness. A phone rings in the distance. I notice that my heart is pounding. To me, notary's offices are always intimidating environments—where the main events of life, love, death, money are dealt with in procedural formulations. This is a society of complete control. Against it, Sarah, oh so vulnerable Sarah, uses the soft crowbar of her imagination, her courage, her telling sentences. Something is being brought to a head here. I see the circle of faces before me: now and then a wrinkle appears, like a ripple over motionless water. Then it's over, and a moment later we're back outside. Stunned, disconcerted. As I cycle away, the angel winks at me. I see that the first stone has moved a little...

From taxi company to prison

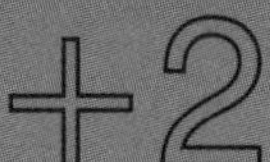

Vtax, a taxi company. Switching from the day shift to the night shift.

Some feedback from Marika, the LFEO collaborator

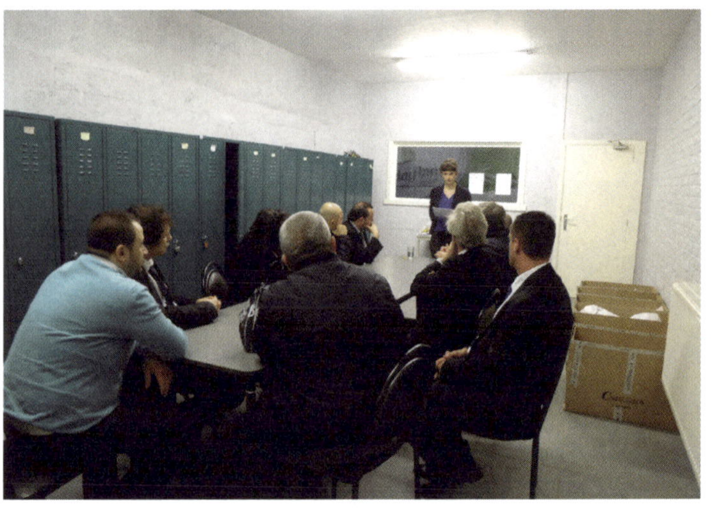

'Immediately afterwards two men came to Sarah, and they pointed out the difference between "us" and Muslims: Muslims are not afraid of death, but have to fear life—if you lead a good life, you don't need to fear death, because you will be rewarded. They also said that Muslims aren't allowed to have credit cards, and can't take out loans—so a banking crisis like the one we went through wouldn't be possible with Muslims.

The taxi driver who drove us back afterwards said that he sees a lot of different faces, a lot of different bodies in his taxi every day. Taxi drivers hear a lot, see a lot, learn a lot about the world.'

GOTHENBURG

Lundalogik, IT company. Weekly informal meeting for all employees.

16.05.2014 | 2:30 P.M.

Some feedback from our contact person

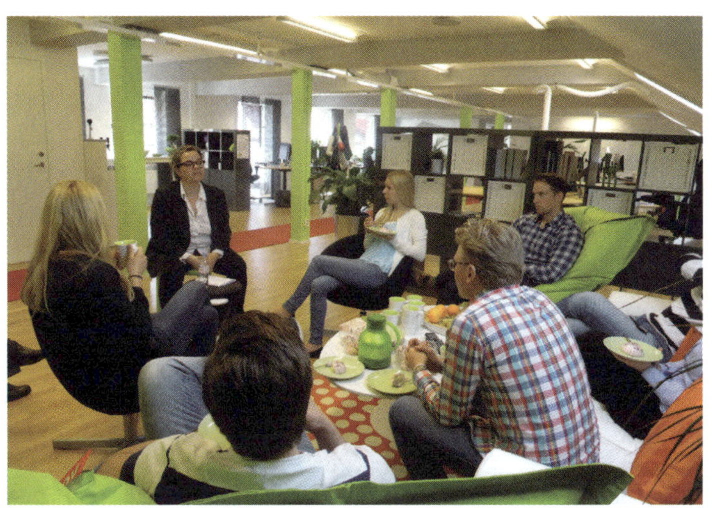

'Some people thought LFEO was thoughtful and interesting, some found it scary. One person said that she almost felt nauseous because it got so deep. Some people found it creepy to be in the situation. Probably that means they usually don't think about themes like in LFEO, and that they were very surprised by the intrusion, therefore felt uncomfortable with themselves and did not know how to handle the situation. Still they appreciated the text, the performer Tove and the surprise a lot.

I think it was good to have LFEO as a surprise because otherwise, if I had announced the lecture, people might have been suspicious and would have felt forced to attend the art project.'

Volvo AB. Farewell celebration for a member of the invoice & cost-control department.

Some feedback from our contact person

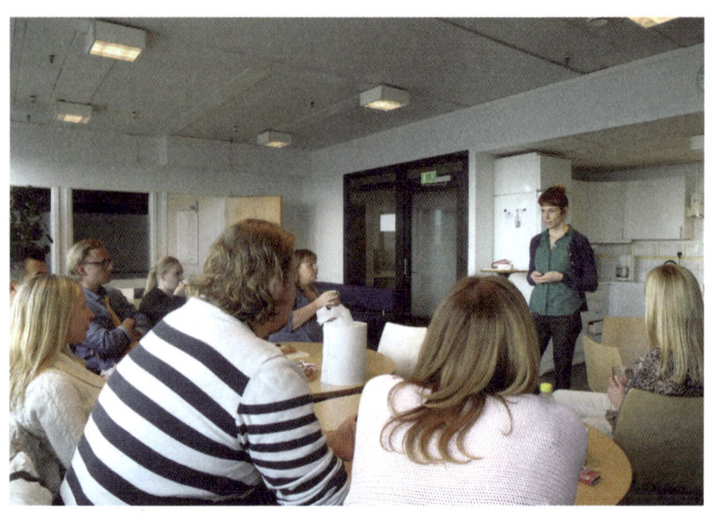

'I thought the group was behaving in a very Swedish way: no one reacted during the lecture, all were very silent. Maybe you're screaming inside but you'd never expose that.

The next day, LFEO came up several times in conversations.

People didn't talk about specific parts of the text. I think this is because everyone took it very, very personally, and felt quite intimately associated with the text—so people wouldn't want to share their exact experience but only express their general appreciation of LFEO.

I'd like to bring LFEO to other places as well—not only to other departments of Volvo, but e.g. to a rehearsal of the band I play in—because we're a group of friends, used to a certain humour and way of speaking to each other, and sharing precious moments of playing music together. I'd like to share LFEO with more people.'

Institut français. Weekly meeting of the administration team.

Some feedback from our contact person

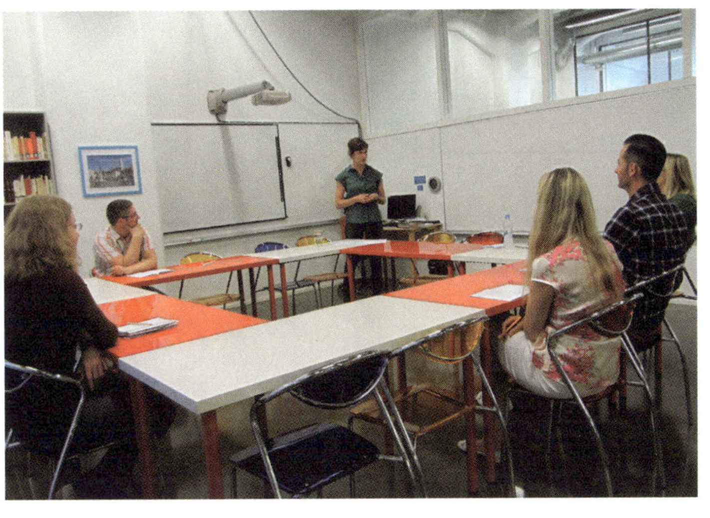

'One comment I heard from a colleague, was, "Well, this was contemporary art", in the sense of opaque, incomprehensible, conceptual, "What's the point?" I saw it as an artwork too (it repeats words, it creates artificial pauses to make people feel uncomfortable…), but I didn't find it "arty".

During the first 5 minutes I felt uncomfortable, also for my colleagues, but then I got "into it" and didn't find it difficult to listen to.

The content of the text didn't surprise me (e.g. the criticism of the consumer society wasn't a surprise), but moving. Most meaningful for me was the reclaiming of the words that easily sound sentimental (like care or love) because I found it presented in a good way, not preachy.

Listening to a text in this situation, being forced gently to listen together with colleagues, produces effects that art doesn't produce in a gallery when you're with friends. First you feel "embarrassed", smiling stupidly. Then it's interesting and you have to get into it because of the intimate setting.'

Anonymous. Regular meeting.

Some feedback from our contact person

‘The lecture came across as rather pessimistic and felt strange. Our team is enthusiastic, positive and dynamic, not the right target audience for this lecture. We’re hard workers who want to move forward and are positive.

We’re also a very close team and share life’s joys and sorrows together—that’s how it is when you’re on the shop floor together five days a week. Certain topics, such as the passage about the catastrophe, were misplaced, especially since some colleagues have been through difficult personal times recently. The passage about suicide was also inappropriate. We found it easier to relate to the passage about care.

Some people in the team thought the lecture had a political tone, they read more into it. For most people the text rambled from one subject to the next, it wasn’t clear what its purpose was, but that’s probably what makes it art.

The lecture contrasted with the clear informative explanation we had received from the director beforehand. We’re used to concrete dynamic proposals that are inspiring.

It would’ve been better if it hadn’t been a surprise, if we had known in advance that an artist was coming to speak. If you know that in advance, then you listen to it differently.’

Vodafone, telephone company. Meeting of the staff of the OSS group Portugal.

Some feedback from our contact person

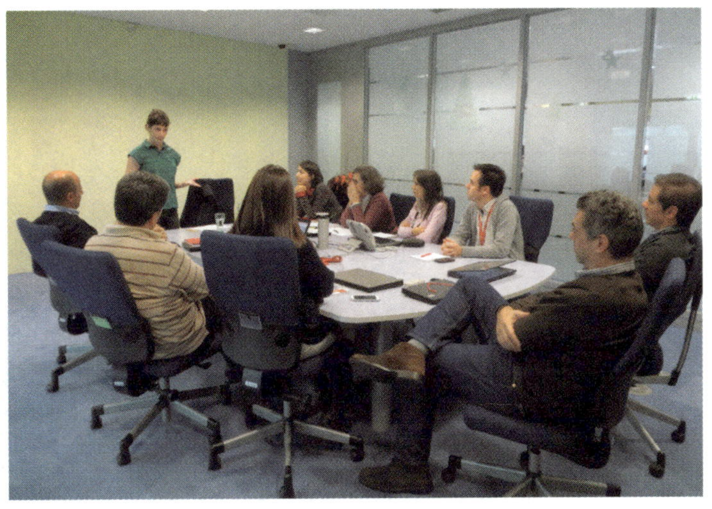

'After LFEO someone had to give a presentation, and that felt quite strange. He said, "Do I really need to give this presentation? After this?" Someone answered, "Only if it's done with a lot of love."

The language of LFEO is not usual for a meeting, it takes you to another place.

I completely related to what was said. As a project manager I have to create a team. I sometimes speak in terms of creating a moment. In my job there's a lot of care and love—this is important because we're not robots. Otherwise people can't function. People need creative space to develop ideas.

The text is at once personal, political, ethical and about society. It reflects on the identity of a group. A group can reject or allow individuals. If you accept the individuals as themselves and as contributing to the group with their own voice, the group can develop in a positive way, it can grow. If the group rejects personalities that are different, then you can't create and the group will die in the end. That's what's happening now in this crisis. When you start saying that people aren't valuable because they're not working, you reject them and that's unhealthy.

Sarah was here, she was in the space, "It is now", and that's very important. It made me think about my life, think about not losing track, about not losing the connection with what I'm doing at work.'

LISBON

Hospital Santa Maria. A clinic session for the Medicine Service ID.

13.12.2013 | 12:15 P.M.

Some feedback from one of the doctors

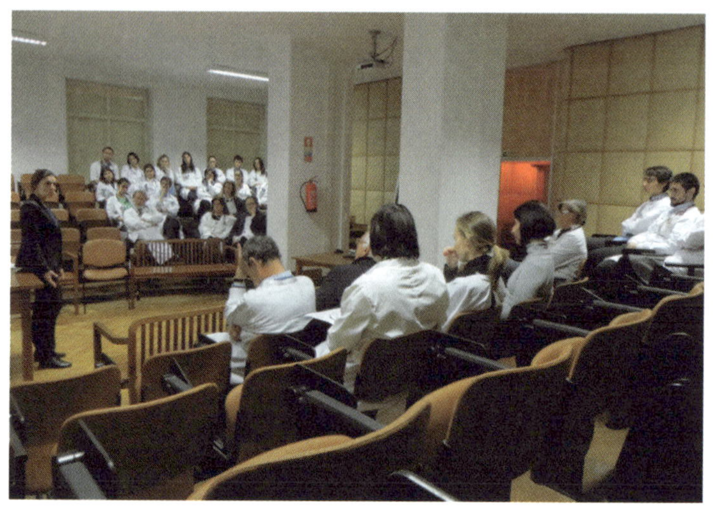

'I heard two reactions. One person found the lecture useless, because she had heard the content a thousand times. Another lady, rather conservative, was moved by it.

Personally I'd be interested in knowing how you measure the effect of this lecture. To quote Galileo, "Everything that is important can be expressed in numbers." Maybe you could invite a sociologist to help find a research method?'

Ballet National de Marseille. Rehearsal.

Some feedback from our contact person

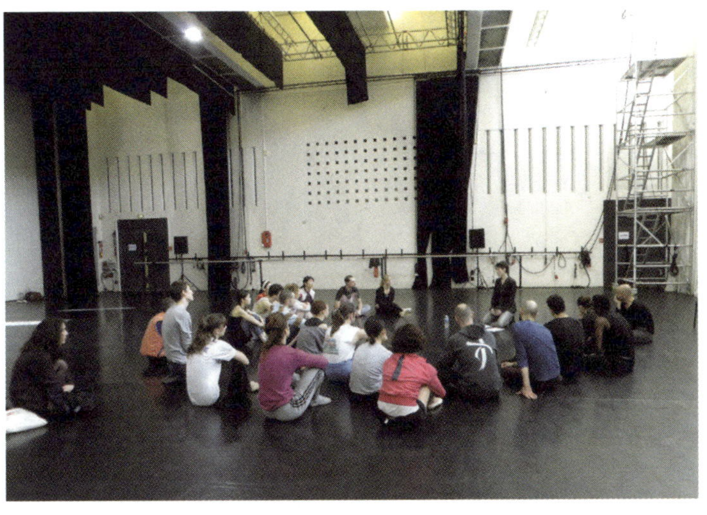

'The dancers seemed surprised to have been "abandoned" without a word immediately after the lecture. There was a long silence, the dancers seemed to be in a state of reflection, some of them talking together in a low voice while gradually resuming their place in the corps de ballet for the rehearsals.

The discussions took place the next day. The dancers all felt concerned and the intervention resonated powerfully with most of them. Some of them would have liked to talk to the author of the text. Some would have liked to be able to reread the text. Some didn't understand the form of the intervention and felt a certain "unease".

One passage in the text that left an impression was "The disaster is within us". We wondered whether the words would have had the same resonance if there had not been the attack on *Charlie Hebdo*. Would we have been less affected?

The text questions the fear in the face of this necessary questioning. Others said that we shouldn't be afraid to ask ourselves questions. Still others thought that they didn't need to listen to this lecture to ask themselves these questions, that they asked themselves these questions spontaneously.'

MINDE	20.09.2016	7:30 P.M.
Atlético Clube Alcanenense, third division football club. Daily team practice.	Some feedback from our contact person	

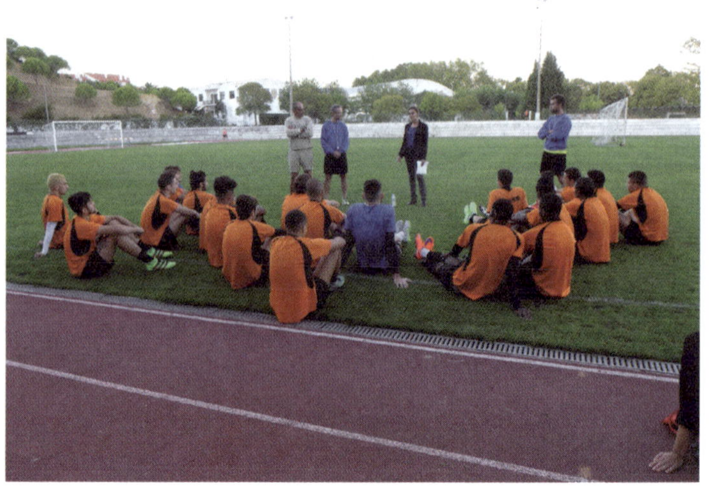

'We talked a little. There was one player who asked if the stories of the train and taxi were true.

We're a club with several nationalities and I took the conversation to talk about the different ways of thinking and acting. As we're a team we have to have one way of thinking. We have to be less self-indulgent.

I think the lecture is about our reality, and that's also what's happening in our lives. We're selfish, we share little, we run around but don't get anywhere, we don't stop to think, to realize what it's worth. Therefore it was a very interesting intervention.

We're part of an association, a community, we're the oldest and most representative association of the county, a major milestone in national football. We don't like to stay closed in our box, we like to share. We felt LFEO could be an interesting situation, and also this way you could get to know us and share what we are. Associations and authorities have an important role to play in sharing and we want to give our strength accordingly.

The text is interesting. I'm someone to who material values are of little importance. I grew up with few material possessions and they were never important to my happiness, on a day-to-day basis I don't think much beyond what we already have. The text made me think of those times when we believe a lot of things and then they don't happen.

Those were words that touched us. We have six or seven nationalities, different religions, different ways of thinking and it all led to us also taking the opportunity to intervene and talk in the sense of being a united group.'

Escola Secundária de Alcanena. Teachers' general meeting for the school-year beginning.

Some feedback from our contact person

'We received two text messages from different people. One said thank you, she appreciated LFEO very much. The other said: "First I was shocked and irritated. It didn't make sense. Then I understood. Then I applauded."'

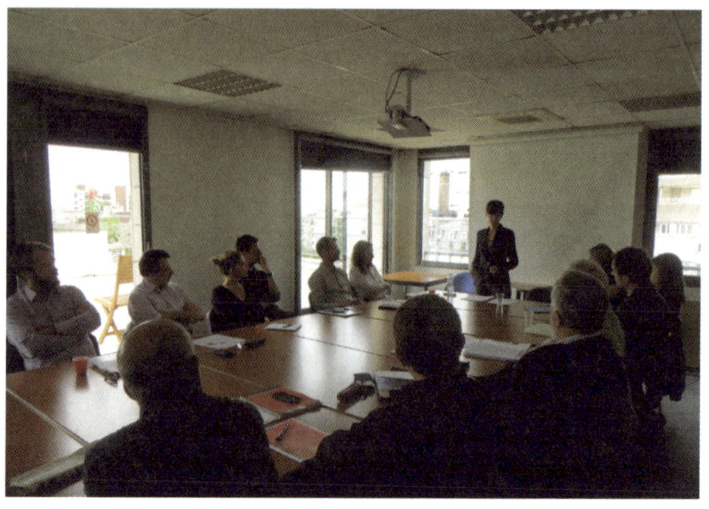

‘We were surprised by the event but also by the speech. Living together is reflected in our logo: “Les HLM, vivre mieux, bien vivre ensemble” (Social housing, better living, living well together).

Everybody appreciated this action. There was a man who found the speech a bit “la-la land-ish”, i.e. a bit soft and idealistic, but he enjoyed it all the same. It’s not always easy to be open to such a speech.

During the meeting, the text was reused: “the moment before”—it’s an encouragement to improve the situation—and “living together”.

The lecture starts with a personal text but becomes more and more political. This text calls for responsibility, it says “there is no system outside us”, it is a positive thought. At HLM we are often confronted with people who are isolated, who are frustrated and angry with the system.’

Espace 19, volunteers' association.
Meeting for knowledge exchange.

Some feedback from our contact person

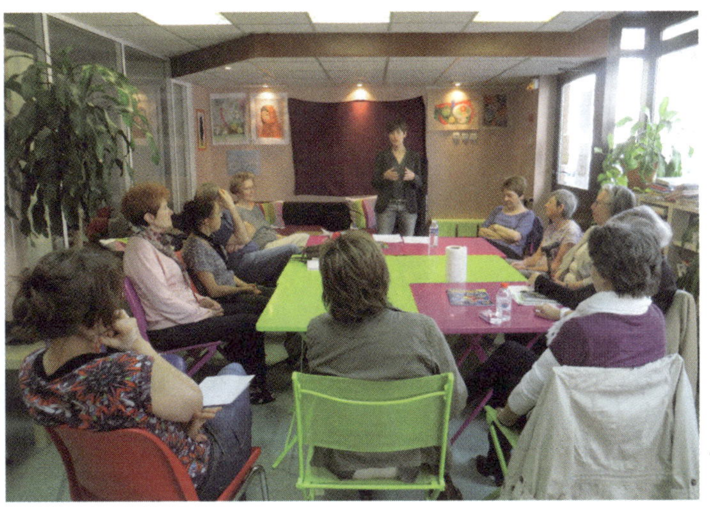

'There was a lot of discussion during the text, people answered the questions and discussed among themselves about the catastrophe, the word love having so little value that it's stripped of its meaning. I liked the thought of a new care policy. Because even in places where "care" or "living together" is the core business, the main thing are the figures, the content is no longer important.'

Caisse des Dépôts. Breakfast meeting of the Finance and Strategy departments.

Some feedback from our contact person

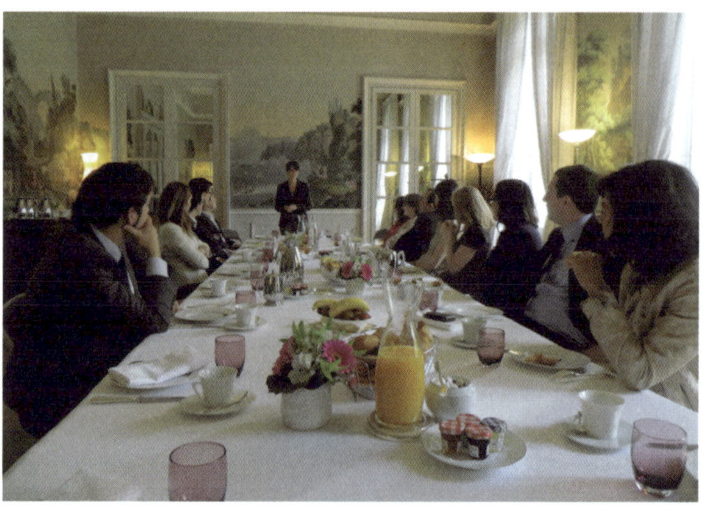

'Some people found the lecture hard: they work at the Caisse des Dépôts where everyone makes a good living. The question itself, "Do you think you have more or less money than me?", already makes people uncomfortable. But it's a good one because it forces you to think about how you relate to the people you live with.

I thought the text was activist, its contents quite familiar, but it was presented in such a way that I really wanted to listen, it was really you. Being surprised by someone, as well as the way the text was written (it wasn't insulting), brings it very close to you.

The sentence "There is no system outside us, we are the system" touched me particularly.'

Roularta Media Group. Board meeting.

Some feedback from our contact person

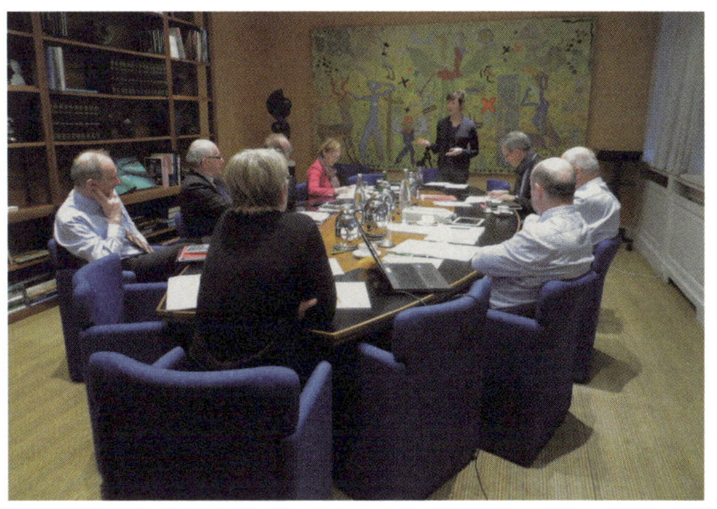

'People talked about it for the rest of the day, I heard. Clearly "something" stuck here and there, if only that story about the Persian carpet.

West Flemish people are very down-to-earth people, even if we say so ourselves, and such an exposition was in sharp contrast to the order of the day: a high-level meeting with policy discussions, so that may not have been the ideal "match".

Personally, I also found it a bit chaotic and it goes so fast and in such a short time that it is indeed not obvious to be gripped by it when, a few minutes before, you were discussing a strategy expressed in millions of euro.

In short, it's actually very difficult to arrive at a conclusive evaluation.'

ROTTERDAM

18.09.2013 | 10:15 A.M.

City of Rotterdam. Meeting of the Executive Board and the municipal secretary.

A few days after our intervention, we were invited to the town hall for a meeting with the deputy mayor and then the city manager. Here is a summary of what was said:

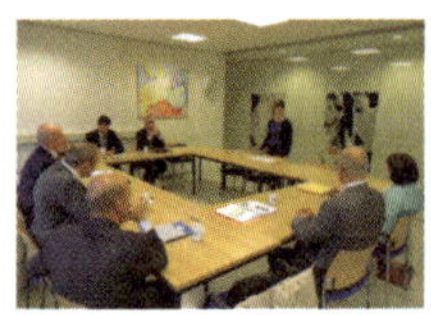

Deputy Mayor

'The group you addressed is a difficult group that is always ready to argue, the city manager has been trying to change this for a year.

When I announced your arrival, it created unease among some people. It is a group that is used to giving answers, not to dwell on questions.

This group has never been silent for more than 3 minutes in a row, and has certainly never listened in silence for 17 minutes. After you left, it was quiet. In the context in which you were guests, it is almost perilous to speak freely. In their function they have to operate mainly systematically, technologically—these are people who are mainly concerned with major, systematic decisions.

We've already made a lot of effort to allow the human element, it had never been a success before, but now it was, because people felt addressed by the questions. I myself was touched as a human being.

We were confronted with the power we have with regard to the system. The city of Rotterdam functions as a company and sometimes you have to make decisions concerning the work of 4000 people. If you then put yourself too much in the place of the people the decisions are about, you can no longer make those decisions.'

City Manager

'It's very nice that Sarah stays away from the ideological in the text, that would be too easy because then you wouldn't allow any dialogue, you can then either only applaud or fend off, go on the defensive. A text that doesn't take a stand makes it more dangerous because what do you do with someone who asks questions?

The text was political because everything, every act that overthrows something is political. It is also a philosophical text. Today ethical questions can no longer be asked. Morality also involves daring to go against a system and following your own moral compass.

My mother, for example, was upset recently because the slow train she always took had suddenly become an intercity. The train conductor, going against the rules, decided to stop for her anyway.

I love theatre, I love poetry, I love unexpected disruption.'

Diaconal centre, St Paul's Church. Support group for people in difficult living conditions.

Some feedback from our contact person

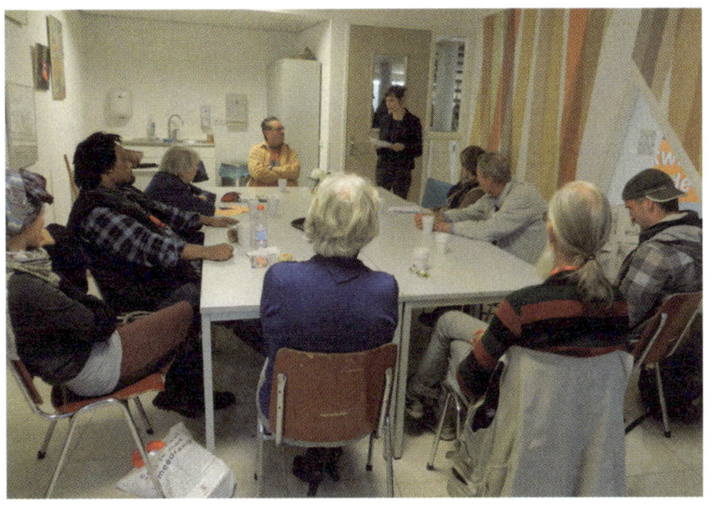

'Your visit left a deep impression, the words were very touching. In the beginning it was difficult to say anything about it because everyone was very quiet.

Afterwards there was a discussion about the questions Sarah asks, such as "Do you think you have more or less money than me?" It was said that you have to accept that some people are richer. Sometimes you don't know. You can think that someone is stronger and it turns out they're not.

I'm sorry I didn't try to get back to you about "We are before" because that's a very positive message. I myself had to think about this a lot: there's always a moment before you take action.

There was also talk about the fact that freedom is always limited by others. What freedom do you have for yourself? There was also talk about the relation between power and freedom.

"Care is not a sexy word." The city gardener, who always makes a good contribution to the group, said: "Care is a tender word". He was reminded of caring for his plants.

What I like about the text is that it appeals to thoughts and images instead of facts.'

ROTTERDAM

Wi Masanga, meeting centre of the Surinamese community in Rotterdam.

21.09.2013 | 6:00 P.M.

Some feedback from our contact person

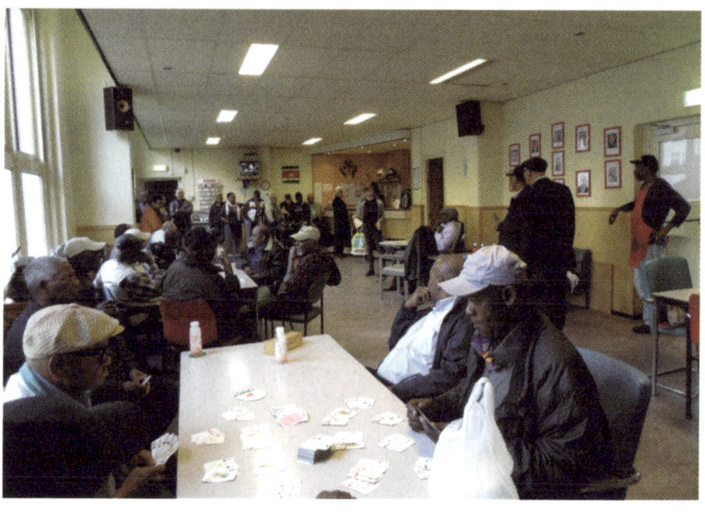

'It brought about more than I expected. In response to the catastrophe they had to imagine, someone in the audience shouted "the closure of this meeting centre". Subsequently, this call opened a positive dialogue/brainstorm. People started thinking about a possible financing of the community centre so that it could remain open after all. It was nice to be able to talk about this because the conversation had become clogged up.

Even a number of negative reactions from the group led to a dialogue: "What is she saying?", "What am I to do with her love?" were echoed back by someone else: "Where is your hospitality then?"

What was greatly appreciated was Sarah's energy, a combination of peace and invitation. And that energy was sustained, despite the chaos and the people calling out their comments. This attitude is very special for the people of Wi Masanga because they're not used to it. They're used to people getting angry or running away.

In this group it's an advantage to speak as a woman but a difficulty to speak as a white woman who, on top of it, has come to do something they didn't ask for.

I was grateful that you had chosen Wi Masanga for an LFEO because we're never really chosen for anything.'

JUST cosmetics. Product presentation and demonstration in a private home.

Some feedback from our contact person

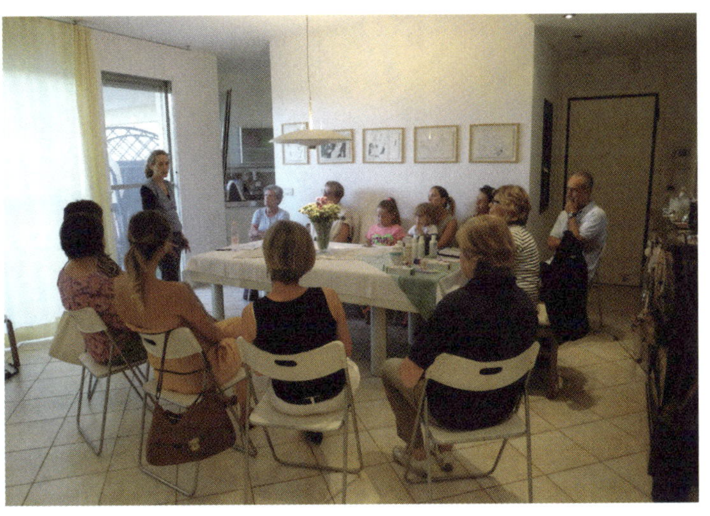

'LFEO could have been a shock but it was something very profound instead. The ladies were thankful for this "beautiful thing".

The text is not pessimistic, it's very realistic and it concerns every one. It's about things we actually already know, but if we don't stay awake, if we don't pause and reflect, these things risk being forgotten.

We can do things if we really want. There are conditions (social, political) that have made us who we are. But on a smaller scale, in our own family, we have choices and we can take steps. At least that's what I hope for my family and daughter.

We all have to do that, on a small scale. Otherwise we live just like atoms, without any concept of collectivity.

My mother was present during LFEO. Usually she doesn't like this kind of thing—art—she's not very attentive. And she's always running around. That's why I thought she would get angry, but instead she called the next day to say, "Good heavens, what a girl [Sara Masotti]! What beautiful things she told us!"

You need to make this project travel, and show it to as many people as possible. If someone says that LFEO doesn't concern him/her, they probably were refusing to listen right from the start already. It's not possible not to be concerned by LFEO because freedom and love are things that matter to everybody.'

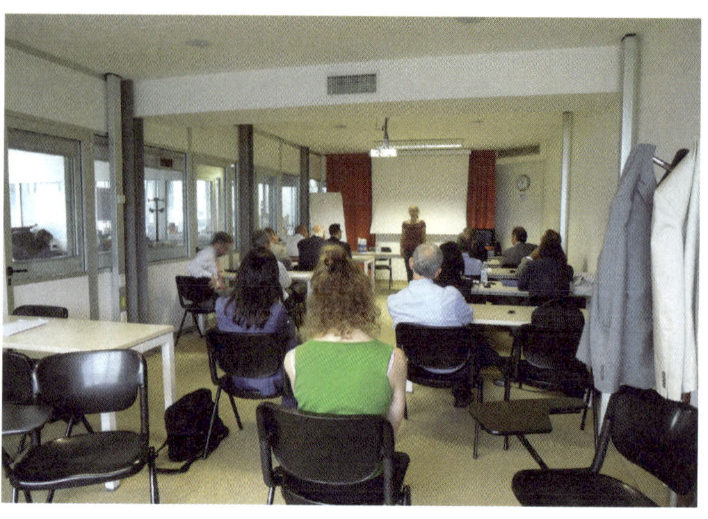

'LFEO was special, it was a magnetic moment.

All of the people present during LFEO know each other, but they're not at all used to speaking together about themes like those proposed by Sarah's text. They are strangers to the artistic discipline. They are salespeople.'

Studio Battistini, housing association. Yearly meeting.

Some feedback from our contact person

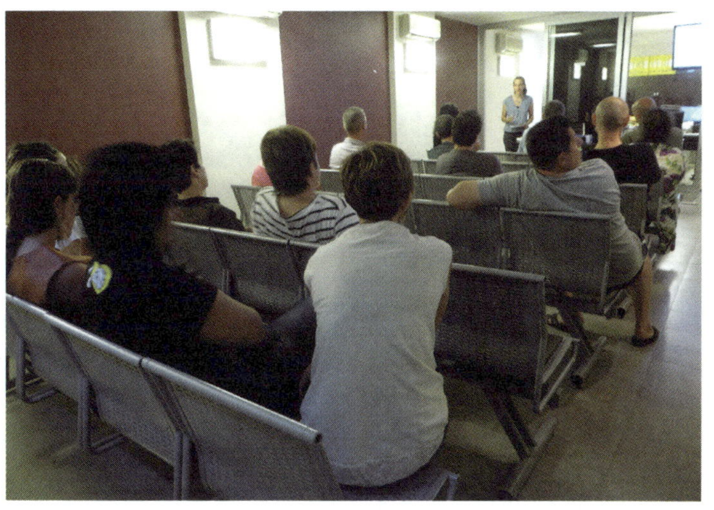

'There was a moment of silence after you had left, the need to digest the things that had been said. LFEO was a moment of reflection, with the right triggers and correct pauses to stimulate reflection. The language of LFEO was simple, but the thoughts were profound. The concept was about reflecting on the meaning of life and on values. We're always running around, asking ourselves who's the strongest, who's the most beautiful, who has more money... but in the end those are not the essential values.

Most significant was the carpet/suicide story. Because this story deals with values, it's about priorities that one chooses. What weight do we give to what values?

Opinions were clearly divided between men and women. Women received LFEO in a positive way, they found it a profound reflection. Some of the men didn't comment on LFEO, others didn't feel concerned by LFEO, they weren't interested, they found it a waste of time.'

SANTARCANGELO | 12.07.2014 | 8:30 P.M.

Society Club. Summer party and handover ceremony (investiture of the new president).

Conversation between Linda (LFEO collaborator) and our contact person

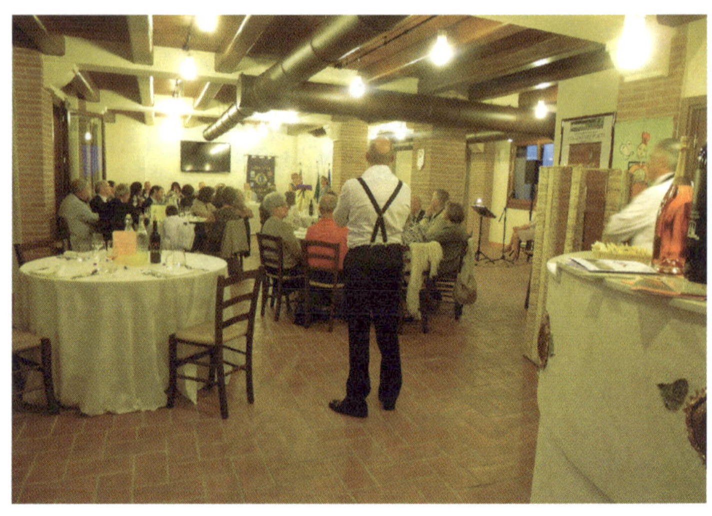

'What was LFEO like for you and your team?

The text speaks about things with a big impact, but a lot of people said it wasn't the right occasion for LFEO. It was a light-hearted evening, whereas the text raises important arguments that are also true, but hard. This was too big a contrast. Maybe a more serious meeting, like a business meeting, would be a better fit.

The actress didn't seem to speak about her personal life, but about the daily life of the author—who was certainly a more mature person than the actress.

Sara and Sarah are about the same age.

Then she must be a very profound person.'

Cappuccini Friars. Moment of prayer and encounter of the Novices with the Friars of the Convent.

Some feedback from our contact person

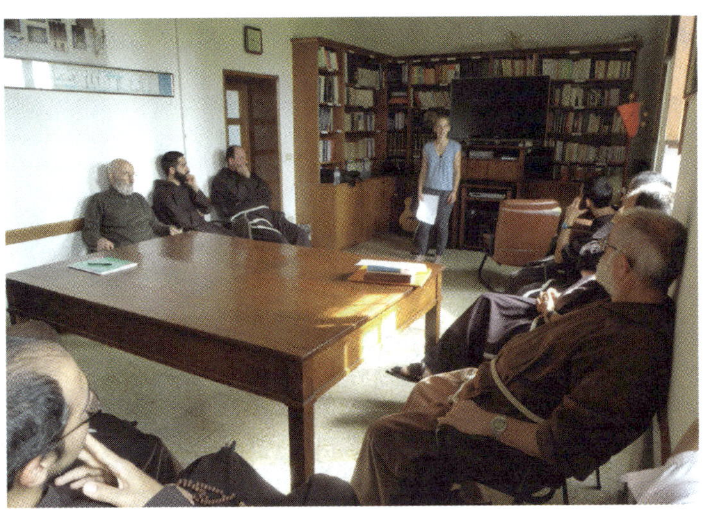

'Some found it a disturbance of an important moment, and not in a positive way. We almost all felt a lack of hope, and (too strong) a pessimism in the text. Even though at the end, the text opened up. Many thought that maybe the author of this text doesn't know God.

Some novizi had been afraid the performer was a psychologist who had come to evaluate and test them.

In the text I noted a quest, but also a lack of God within the author. I think LFEO could be useful for the *novizi,* because it can be provocative to be confronted with a text representing a lack of God, while oneself has a totally different vision.'

STOCKHOLM	12.06.2015	1:30 P.M.
Environmental department. Informal staff meeting.	Some feedback from our contact person	

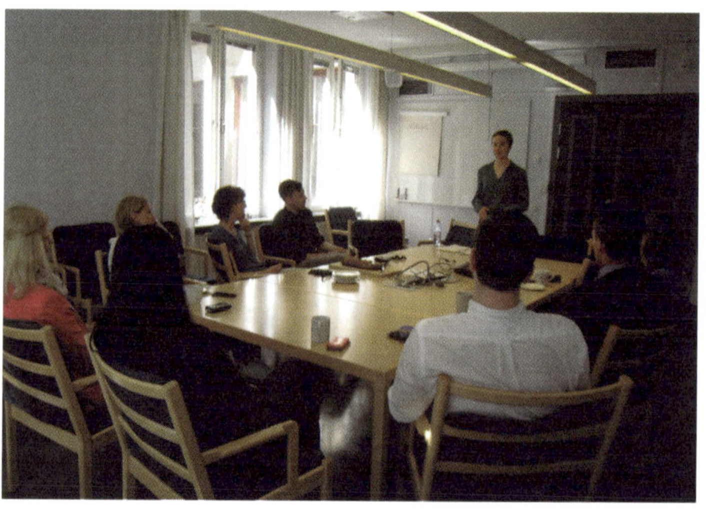

'It was fantastic, it went straight to my heart. Everyone was overwhelmed by the happening and very positive. We were surprised and shocked in a positive way, both by the fact that the lecture came as a surprise and by the content of the text.

You're in the middle of your daily life, which is very, very busy, and then there's this pause, this moment to reflect on the big issues. It was a significant change of mode: someone speaking slowly, looking at you, offering you these questions...'

STOCKHOLM

POOL, advertising company. An afterwork.

12.06.2015 | 3:00 P.M.

Some feedback from our contact person

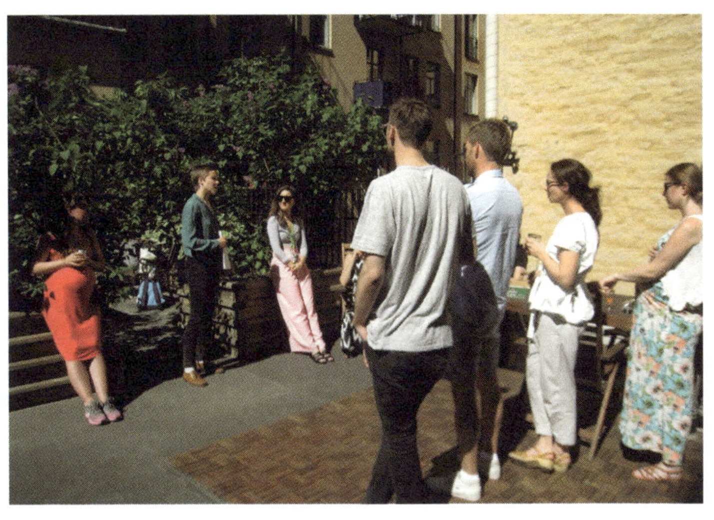

‘It was very touching, some of us almost started crying.

Someone wondered who the “sender” of the text was, whether there was an organization behind it like the Red Cross or something. We were even prepared to donate some money to this organization.’

TALLINN

KAFO, coffee enterprise. Weekly team meeting of the sales department.

25.08.2014 | 10:00 A.M.

Some feedback from our contact person

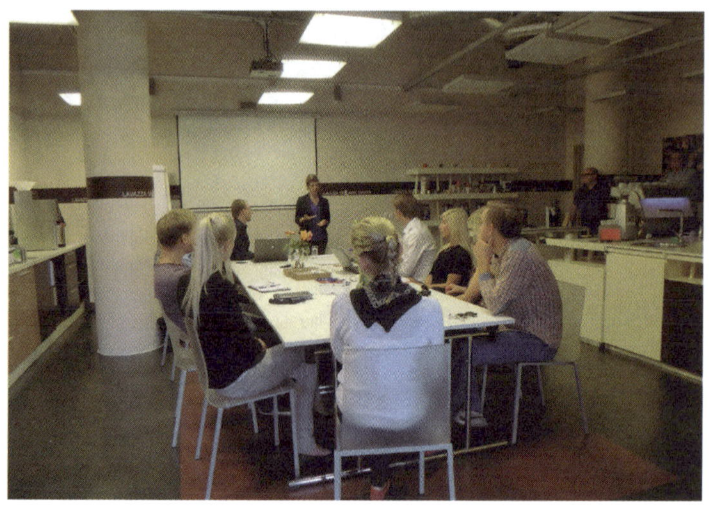

'LFEO was an extraordinary event, a spiritual event. Sarah was authentic, she reflected her inner thoughts, her real emotions in an authentic way.

The most critical topic to Estonians is probably the passage where the key words "surveillance" and "feeling unsafe" are mentioned. They are linked to questions about security, linked to Russia as the former power and Russian control of Estonia for many years. And therefore it also reminded the listeners of the current situation between Russia and Ukraine. Security, defence, occupation by Russia (and others) are topics we have to deal with. Those topics are very much part of the history of Estonia.'

An insurance company. Management and key stakeholders meeting.

Some feedback from our contact person

'It was good to have LFEO as a surprise. It is a special moment in your very grey, daily work life, it puts you in a different situation.

LFEO is very different to the life in a corporation and all the bullshit that goes on in corporations. Fake stuff. Fake people. People playing roles they think are necessary to play. People are conservative, worried about what our bosses somewhere over the ocean think of us. I hope that thanks to LFEO, some of my colleagues have had a moment to think, "Oh, I forgot about those things".

I try to wake them up sometimes. LFEO makes you think of how far from real life corporate life can be.

Corporate life has a lot of rules about everything—political correctness, gender equality, etc. It makes the world look very flat.

These big glass houses are filled with hypocrisy and with boring people.

In the part about "the system", I see a political link. I wasn't sure if it was just a performance or if Sarah really thought what she was saying, but I feel very much the way Sarah described it. Not only during LFEO. I often think about how kindergartens, schools, universities are producing the grey mass, the workforce. The social system pushes people to become those who pay taxes, who don't do crazy things, who don't complain—which is all good for the system. We are being driven more and more towards a certain way of life, as Sarah says: "The list of abnormal behaviour is getting longer." But actually that is what gives life its colour, like playing crazy music, doing surprise lectures... It should happen more often.'

Toggl, time-tracking software development. Weekly informal 'kitchen talk'.

Some feedback from our contact person

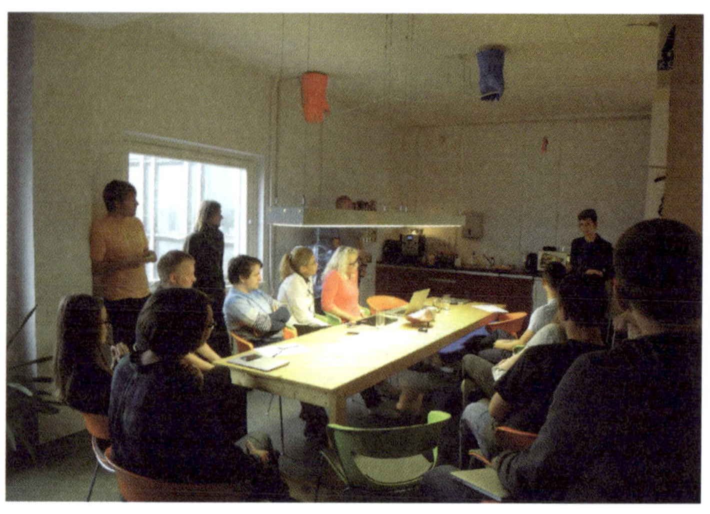

'In the evening I had trouble falling asleep, some of the sentences of LFEO kept popping up: the moment, we are before… The timing was very strange, late at night. But interesting that it happened, because I realized that somehow LFEO had worked on my subconscious, somehow strange connections were made. It's hard to tell what impact LFEO had on me. Somehow many of the ideas in the text were familiar to me, but subconsciously it made me think about things I hadn't thought about before, something I wasn't used to.

Not technology, but consumerism is a troubling thing. Technology makes it easier to connect to each other, to find people with the same thoughts, to create niche things (enterprises, e.g.). Technology actually can help to overcome consumerism. Maybe because we have the heritage of socialism, me and my generation are less inclined towards consumerism.

It was good to speak about care and love, because when life is fast-moving, like nowadays, it's easy to forget about these things.'

A political institution.

Some feedback from our contact person

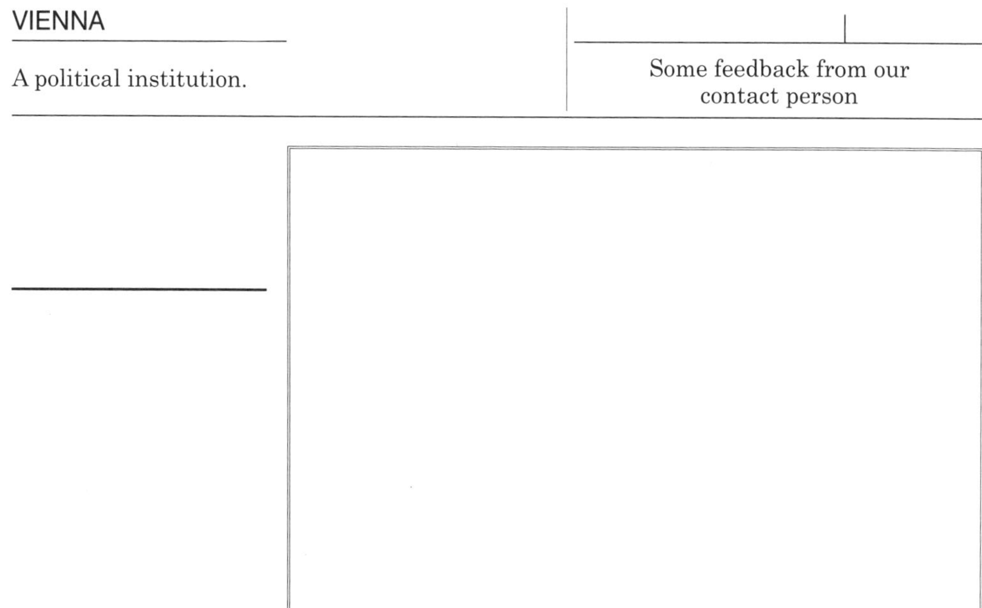

'Personally I could understand if someone refused to let LFEO come too close, because it's somehow an impertinence to have to listen to a text without being asked before.

We didn't talk about LFEO afterwards, we don't have a culture of exchanging personal opinions.

I had been afraid that LFEO would be embarrassing or too provocative, and indeed I found Sarah's questions provocative. That moment I had goose bumps—I felt responsible and hoped the text wouldn't get more and more provocative. But after all LFEO was thought provoking, and so were the questions, which is actually good.

The boss said it was more a psychological conference than an art project.

I'm not an "art freak", I think none of my colleagues are. This project seems to be very intellectual, the structure of the text is unusual, very interesting. Also the aesthetics of the website is interesting, with all those empty rooms.

The part on the system was touching: of course I'm part of a huge system here. Everything is totally formal and structured. So to speak about a system touches a nerve.'

VIENNA

MSC, Mediterranean Shipping Company. Biweekly meeting of the management department.

12.03.2014 | 2:00 P.M.

Some feedback from our contact person

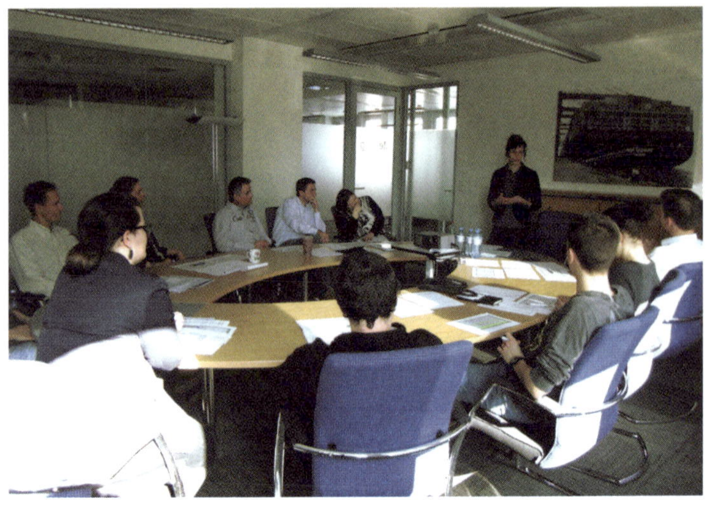

'You could see that people were at first sceptical, then interested. After LFEO the group decided not to continue the meeting. People agreed that a lot of input had been flowing in. The meeting would take place another day and everyone went off to let LFEO settle, to take some time for themselves.

Everyone described it as an interesting experience that had made them thoughtful.

I didn't think about LFEO "only" as an art project. Words were said that we're not used to talking about in daily life, such as "love" or "care". The culture at MSC is warm, people can exchange personal thoughts but of course the business world isn't fun in general. There's always too little time. One woman who had also attended LFEO came to my office today, crying.'

VIENNA

Best in Training, language school. German class.

13.03.2014 | 8:00 A.M.

Some feedback from our contact person

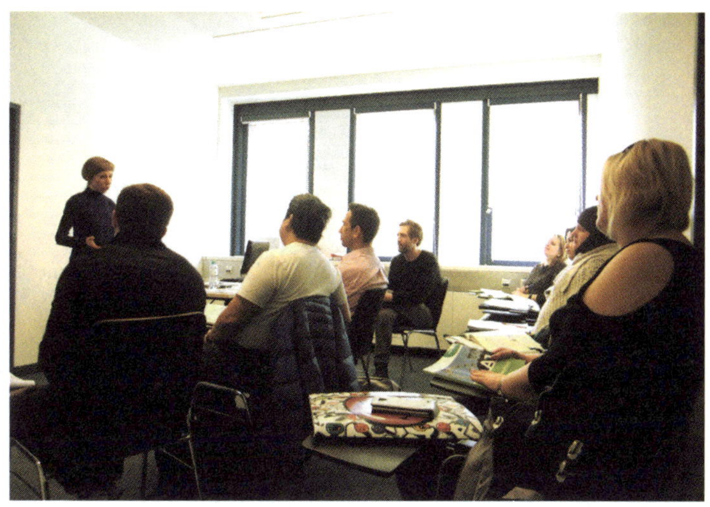

'The students didn't understand all that much of the text, so afterwards I had to explain it to them. This explanation was followed by an intense, emotional discussion (in broken German!) about freedom, money, media and surveillance. Some people almost started fighting, their opinions were so different. In order to do a bit of my German lesson, I had to interrupt the discussion after a while.'

VIENNA	13.03.2014	2:30 P.M.
Haus Rossau, home for the elderly. Before a mandolin concert for the residents and staff.	Some feedback from our contact person	

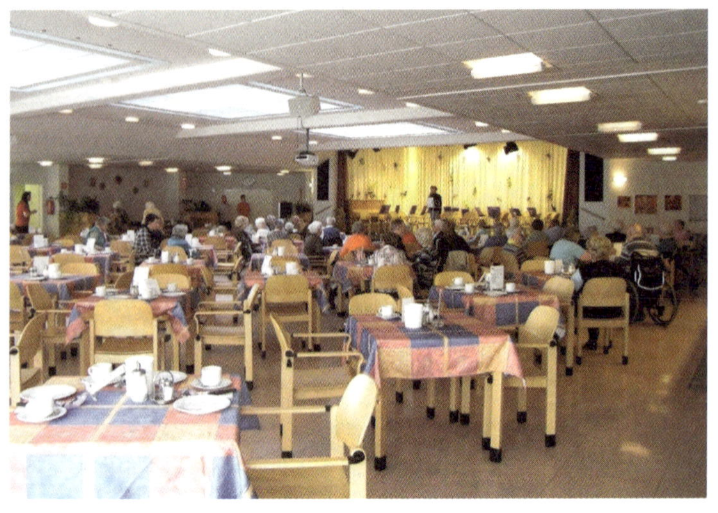

'I heard from residents that they didn't know what to do with LFEO or think of it, even though they're very open-minded in general. I think it's because the text doesn't have to deal with the reality of the residents. Some were scandalized by the part about sex. People were expecting the mandolin concert—having a break in their programme was disagreeable to them. It was an adventure, but we wouldn't take LFEO into our usual afternoon programme. LFEO is "modern art" and therefore it provokes discussions. If your aim was to create an exchange between people, you succeeded. People had things to talk about afterwards.'

Linda, the LFEO collaborator, adds:

'I personally spoke to an elderly lady afterwards who found LFEO very inspiring, it made her reflect. She said it was like Seebacher's poems—it makes you think about interesting things.'

VIENNA

Josefstadt Prison.
Informal meeting of the prison board.

20.03.2014 | 2:00 P.M.

Conversation between Linda (LFEO collaborator) and our contact person

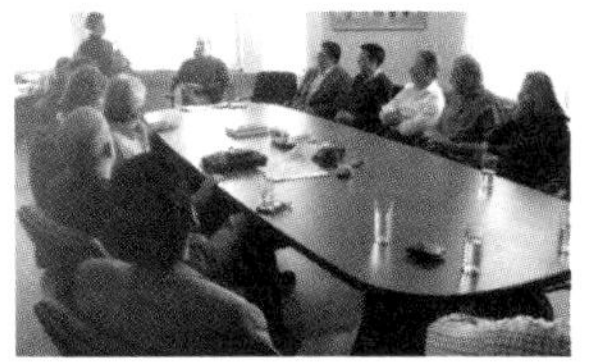

'What was LFEO like for you and for your team?

I liked it a lot. The reactions were very different: a third found they were forced into it (especially the prison officers); a third said it was something new, that they would think about it; a third liked it a lot (mainly those with a higher education, psychologists, etc.).

After the lecture there was a long silence, people dwelled on their thoughts. After a while they started conversations in smaller groups. Later, in a restaurant, people were quite thoughtful, it took longer than usual for them to get into a celebratory mood.

Was the text perceived as critical, political, personal…?

Mainly personal, especially the topic of sexuality. The carpet was a big hit, but it's always easier to make a joke than to talk about your own personal thoughts. I think everybody had their own thoughts about 'love', but nobody really talked about it. Some thought it was political and said things like, 'Well, that's leftists for you'.

What part of the text was most meaningful for you/them?

'We are before …'—the reaction was that somehow we are always before. The next morning, some people brought up examples of how they are before, so the text really seemed to have an effect on them. I think 'freedom' was also important, because everyone here works in an environment where people are not free. This is part of their job. Anyway, freedom always has its limits and it should have. If not, we would kill each other, even more than we already do.

About 'the system': I always try to show my employees that everyone can shape things on their own within the system. Everyone is responsible for him/herself and can change or influence things. The Justizanstalt is very hierarchical. A woman in a leading position is a big break. But it needs this break for higher esteem for everybody.

Would it have been different if the performer had been a man?

I think it would have been a difference for the men in the team—maybe there would have been more acceptance. But more interesting for me was Deborah's appearance, which seemed inappropriate for this environment and reminded me of my own situation. The size of the body is very important for the prisoners, also for the staff. For a small woman it's much harder to get attention.

I'll still think about this project when I'm retired.'

Logistics

Kristien Van den Brande,
Marijke Vandersmissen,
Marika Ingels, Linda Sepp
and others

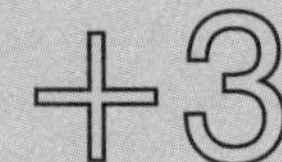

A Few Figures

Lecture For Every One was and is a collective and tentacular project. **From 2013 to 2018,** we infiltrated **328** different meetings with LFEO. On only 7 occasions was LFEO cancelled at the last minute. Since the lecture always takes place in the language of the respective meeting, the text now exists in **12** different languages: Dutch (Flemish), English, French, Finnish, Portuguese, Austrian German, Swedish, Italian, Estonian, Swiss German, Greek and Icelandic. The text was sometimes translated simultaneously on site, among others into Turkish and Arabic. **16** different performers performed LFEO over time.

In total, **7873** people have listened to Lecture For Every One. LFEO was produced and distributed by the arts centre CAMPO; **4** freelance collaborators also worked specifically on LFEO.

LFEO was supported and distributed by **27** different art organizations/institutes. These organizations paid CAMPO a fee with which the performer and the assistant were paid to carry out local LFEO interventions over the course of several days or weeks. Because each LFEO series had to be created each time a new on site, a rider was put together for the local organizations. The rider comprised **8** pages and several attachments.

Locations

Kristien Vandenbrande has drawn up a **13**-page list seeking to sketch the sociological background so as to be able to address ‘everyone’ and ‘every one’. It’s an attempt to think about the city in terms of the mobility between the different communities/gatherings versus the movement of individuals.

The LFEO is intended for gatherings of people who come together for various reasons. The LFEO is inserted into the existing gathering as a foreign object to which every individual can relate differently. It is a form of intrusion in the local fabric, a friendly stranger that asks for 15 minutes of their time.

People come together for all sorts of reasons, at their place of work, in their free time, for family reasons and so on. The LFEO could be given during **a team meeting, information or advisory session, debate, congress, lecture, discussion group, in-house training, editorial meeting, members' meeting, open day, introductory evening, personnel party, an account of a journey, consultation, (educational) study day, assessment or advisory committee, evaluation, board of directors' meeting, annual general meeting, crisis meeting, top management meeting, shareholders' meeting, company party or outing, international company summit, inter-sector consultation, networking day, showcase, guided tour, expert group, lobby group, seminar, jury, First Aid course, conference, study trip, drink, press conference, gala, dinner, premiere, skybox gathering, exhibition, book launch, working breakfast, thematic gathering, think-tank, celebration, workshop, reception, briefing, etc.**

There follows a non-exhaustive list of possible settings for an LFEO. In most cases the project will tour a series of venues. In this respect it is important to ensure a sort of dramaturgical distribution: both large and small groups, private and public, in the languages of local communities (e.g. in Brussels an equal division between Dutch- and French-speakers), in the various boroughs of a city, from prestigious meetings to informal gatherings etc. The list helps avoid such things as a preponderance of hobby groups in one and the same city.
We are not so much looking for the most unusual groups as for the groups that have some significance in a town or city, and how a city moves from one gathering to another, of completely different types.

An arts centre, festival or cultural centre may be able to help find contacts who can introduce us to the group or to someone in charge of the group who can introduce the LFEO. Much is expected of the grapevine.

Possible settings for a LFEO
General categories:

National groups
Religious groups
Service clubs
Good causes
Large private companies, multinationals
Telecom
Press
Independent professions
Banks and insurance
Leisure activities
Housing
Law
Public institutions
Government departments
Education and employment
Political movements and activists
Politics
Science
Congress centres and trade fairs
Care and medicine
Social care and welfare

Special occasions
Others

Distribution

Programmers (i.e. arts centres, cultural centres, theatres, galleries, festivals, biennales, etc. – simply referred to hereafter as 'the arts centre') can present the LFEO as an artistic intervention at 'gatherings' (which may or may not be familiar to them), micro and macro, temporary and sustainable communities, from family to society, from city to country.

An important aspect is that it is possible to devote a minimum level of attention to the LFEO (in this sense anything like a market or a party is unsuitable because the concentration is too meagre). Any gathering of people who 'have come together to...' is a potential audience for a LFEO.

Broadly speaking there are two possibilities: the LFEO goes on location or takes place in the arts centre. The vast majority of LFEO takes place outside the arts centre. Generally Sarah presents one or two announced lectures. More public presentations are subject of negotiation.

1) LFEO on location

The LFEO breaks into existing groups (preferably min. 10 people, unless very important meeting with less people), especially gatherings that are not necessarily familiar with an artistic intervention, for example a town council, a meeting of company shareholders, a family gathering, a union meeting, a support group and so on (see the website for more examples). Both the arts centre and the makers of the LFEO can put forward proposals regarding 'presentation venues'.

Note: This is private and not open to the public.

2) LFEO in the arts centre / 'announced lecture'

People come to the arts centre to see a presentation of LFEO. This is organized by the arts centre.
In the 'announced lecture' LFEO is shortly presented as a project (integrating the places where LFEO has been or will be in the respective city) and as a text (about 30 minutes). It is nice to have a Q&A immediately after this presentation, introduced and/or moderated by someone from the arts centre. It is also possible to organize an after talk or Q&A separately, eg. at the end of the series of LFEO in the city.
The 'announced lecture' is presented in a theatre or other suitable space in the arts centre (to be decided in consultation).

For announced lectures, the arts centre should provide technical support. For a technical rider, see the annex.

About planning

It's important to start looking for gatherings 3 or even 4 months beforehand, as it takes quite some time!

The overall planning of all lectures should be ready the latest 2 weeks before the first LFEO takes place. By then we should also have pictures of all locations for the website.

A maximum of 2 performances per day per performer can be given (only exceptionally 3 performances is possible).

There should be at least 2 hours between 2 lectures (an important factor is of course the distance between the locations).

FIRST CONTACT HOST ORGANISATIONS : EXAMPLES

EXAMPLE LETTER 1 / ENGLISH

Subject: inquiry on possible performance in May

Dear Sophie

As promised I send you more information about the project *Lecture For Every One*, a text by Sarah Vanhee, invited by Kunstenfestivaldesarts 2013. The text will be performed in 40 different situations in Brussels, between May 3 and 25.

Sarah Vanhee is a Belgian artist, working in performing arts, visual arts and literature (http://www.sarahvanhee.com/about). She has been invited by the Kunstenfestivaldesarts, with the idea of developing a lecture-performance on the current state of the human condition and the different forces acting upon society. How to live together with others, being an individual citizen/private person, but also being part of society and it's collective structures and organisation. How to find a vocabulary, a narrative, a reference frame that addresses this living together, between the singular and the collective, within a society that becomes increasingly atomized?
The text consists of personal anecdotes, (rhetorical) questions, humor, some more philosophical thoughts. She tries to speak "freely", as a citizen amongst other citizens, considering society as a co-creation on a daily basis.
It will be performed in Brussels in 40 different situations, in different languages, but she will always say the exact same text in every situation - whether that is a conference at KBC, a debate at Cercle Gaulois (society club), at football training, a Untion meeting, a weekly meeting at Nestlé, a training course of expats managers,... or a meeting at Médecins Sans Frontières?

After Brussels, the project will travel to Helsinki, Leuven, Gent, Rotterdam, Berlin, Amsterdam etc.

The lecture takes 15 minutes. It can be performed in French, Dutch or English. There's no cost, no technical set-up, no external audience or press.

Short description of the performance in French:

Lecture for Every One n'est pas un spectacle. C'est un intrus, un cadeau, un gentil virus qui se répand dans le tissu complexe de la ville. Avec cette création, Sarah Vanhee s'échappe du théâtre et entre dans le monde. Comme un "friendly stranger", l'artiste détourne des rassemblements communautaires – un comité d'entreprise, un conseil municipal, un comité de quartier... – pour y donner une courte conférence, et cela non moins de quarante fois durant le festival. Elle infiltre des contextes aussi différents qu'il se peut en posant toujours la même question : dans notre société fragmentée, est-il possible de s'adresser collectivement et individuellement à tous les citoyens ? Et cela, autrement qu'au travers des règles et des lois, des messages politiques, des médias de masse ou de la publicité. En vérité, existe-t-il aujourd'hui un cadre de référence partagé ? Ambitieuse et généreuse errance artistique à travers la ville, Lecture for Every One est une tentative de parler « librement » dans un geste qui combine le singulier et le public.

Sarah is very interested to bring this text within the context of MSF. This could be during the annual heads of mission week between May 20 and 24, or the general assembly on May 24.

I would be happy to meet you next week, to discuss this proposal live.

Could you please reply before March 7 if there is an interest? At the end of the week we try to set our agenda of May.

Thank you for your attention
and looking forward to hearing from you and a meaningful exchange,

Kind Regards,
Kristien

Kristien Van den Brande
artistic collarator Sarah Vanhee

CONVENTION / CONFIRMATION LETTER HOST ORGANISATIONS (examples: Brussels, kfda)

EXAMPLE CONVENTION / ENGLISH

Brussels, ... April 2013

Confirmation *Lecture For Every One* by Sarah Vanhee

Dear Sir / Madam,

Hereby, we are pleased to confirm that Kunstenfestivaldesarts and arts centre CAMPO are offering you, (name of the organization), an exclusive performance of *Lecture For Every One* by Sarah Vanhee. The presentation fits in with the programme of Kunstenfestivaldesarts 2013 in Brussels, which runs from the 3rd to the 25th of May.

The performance will be taking place on the ...th of May 2013, at ... o'clock in (exact location). The spoken language is (language). The performance is offered free of charge.

Sarah Vanhee (performance in Dutch and English) or Mylène Lauzon (performance in French) and 1 or 2 assistant (name(s)) are welcomed about ten minutes in advance by (name of the contact).

The lecture takes place within the existing setting and takes approximately fifteen minutes.
A picture will be taken (unless permission to do so has not been granted).
Neither of the parties is allowed to film during the lecture.

The name of your organization will be mentioned on the website of *Lecture For Every One* (www.lectureforeveryone.be). The picture of the lecture will be posted on the website as well.

After the lecture, attendants will be given a leaflet with information about the project.
On the 25th of May at 12 o'clock, Kunstenfestivaldesarts is organizing a discussion in the Beursschouwburg about the project and the experiences at the forty gatherings where the lecture will have taken place during the month of May. Everybody will be kindly invited to participate in this discussion, over a cup of coffee.

We would like to take the opportunity to thank you again for welcoming *Lecture For Every One* into your organization, and we are very much looking forward to it.

I will contact you again during the month of April to settle any last practical matters. If you have questions yourself, do not hesitate to contact me.

Kindest regards,

Kristien Van den Brande
Artistic assistant to Sarah Vanhee
On behalf of Kunstenfestivaldesarts & CAMPO

CALLSHEET LFEO – EXAMPLE / ENGLISH

DATE & TIME	23 May, 10 am Meet & leave at 9:30 am
WITH	Performer: Sarah Assistant: Linda Report: Linda Eyewitness: Mikael
WHAT	German Embassy Employees meeting 15 people – English
WHERE	Rue Jacques de Lalaing 8-14 1040 Brussels
CONTACT	Henrike Radermacher
PLAN	MEETING AT KUNST - WET

9:30 Meeting at Kunst-Wet
9:35 Walk to Rue Jacques de Lalaing 8-14 – 450m 6 mins

1. Head south on Av. des Arts/Kunstlaan toward Rue de la Loi - 26 m
2. Turn left onto Rue de la Loi/Wetstraat/N23 - 280 m
3. Turn right onto Rue de la Science/Wetenschapsstraat - 90 m
4. Turn left onto Rue Jacques de Lalaing/Jacques de Lalaingstraat - Destination will be on the left - 80 m

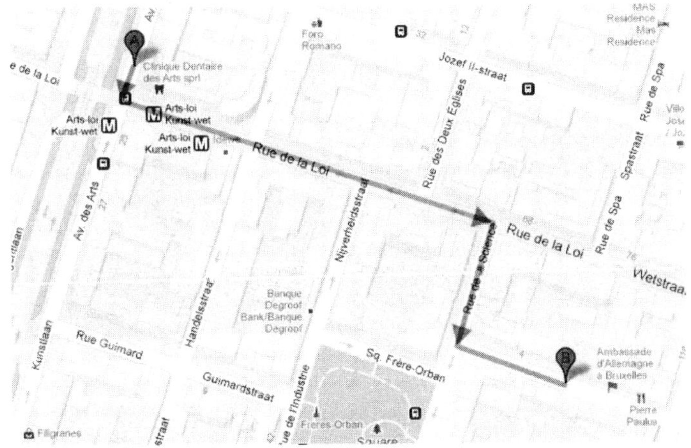

Tabelle1

Date	Place	Perf.Time	Meeting	Persons	Assistant / Eyewitness
SUNDAY 11.	Dance Atelier	12:00 to 17:00	Rehersal -	Sarah, Bryndís, Aude (Aude whole day?)	
	Dance Atelier	16:00-19:00	Rehearsal -	Sarah, Marta, Aude	
	Dance Atelier	Space booked from 9:00 to 21:00			
MONDAY 12.	Dance Atelier	10:00-15:00	working session	Aude and Sarah	
	Dance Atelier	16:00-20:00	Rehearsal	Sarah, Bryndis	
	Dance Atelier	17:00-19:00	Meeting, prep+ call the choir and University	Marta and Aude	
TUESDAY 13.	Dance Atelier	10:00-13:00	Rehearsal	Sarah, Bryndis	
	TRY OUT-Icelandic Academy of the arts	10:00	University meeting - meeting between all head of departments. Talking about the scho 9		
	TBC	16:00	Marta calls Atli from FG, Dísa from School dept and Ósk from Cheerleading team		
WEDNESDAY, 14.	High school FG-	9:00	End of the mathematics class. They are now in exams time so that breaks a bit their exam routine.	About 20 students aged 17-19	
		At the end	Marta sends Linda the picture		
	School department of the city	13:00	Executive commitee meeting	10-12	
		At the end	Marta sends Linda the picture		
		11:00	Marta calls Zoe from Red cross		
	Cheerleader team in Iceland- Valkyrjur	20:00	Rehearsal/training-starts at 19:30 we come at 20:00	about 9- strictly female	
		At the end	Marta sends Linda the picture		
THURSDAY, 15.	Dance Atelier	kl.16:00-17:15	Marta Kristjana from Orkuveita RVK+ æfa me Bryndisi með þýðingu		
	Red cross	17:45	One of the weekly meeting at the red cross office, they go to cook together and then play or go to the cinema etc. Don't speak very good icelandic. Most of them speak easy English, a RC volunteer would translate simultaneously	about ten- mostly male	
			Marta makes feedback calls from the three places and calls		
		At the end	Marta sends Linda the picture		
FRIDAY, 16.	City energy department	9:00	Organisation meeting for quality and security matters. Go over the measures and over the projects of the week.	6, 7 persons, Quality manager, security manager and their staff.	
		At the end	Marta sends Linda the picture		
	Arts Academy of Iceland	9:30-10:45	Driving to the Arts academy and break		
	Arts Academy of Iceland	10:00-11.00	Aude meets with tech		
	Arts Academy of Iceland	11.00-14:00	Public presentation rehearsal in the space		
	Arts Academy of Iceland	14:00-14:40	Break		
	Arts Academy of Iceland	15:00	Public presentation		
	Arts Academy of Iceland	16:00	Marta calls Sveinn from Matís and makes feedback call from Red cross volunteer (can happen before during the day if space)		
MONDAY 19.	Matís - Stjórn on Monday / FoodProcessing Company	09:00	Administration and management board, go over the week and its events and projects	12- 14 persons, managers	
		At the end	Marta sends Linda the picture		
		09:30	Marta calls Kristjana for feedback		
TUESDAY 20.			Marta calls Sveinn for feedback		

This will take 15 minutes, I will ask you to listen, and then I will leave again

A conversation with LFEO performers

+4

LFEO has been performed by 16 different performers in 12 different languages. Sometimes the local performers were proposed by the art institution, other times by Sarah.

Mylène Lauzon performed LFEO in French in 2013–2015 in 4 different cities. Katja Dreyer performed the German version in Darmstadt in 2014. Christine De Smedt performed the Flemish version in Evergem in 2015. Sarah Vanhee performed the Flemish and English versions in 2013–2019 in 24 different cities.

The following text is the result of a conversation between Mylène, Katja, Sarah and Christine that took place in Brussels on 17 October 2019.

S

What did it mean to you to say, to perform the text in all these different contexts?

K

It was so nice to extend my job as a performer outside the theatre, committing this friendly act of invasion. You just say, 'This will take 15 minutes, I will ask you to listen, and then I will leave again.' And through the words, you build a layer of energetic communication with the people there.

S

In what way did you feel you were doing a job?

K

To me being a performer is not a 'job', but something I need to do, it's part of me. I often do it in a black box, where people come to see it. This time it was possible to be a performer with this text as the ticket. 'Job' is the wrong word here.

M

For me it had more to do with the sense of using a universal language. The idea that what I was saying were actually words and thoughts that were meant for everybody. It was hearable, receivable for everybody. You don't have many occasions in your life to do that. This text positioned me in that place where I had this language, this meaningful, profound communication with a lot of different people.

C

I agree with the fact that these words connected me with them, and at the same time with many others who were or will be in the same situation.

The fact that I spoke Flemish was very special to me. I usually speak English in the performance context. Also, it wasn't in the city—which is the environment I mostly work in—but in an environment where they produce carpets and all kinds of industrial things. That context was very particular to me: to go from the city to the province and speak my native language. And then to get them to think about things unfamiliar to their work situation. The text moves from one thing to another. You 'get' them, and then there is a shift in the text and they have to think about something else. That situation is disturbing. It's a disturbing project. But it's also very soft. You're introduced by someone else, the contact person—like someone who places an invisible mental stage there for you. The introduction is super important. So the project does a lot to make them comfortable, and then uncomfortable. First you give them 'coffee and croissants' and invite them to 'make themselves comfortable', and then pfft, a smash in the face! And then 'ciao!'

M

'Deal with it!'
(collective laughter)

S

When you were in those places, did you feel that the intervention, the text, your presence had an impact? What did it produce?

K

I sensed different things from different people. Of course, my sensations may just be in my fantasy, but I take them for real, otherwise I can't work with them. Some people were resentful, curious, welcoming, happy; some felt you were feeding them with something… Some people were very grateful, others really rejecting… But all of them have to negotiate how to deal with this surprise. And that's something really nice to witness from so close, as a performer.

M

They form a small collectivity that has come together for a specific aim, right? And then you go there and open up something within that group. Whether the experience was meaningful or not, still they had an experience that is really different from what they are used to experiencing together. So that is something that stays there.

C

It's always a rupture, in any case.

S

How did you negotiate your own presence?

M

I don't have a career as a performer like you three. So maybe for me it's different. But I remember clearly that I wasn't trying. In a sense, the question is: who are you working for, the resistant ones, or the people who are 'with you' and open? I wasn't forcing my gaze, or trying to… It was more like, 'Ok, we're meeting each other here'. The text already makes people a bit uncomfortable, so I was trying to be as fluid as I could, not trying to grasp, or to force. If people retreated, I would just let them… That was more or less my 'tactic'—and to embrace everybody, even if they seemed absent.

K

The text is so strong that you can't put too much in it. You have to be the medium, you have to be present, but it's the text that's doing the work.

You were very clear, Sarah, in the way you wanted the text to be done.

S

In the end it became extremely scripted.

C

The context and the text demand a very specific performativity.

K

An attitude, something like, 'Well, are you ready? You're going to deal with me now. We're going to start, and I'll be gone soon.' There is a touch of violence, because they didn't ask you to come.

C

In that sense it requires a sort of neutrality, no? But being neutral and embracing, what do you do with your body to do that?

M

What helped me was to really focus on the partition, the space, the time, so that you don't really have to deal with the individual. The job is there.

But then we're human beings, and of course, if people don't give a shit, you can feel the tension, and then what do you do with that?

K

This, anyway, is something you cannot deal with when you are a performer.

C

It's not an interaction. I don't say these words because I think you're stupid or need to hear these words. And I don't take on a moralistic attitude either. That makes it very neutral.

M

You just leave it there, you just give it to them there, in the middle of the table and then they're responsible for whatever they do with it.

C

At the same time, the content of the lecture is not neutral, not at all… To talk about care, for instance…

M

It's really personal.

K

Because it's so strong, the words demand space. And the performer has to give the words the space, and the space between the words. It's really interesting… In fact, I'd like to do it again! *(laughs)*

S

Did you ever feel it was misplaced or did you ever feel uncomfortable imposing yourself on people?

C

Sometimes, yes. You stay neutral, but at the same there is so much going on in your head, in your body. When you leave you say, 'Phew!' Like in the municipal council, where I felt quite uncomfortable… and mostly in the bigger groups. In the smaller groups I had the feeling I was on the same level. But in the bigger groups… they have more options to not listen, and then you can get a little bit upset…

K

There are a series of problems to be solved when you arrive. The most difficult experience I had was a choir who wanted to rehearse a Stockhausen piece and the première was three days away. These people really wanted to sing together, and so I thought that was really a mismatch. The people were forgiving, it was totally fine, but in that moment, I had a really hard time. With people who are paid to be there, whose job it is, I don't mind stealing 20 minutes of their time. But with people who have paid babysitters to go and sing together…

M

The contact persons are really important. They have a lot of influence on how the experience will be received. When they introduce you, you feel it.

S

Christine, you said something striking to me earlier: 'You go there to get them to think'. One of my sources of inspiration at the time was Isabelle Stengers' *Capitalist Sorcery*. She emphasizes that, literally, today we have 'to get people to think'. To what extent was this also a political act for you?

C

It's also the crack in the wall letting some light in. I mean, it's not that we are the light—but somehow it helps to shed some light from a different perspective. And I think that's what we do with our work: we make people think. That doesn't mean it's only an intellectual thing. It's also sensorial, communication, how you stand in life, in your work, in relation to others. Is that political? I would say yes, to a certain extent.

M

For me, it's totally political. But I would turn it around. I wouldn't say it's turning a light on things, but rather revealing what's underneath, in the dark. You don't go there with a sense of authority, saying 'This…', and 'That…', turning a light on things. It's really like something super organic, personal, underground, which usually isn't discussed in society. We are all made of these preoccupations. It's really intimate. We usually don't go to work and put ourselves, our intimate selves out there. And yet we're not machines, are we? We go there as mums, as dads, having problems with our family, whatever. You're also busy underneath the surface of your function inside the group. So it's like saying, 'We're in it together, we're inhabited with all these things, and how can we make room for it? Care…' In that sense it's totally political: restoring intimacy as something we also share together.

S

The first thing we do in the text is to talk about the bodies and the faces of the people. To my feeling, this makes them utterly uncomfortable. Then, when we start the second page, the story, they start to relax. But addressing the bodies and the faces is something that's never done in these meetings. Saying, 'We're people, we're human, with real faces and bodies' is not something you ever start a meeting with.

M

And how you read the other, 'He looks tired', or 'She looks happy...' How do we really look at the other?

K

It's political but it's also subversive. That's what I really like about it. It's not activism, but almost.

M

And why isn't it activism?

C

Maybe it's a soft form of activism...

K

It's not such a soft form.

M

It's not a political discourse, but a political form, aesthetic—it is utterly artistic, right?

K

What politics are there between us? Between me and you. It's turning what is political into something very understandable.

C

In that sense, it connects to their eyes, their bodies, their money, their time. It connects immediately to the basic stuff. Plug in, plug in, plug in! You're constantly connected with what you're saying. It's not abstract.

M

It's not discursive.

S

Is there any situation, person, space, moment, emotion, energy, that you remember in particular from LFEO?

C

I remember someone crying, but I don't remember where, in which context. Some were completely emotional because of the text. It was probably in the meeting with the school board and teachers. People who were already much more connected to these kinds of questions, I think.

I can imagine—I'm projecting—that you can get emotional only because this person is standing there: the beauty of the situation, the beauty of someone making the effort to come and say this to us... Wow... It's like Aretha Franklin singing 'Amazing Grace'.

M

I remember this meeting of a group of people in precarious living conditions who didn't always have a home. They gather in this place, and they play football together, and after they meet in the cantine. There my intervention lasted very long. It was the first time I had to deal with people who were actually answering my questions. They were really attentive and listening. It really was a gift for them, an opportunity. It was almost like they were hearing the words and were touched and wanted to say something about it. As if they hadn't had any former occasions to have these types of reflections. It was really warm and quite astonishing, in a boys' club there. I know that when we left, something resonated and stayed with them.

And then there was the meeting with the old ladies in Paris. That text, for older people... How do you make a revolution in your life when you're past 70? They were really touched. All of them listening with clear eyes, some crying, some not. I don't know what it meant for them to have a young woman come there and say those words to them.

K

I also think that someone started crying, or else people were starting to hide behind each other, because they were feeling emotional and they didn't want their colleagues to see their vulnerability. Like with the architects, who started giggling. It's as if you tap into some emotion—they're so afraid they're going to explode. But that's my interpretation, of course.

S

How did you, as performers, feel about that, dropping the text and then just leaving?

K

I liked that a lot, because it gave them space to deal with it, and I hoped they didn't need me to deal with that space.

M

That's yet another political dimension. For me the why was so clear that I never felt uncomfortable. There is no superiority or hierarchy to what this text is, so it's a shared responsibility between you and the people in the meeting, as a group and as individuals, as to how you take care of the experience together.

K

You feel as though you're abandoning them, but with a warning. You give them space, leave them and relieve them of your presence: 'At last, she's gone!'

C

I agree with everything but I can still physically feel the abruptness of the situation. Like the municipal council, it was like, phew! You have to go and run and let the energy out, because there is an energy circulation. It's a little shock, each time.

M

Even in a small group, it's abrupt.

C

It's abrupt, and it did something to me. The presence of Marika, the assistant, was so important there—the care of the project towards the performer: when you leave, you have someone to take care of you. I've done solo work where you're completely alone, and being alone is horrible.

S

Did you take something from the project for yourself, as a person or as a performer?

M

It's linked to where I am at today, as the director of La Bellone… You address something, you give something, you know why, but you don't need people to understand right away. To be confident in the material and in time, it will 'make its way'. Now that I have to lead people, am responsible for them, it's like, ok, I open up stuff and I'm confident that it will do its work by itself, that you can let people do their thing with their own temporality. There's something fluid about it. It's not phallic, it's utterly feminist.

S

It's nice to see the project in terms of longevity. We don't have to be fooled by the belief that we do something and that we can immediately interpret a reaction.

K

What I learned as a performer is this special thing: you enter and you have to switch on your presence, without becoming an actor. We always have to be present, but what kind of presence? How can you get the attention… through changing something within yourself, a certain concentration. Connecting with the people, and the situation in the space.

C

We were talking about the solo before… I thought, if I have to do a solo again, it's not OK to just do it alone, to go out alone. It's not because it's a solo that you can't share it.

And the second thing that I got out of it is that I had the chance to be in all these different contexts. As you said, Katja, it's a ticket into these situations. This was so important.

S

What does it teach us about people coming together today?

K

There's always a big table somewhere!

C

Not always… My first time, some people were standing, others sitting, it was a more contemporary way of meeting, like at a bar, for entrepreneurs.

K

Most of my meetings had big tables—maybe for people to protect themselves behind.

I found it interesting that people meet so often. What do they meet for? Is it a formality? What does this formality represent for them?

M

Doing LFEO helped me to get this job. My interview for this job was with 12 persons in front of me. And seriously, I did the same sort of breathing and focusing like before performing LFEO.

K

I had a talk last weekend in Warsaw, with a woman running a festival. It was before the elections, and she kept saying, 'It's so good that you show this, it's exactly what we need', because 'We are before', 'We are before'… That's such a strong sentence in the text.

S

We will always be before.

K

How is it received or perceived as art?

M

I'd like to ask: where was the acting part in it? Because for me it wasn't acting. It was choreographed, I had directions, the concept and the aesthetics were super clear and we were prepared for it. But I was myself, talking to these people, with these words. And at some point, Sarah's words were so integrated…

K

Yes, I think there was no acting in there.

C

Or acting in the sense of non-acting. Yet I didn't feel these were my words. For me, thanks to Sarah's words I could be there. Otherwise I wouldn't get into this situation.

K

'We are together with these words.' I am saying the words, but I am also with them. That's different than saying, 'I am the author'.

S

Yet I felt the same. That's the reason I could keep doing it. I was telling myself, 'I'm just carrying this out', because I would sometimes feel resistance in myself after doing it ten times in three days… then I would tell myself the same kind of directions I gave you, like, 'OK, I'm also just doing this, lending myself to these words.'

K

If you're the author, you have to make the opposite movement. But it's the same movement—a distance you take from things.

Conversations with contact persons

Jan
De Brabanter

Taziana
Pyson

Anton
Wilsens

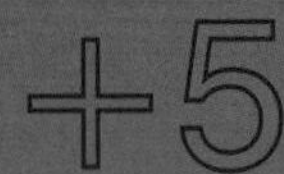

Jan De Brabanter

Is a boring meeting about trade the place to listen to art?

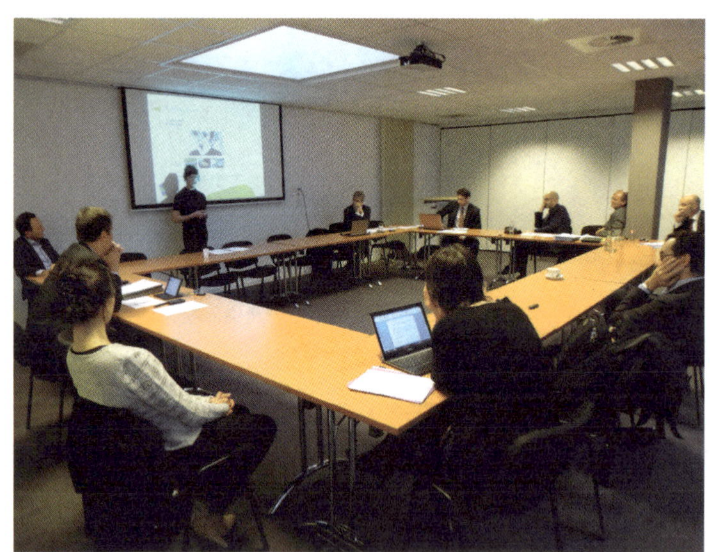

Jan De Brabanter is the secretary-general of BECI. He was the contact person who helped us to get into a meeting of the board of directors of BECI on 15 May 2013 in Brussels.

The following text is the result of a conversation between Jan De Brabanter and Sarah Vanhee that took place on 8 October 2019.

S

What is BECI?

J

BECI (Brussels Enterprises Commerce and Industry) is the Chamber of Commerce of Brussels but also the Union of Enterprises of Brussels, the defender of Brussels enterprises. You were the guest of the board of directors, which had to be convinced to let in a new element, an intruder! I'm not saying it's a conservative environment, but it is an environment in which expectations have been standardized. I attend the board of directors to learn what the priorities are for Belgian enterprises, how things stand as regards relations with the Brussels government, what the topics are, what the financial situation is... And then suddenly there was someone new playing with language. It was difficult for some, but it was nice. Some of the reactions I heard were quite good.

Before the meeting it was in fact quite difficult to convince people. People in the organization were asking, 'Isn't this going to make a poor impression? Alright, we love art, people are excited about it, but is a boring meeting about trade the place to listen to art, to do or experience art?' People from our environments go to the theatre to experience art; a meeting room as venue is a new element. But hence also the positive reactions that I got subsequently: 'That was refreshing', 'A moment of pause or a moment to reflect', 'Yes, I'm going to think about that'. To me it was in fact comparable to the violinists during lectures in the past. When a serious lecture was given in an auditorium, a quartet or something would perform during the break... A pause in a boring meeting.

S

Do you remember the moment when you were first approached about the project?

J

Kristien dropped by to see me. I found it amusing, also from my professional deformation: culture is also economics. I'm convinced, especially in Brussels, that culture and the arts are really a part of the city's activity. People all too often like to pigeonhole culture: 'That's something for the weekend or the evening'. Or at a light-hearted event, at a corporate event, etc. But it is precisely that interlacing that seems interesting to me. People who are engaged in culture are also confronted with issues of financial support, political trends, urban development, mobility and other things. So to me that connection is very useful. That is why I quite enjoyed suggesting to my CEO to hold the lecture during a meeting of the board of directors. I also played on the element of guilt. Imagine if we had said, 'We're not doing that'. Why not? How can you disillusion people by saying, 'We're not doing that'? And that was easy: I suggested that to my CEO, and indeed he said, 'Why not?'

S

Was it difficult for you not knowing what the content of the text was precisely?

J

Yes, of course! But that element of surprise is in fact typical of our business too. You always go to a meeting with a certain bias. In our environments, in a meeting of the board of directors, the work is done in advance. You are there to confirm decisions that you have in fact prepared in advance, which have been 'pre-chewed'. But sometimes things can suddenly take a very different turn. You think that everyone has agreed on the decision, and then suddenly you get resistance from an unexpected corner. A debate can then ensue leaving you facing some serious criticism. That is naturally the experience that I may have feared, with reactions like, 'Jan, you're nuts, don't ever do that again!' Then again, nothing ventured, nothing gained.

S

And do you remember anything about the content of the text?

J

Above all the *Spielerei,* the playing about, the wordcraft. It was a painting, a cascade of rhetoric! It was nice to listen to. I also found it exciting that you used terms taken from the world of meetings, with some puns, including on decision-making… Yes, I remember thinking at the time that you had adapted it to a sort of vocabulary that is typical of boring meetings, decision-making processes.

S

We have been to many different environments, and there's a question I often asked myself: what percentage of you as a private person is listening there?

J

I'll just speak for myself. If you have to operate in professional environments where it appears that the things you do clash with your own beliefs or with your private life, then something's wrong. Then you need to get a new job. That holds also for people who sit on a board of a directors. The board of directors of BECI consists of people who are not being paid. They are there because of a sense of social responsibility, or a certain self-interest, sometimes also because they are ego-driven and think 'I'm a on the board of directors of such and such'. But they're not paid, so there is a commitment. These are people who are really interested in the subjects that are being discussed. I see a lot of people there who want to do that on the basis of both their private life and their business concerns. That has to do with integrity. If I were to observe that the job I do today contradicts my principles, my beliefs, then I'd have to do something differently.

S

To what extent did my appearance as a young, white woman make a difference?

J

That's a pertinent question. It reminds me of the evolution in recent years. Some people might have thought, 'What's that young thing doing here?', with the idea, 'Is she a student? Or someone's daughter?' Listen to me, I'm talking like an old man! I think that today, more so than six years ago, it would raise far fewer questions. For instance, I notice that there are a lot of young women and young men too among the directors. That caste of directors of the Chamber of Commerce, with all these old men who still have some free time and are given the freedom by their enterprises to go to meetings—that has changed a bit. Brussels is a city of start-up companies, which we cherish because that's the future of the economy. So there has been an evolution there. Ten or 15 years ago, you would have seen far more old men and far fewer women on that board. The contrast with you might then have been even bigger.

S

The last word I pronounce is 'power', and then, 'this is for you'. So that's also what I tell every one. How do you deal with this power, within such a board of directors?

J

Everything is relative. You can perceive that negatively or positively. Within a meeting of the board of directors of the Chamber of Commerce, you have to assume a certain power, or let's say influence. Owing to a matter of representativity, we have members who have political or economic clout. Because we represent a specific group that does indeed want to have some say, and which, like a political party, has power because of an electorate. It gives an organization or an association power to discuss certain matters and to decide, according to the KPIs, as we call them, on objectives you have to achieve; that can go from the pure pursuit of profit to an urge for further development, or a higher level of employment, or new production lines. That's power. You have to describe it positively. 'Power over people' within enterprises would be negative. But that is so passé, because at the end of the day, people within their enterprise, also on account of their representativity, sometimes have more power in the company than the entrepreneurs themselves. Trade unions, for instance. So everything is relative.

S

If you yourself were to do an LFEO, what would it definitely have to include?

J

Firstly, I wouldn't be able to. I have great admiration for rhetoric and wordcraft, but I couldn't do it… But for myself? Consistency, being able to look yourself in the mirror. Not to do anything that clashes with your own beliefs or your own interests. Honesty, for sure. Authenticity. Professionally we are busy building bridges, bringing people in contact with one another. Allowing something new. I find that important.

Taziana Pyson

The margin is valuable

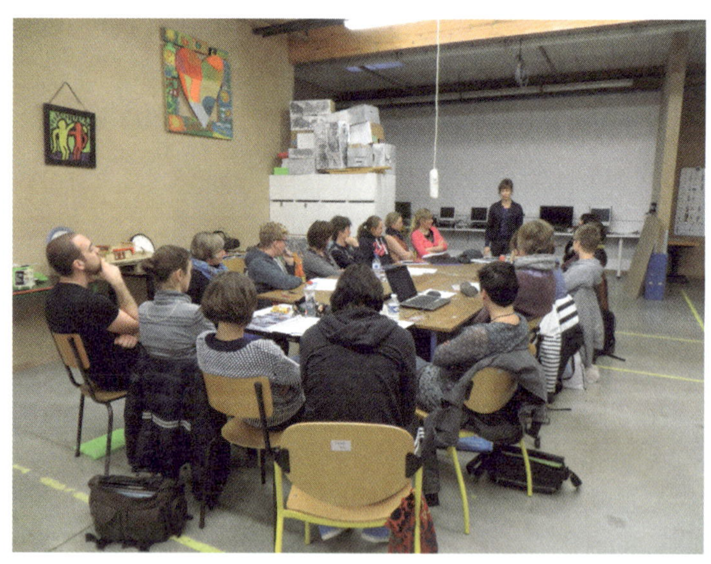

Taziana Pyson is the director of the special education school Dominiek Savio in the village of Gits. She was the contact person who helped us get into the school's staff meeting on 6 February 2014.

The following text is the result of a telephone conversation between Taziana Pyson and Sarah Vanhee that took place on 18 October 2019.

S

What do you remember about LFEO?

T

It was an exceptional gift that you gave to the team. Something that carries people to a different world in an unexpected manner. And the way in which it happened was exciting. I had no idea what it would be in terms of content. Nor what its impact would be. There were a number of people at the meeting who were culture-minded, but also a number of others. It took them out of their comfort zone. So at the time I asked myself, how are people going to experience this? Just now I asked someone I happened to bump into. He said, 'It was wonderful'. It was so long ago, but his face lit up at the thought... He was so happy! He could immediately visualize it too. And the same holds for me. When I think back, I see us sitting there, and I feel that same atmosphere again.

S

Can you try to describe that atmosphere?

T

At first people were like, 'What's this about?', 'Is this serious?' They only gradually stepped into your story, but were then fully immersed in it.

S

Did it leave any traces?

T

Mark referred to the story of the carpet... and then I remembered it too. But that wasn't something that I remembered specifically, for me it was more about the unexpected, about suddenly entering a different world... Less the content than the form of the performance—if I can call it that—the medium, the surprising nature of the medium... The opening up of your mind at that moment, but don't ask me what the precise contents were now. But that may have more to do with my memory. I have more of an emotional memory than a factual one.

S

How important was it that it came as a surprise to you and the people?

T

To me that's precisely the power of the medium. You can't have the effect of something that opens up your mind, but then first define the borders of how far it can be pulled open! You can't say, 'We want to be open-minded, we want to be open, but we want to ban a type of content'.

S

Do you think that I was there for those people as an artist or also simply as a person or a citizen?

T

It's a question you'd have to ask them, but I think that they really experienced you as an artist. So did I.

S

Is that easier than if I had been there as, say, a politician, an activist or a student?

T

Yes.

S

What then, to you, is the role of the artist?

T

That's a good question... *(long silence)* It reminds me above all of an image... Someone once told me that if at a certain point an anthill collapses, then it's always the ants that were on the edge of that hill, in the margins, that can keep going, that will survive the collapse. They can continue what was in the group. So you sometimes have to stand in the margins to be able to have that distance, and also to see the most vulnerable things in the group. You can accept things from an artist and let yourself be moved because it's someone who makes connections from a certain margin. Indeed, that also depends on who every artist is in him/herself, as a person. It's not a role, but it is the medium that determines whether 'I can act from the margins'. That's not the same as the mandate given to an activist or so. The margin contains something very lively that belongs to a culture, a structure. In that sense the margin is valuable rather than marginal. And art is a part of it too. If you are moved by something that is put on, it's because you are ready to listen to that person speaking from the margin. With you that happened from a position of vulnerability, not offensively. By contrast, activists often want to draw you to an opinion, or push you away from one. But touching from the margins, or drawing in from the margins, is another position, I find.

S

If you yourself were to do an LFEO, what word or concept would definitely have to be included?

T

Vulnerability.

S

One of the most important sentences in the text, and one that is constantly repeated, is, 'We are before'. Is that something that you can subscribe to in your profession or in your private life?

T

Yes, absolutely. I think that you can make a difference in a work environment and that that gives you power, no matter where you are in society, to act in a way that is focused on taking responsibility for others. A lot of things can make you feel powerless. But that's no excuse to let your daily behaviour be dominated by principles, evolutions or trends which you don't support. Even if you don't take direct action, through your resistance or in your behaviour, you can still play a part in society.

Anton Wilsens

They were caught unaware

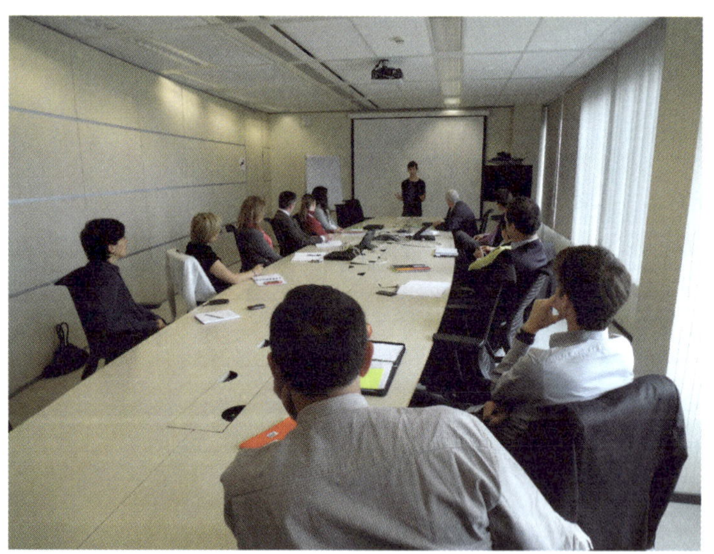

Anton Wilsens is head of Transition and Transformation at IBM. He was our contact person at IBM and helped us to enter with LFEO on 14 May 2013 at a meeting of the sales team for the Financial, Industrial and Distribution sector.

The following text is the result of a conversation between Anton Wilsens and Sarah Vanhee that took place on 16 October 2019.

S

What exactly do you do at IBM?

A

IBM offers outsourcing: we take over the IT of companies who no longer want to manage their IT themselves. The first phase of the takeover is called the 'transition'. After that we generally carry out a 'transformation': we make the IT more efficient, among others by applying our own standards, which we use around the world and which we've perfected over time. Outsourcing can concern not only equipment, but also people. I'm currently the director of the team for the Benelux, France, Spain, Portugal, Greece and Israel.

S

Are the companies you take over always of a certain size?

A

Not necessarily, they can be large or small. IBM is best known for the large ones. There are only a few that can do that. We can integrate two, three or four hundred people, because we are more than 350,000. And in my department, in the supply of IT services, we are more than 100,000. So when we integrate four or five hundred people, we'll feel it, but we can manage it.

S

Let's go back to 2013.
What exactly was the meeting we entered?

A

A biweekly team meeting which gathered all my colleagues of the time and our boss. I had suggested to my boss that we disrupt that pattern for once by bringing LFEO. Outside him and me, it was a complete surprise for everyone. It's something very unusual for IBM. As far as I know, it hasn't happened since.

S

Was it important that the request reached you via Eva, your sister, who was working for the Kunstenfestivaldesarts at the time?

A

That certainly helped. If Eva proposes something to me or recommends something, then I'm going to pay close attention. And the name Kunstenfestivaldesarts is kind of a quality label. But the proposal you were making had to be good on top of hat. So there were three criteria.

S

Do you remember anything of the contents of the text?

A

It's strange. I recently tried to remember, and so did my boss, but neither of us managed to recollect anything of the contents of the text. The only thing I remember is that it wasn't a classical text, no standard recitation, poem or prose. It was quite surprising and unexpected. People reacted differently to it. Not everyone could assess its artistic value, some took it too literally or too personally. But that's the thing about art, everyone takes it his or her own way. We knew that it was going to happen, and they didn't. They were caught unaware.

S

Do you remember anything about the kind of language I used compared to the language normally used in meetings?

A

We felt that the text wasn't a text that you would normally hear in a meeting. It was more expressive. I think that emotions in many business meetings are still avoided, you have to remain factual—although people do raise their voices sometimes—and some people can do that better than others, but the intonation here is a lot more monotonous, I think.

S

So you normally try to keep meetings free of emotion?

A

Yes, in the past especially. I think things are slowly beginning to change. We are working on 'engagement': how can you get your staff 'engaged'. People must feel that they can be themselves, that they can bring their emotions to IBM. Our slogan is: 'I believe, I belong, I matter'. The purpose is that people *believe* in the company and the strategy, that they feel that they belong in the company, and that what they do *matters*. That's not so simple, because in large companies people can very quickly feel like a number. So we try to ensure that everyone has the feeling—when he or she goes home in the evening—that he or she made a difference.

S

In short, the text argues that society is co-created by everyone. To what extent do you find that you are also giving shape to society by being a part of this company?

A

We see ourselves as a company that really wants to bring about change in society. For a lot of people, that's an important reason to work for IBM. IBM is an IT company that is more than a hundred years old and has always believed that we are doing IT to make the world a better place. For instance, we have a lot of AI solutions, which we use to cure cancer, for example, or to solve traffic problems. I personally believe that a lot of people are looking for a bigger goal in life, more than just working from 9 to 5 and then going home. The strange thing is that we are all working together here. We're a mini society, but we don't always know each other very well personally, and we can also be very different. At school your friends are a lot like you, listen to the same music, wear the same clothes. That's not the case here. Almost everyone wears a suit. It's not a written rule, and no one says you have to, it's just a custom. I find that exciting: you can't judge someone on the basis of their appearance, which does happen in everyday life. There are artists among us too, but you can't see it. One of the people in that meeting you were at is in fact a philosopher, but here he's just an IT expert. It's only when you get talking to him that you notice that there is in fact a lot more behind the façade. You actually make an abstraction of who the person is at home. My family had trouble with that, they didn't understand why I wanted to 'conform'. But I don't have a problem with that, I see that more as an instrument, a bit like a school uniform.

S

When I came to your meeting, did my appearance matter in any way?

A

As you noticed this morning, I think you stood out. That's the disadvantage of having everyone wear a suit. There is a certain uniformity, and then someone like you stands out, and people get piqued, 'What's she doing here?'

S

And yet I'd gone out of my way to wear something neutral. *(laughter)*

A

That's funny. One of my best friends works in the advertising sector, where he has a rather high function. He dresses a lot more individually than me, but he's seen there as 'the goody-goody'. While here he'd stand out. As they say, it's all about context. In advertising, they want everyone to be able to express themselves and decide for themselves what that means. The norms are different there, but they also have norms. When we talk about it, there's just as much pressure on people there to behave in a certain way.

S

You said that your company wants to bring about change in society. How do you evaluate whether change is really an improvement? To what extent does the company think about these things?

A

Yes, there are people working on that in special teams. They're working on data collection, for instance: a big issue is data collection and whether it's good or bad for humanity in terms of privacy. We have been the driving force behind having an ethical committee on the subject. We're also engaging in dialogue with the European Commission and with the US and other authorities to see how we can find a balance between creation and destruction. We also have very strict guidelines. There are a number of countries and entities with which we are not allowed to do business, often countries that violate human rights.

S

One of the sentences I use in the text is, 'There is no system outside of us', 'I don't see a system here, I see us'. Is that something you can relate to?

A

I can certainly relate to that, and I often say that to my people if they have a problem with the company. I tell them: 'We are IBM'. It's not 'me' or 'the company', we all make up IBM together. People sometimes have to stop playing the victim and see themselves as part of the whole instead of outside it. The classic example is 'I'm stuck *in* traffic' vs 'We *are* traffic'. You're not stuck in traffic that was organized by others for you. But people find that difficult. It's also a lot more comfortable to lean back and to say, 'I want to do it, but the company's making it difficult for me'.

S

Is that also a feeling you have with regard to society at large? Do you also feel like, 'We're creating it'?

A

I'm a bit lazier in that regard, to be honest. *(laughs)* In everyday life I'm more like, 'Guys, you solve this mess, I'm just going to keep running my own life, which is challenging enough in itself!' Because I work so hard here now, I leave things in my private life to others.

S

Is it not attractive enough?

A

First of all it comes down to a lack of time, and secondly to a fear of not being able to achieve enough concrete things. I have the feeling, but it's probably just a prejudice, that if I were sitting on the municipal council tomorrow, I'd be frustrated with the lack of progress. I've sat on management boards, and I already found them frustrating. They would literally say to me, 'Anton, you're from the private sector, but it's the public sector here, things can go a bit more slowly'. I have trouble with that.

S

Do you have the feeling that you can have more of an impact as who you are within the company than as a citizen?

A

Yes, absolutely. Also because I acquired that recognition here, grew within the company, and I also feel that I've acquired a certain impact or power—but I find that a strange word. When you feel that people believe in you, it's an extra motivation to keep growing within that context, and perhaps to do less on the side as a result.

S

When I entered your meeting, I was announced as a 'mystery guest'. And examples were given of where we had been already. These were quite similar companies: Nestlé, BNP Paribas, etc. I found that striking because I've gone with LFEO not only to companies, but for instance also to a municipal council, a meeting of homeless people, etc. Was legitimization necessary to say, 'Look, other companies are doing it too'?

A

I don't know why the boss chose that, I wouldn't have done that. But yes, it probably was an attempt at legitimization, to say 'This is serious stuff, boys'. That wasn't necessary, I think. I would have done it the opposite way, precisely. I would have said, 'They've just been in a metro, or a park, or a municipal council'. That would have been a more powerful signal, I find.

S

Is anyone in this company taken more seriously depending on age, skin colour, gender?

A

Difficult to say. The company is working hard on equality. IBM was one of the first companies worldwide to hire black employees in the US in the 1950s. The first black manager was, I think, also at IBM. We also have a very strong LGBT policy, diversity is very important. But people are people, so I can't rule out that some people think differently, but that's not what the company stands for. We see that women are still underrepresented in tech, and other minorities too. For instance, there are fewer migrants here. It's not entirely clear to me what that's due to. There is nothing formal opposing it, the situation is probably the same in society. There's no official guideline to the effect that 'hiring migrants is forbidden'. But there aren't any here. I don't know what dynamics are at play in this regard.

S

Is LFEO an artistic project, or a political one, or...?

A

I found the project artistic by definition, because it's an expression of a specific message in an artistic manner. I think that it is important that it was artistic, because not everyone can necessarily relate to the text. If the people know that it's art, they can also distance themselves more from it. It's not like you're a professor coming to tell us what *the* vision is, and where I would then feel bad because I don't share that vision.

And in any case you're on political ground when you talk about how people stand in society and how society is organized. That's why I find the artistic side more important, because in large companies especially, adopting a political standpoint isn't always encouraged, because you have to work alongside everyone, and you want everyone to feel open. So IBM is never going to adopt a strong political standpoint, except if it regards something extreme.

S

If you had the opportunity to do an LFEO, what would you put in the text?

A

An important point, I find, is the work/life balance. I think that society has pursued capitalism's model of 'constant growth', which I absolutely don't believe in—even though I work in a very capitalistic company, but that's another discussion. I'd like to advocate greater balance in the way in which we do things. But I don't know how I'd put it… How can it be tackled differently, be redistributed? Insights à la Thomas Piketty, in a sense.

S

There is a big question there, from an ecological and human perspective too: is that 'constant growth' necessary? Is that a question that can be raised within IBM?

A

I think that I'm one of the few, at my level, and in my own fashion, to be able to do that, although that may be a preconceived idea in itself. Most people may have a slightly more traditional or more capitalistic approach to life, but the question is worth raising. IBM is working hard on home office and flexibility. But you can tell that the higher up you are, the higher the expectations rise regarding your reachability. In formal terms you can be flexible, but in practice you have to put in long, unflexible hours. IBM is embedded in the narrative of eternal growth because we're listed on the stock exchange and every quarter we have the obligation to show that we have continued to grow. There's not much pity for a company going through a temporary dip. But what I saw as a very strong signal a month or two ago is that a charter was signed in the US between various large companies, where it said that we have to stop focusing only on shareholder value. The shareholder is one of the stakeholders, but the others – management, employees, clients, society—must also benefit. Our CEO, Virginia Rometty, was one of the co-signatories. At last, people are thinking along those lines at the highest level. I find that to be a very good evolution. I actually think that this is the only possible evolution that we as a company can make. We are all too focused on the financial objective, we have to take a broader perspective. Implementing this won't be easy, because pressure from those shareholders remains very high. But I'm proud that IBM was one of the co-signatories.

Lecture For Every One: political action as virtuoso performance and the redemptive potential of art

Gurur Ertem

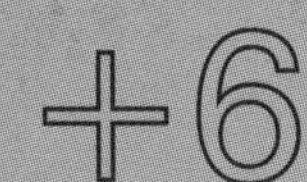

Gurur Ertem is a social scientist and performance studies scholar specializing in the sociology of the body, arts and culture. Sarah Vanhee invited her to write about LFEO on the basis of their long-term exchange as artists and researchers. Istanbul, November 2019

> The urge toward self-display—to respond by showing to the overwhelming effect of being shown—seems to be common to [humans] and animals. And just as the actor depends upon stage, fellow-actors, and spectators, to make his entrance, every living thing depends upon a world that solidly appears as the location for its own appearance, on fellow-creatures to play with, and on spectators to acknowledge and recognize its existence. Seen from the viewpoint of the spectators to whom it appears and from whose view it finally disappears, each individual life, its growth and decline, is a developmental process in which an entity unfolds itself in an upward movement until all its properties are fully exposed; this phase is followed by a period of standstill—its bloom or epiphany, as it were—which in turn is succeeded by the downward movement of disintegration that is terminated by complete disappearance. There are many perspectives in which this process can be seen, examined, and understood, but our criterion for what a living thing essentially is remains the same: in everyday life as well as in scientific study, it is determined by the relatively short time span of its full appearance, its epiphany [...] We, too, are appearances by virtue of arriving and departing, of appearing and disappearing; and while we come from a nowhere, we arrive well equipped to deal with whatever appears to us and to take part in the play of the world.
>
> — Hannah Arendt, *The Life of the Mind*

Who is this figure, this female 'alien', an intruder of sorts, who pops ups in diverse gatherings ranging from a meeting at the European Parliament to a choir rehearsal? Alone, exposed and vulnerable, she asserts herself in groups whose codes of conduct and expertise she is not familiar with and demands to be taken note of by daring to appear, carving herself a space of appearance within semi-public spaces of assembly. She delivers a text of about 15 minutes that speaks of care, freedom, love and power, or the lack thereof. She is alone yet polyvocal, embodying diverse voices collected through encounters with others. She does not preach. Neither does she launch a manifesto. Instead, she incites onlookers and witnesses to think about who she is, what she says and why it should matter. She addresses what it means to live together at a time when notions such as 'togetherness' and 'collectivity' have been emptied by politicians and countercultures alike. She also speaks about that which she could have said but did not. Her language is 'deceptively simple', yet one wonders if she is understood, even if she is heard.

Sarah Vanhee's performative intervention Lecture For Every One resonates with numerous concepts and concerns I have been grappling with in my recent thinking, such as the exilic condition and the arts, the figure of the artist as a perpetual stranger, the relations between aesthetics and political action, and the possibilities for maintaining our love for the world in dark times when reality has been rendered wobbly by attacks on factual truth, destroying our common, shared world. The performance adds layers and nuances to our thinking about political action, its affinities with aesthetics, and art as a commoning, i.e. world-building activity of the human condition.

For the purpose of this essay, I would like to narrow my focus to a few of the many intricate issues LFEO raises, namely the relation between *poiesis* and *praxis,* and the significance of the concept of 'appearance' for public life and politics. Under the light of Hannah Arendt's thought, I propose to think of LFEO as an instance of political action. Furthermore, I want to elaborate on the similarities Arendt draws between political action and virtuosic performance. Yet, again, thinking with Arendt, I would like to argue that LFEO is an example not only of (political) action *(praxis),* but also of 'work' *(poiesis)* as it is, ultimately, an artistically conceived performance. Thereby I would like to assert that LFEO is a prime example of the complementary nature of *poiesis* and *praxis.*

Much of what Hannah Arendt wrote on themes such as truth and politics, plurality, action, public freedom, and the revolutionary spirit resonates with and befriends our thinking about some central themes, perplexities, impasses and potentialities of the current political moment. Arendt sought to re-envision a positive concept of politics and restore the dignity of political action by going back to the pre-philosophical Greece and the revolutionary moments of the nineteenth century in the manner of a pearl diver, uncovering certain moments from the ruins of history.

I would like to continue by laying out the distinctions Arendt draws between the activities of 'labour', 'work' and 'action' as components of the *vita activa,* active life, and concentrate on her theory of political action to describe its affinities with performance. Given the ephemerality of action-as-sheer-performance and the unforeseeability of its outcomes, I analyse the significance of narrative, storytelling and the arts. That is, although some critics and commentators note that Arendt establishes a hierarchy between these three distinct realms of the *vita activa,* I would like to focus on how they are conceived as interdependent. I pay particular attention to the complementary nature of 'action' and 'work', *praxis* and *poiesis.*

In *The Human Condition* (1998 [1958]), Arendt outlines a positive concept of politics by weaving a web of concepts such as action, plurality, natality, space of appearance, public freedom and political judgement. She focuses here on the *vita activa* (active life), which has traditionally been contrasted with the *vita contemplativa* (contemplative life) and distinguishes three types of activities that characterize it: labour, work and action. 'Labour' is the type of activity that is required for survival: it is associated with biology and life itself. The products of labour, such as bread and clothes, are things that do not last but are necessary for survival. These are temporary things used up in consumption; so, arguably, the products of labour are not 'worldly' for Arendt. 'Work' is the activity that creates an artificial world that has some durability and permanence. It is with the activity of 'work' that humans create 'worldly' things such as objects, institutions, judgements, states and artworks. The products of work are lasting, and thus they create a common, shared world across time and space. For Arendt, the 'world' is something we make, something we fabricate. It is made up of the things that remain such as buildings, institutions, poetry, language, artworks. In other words, it is made up of the things that create the public realm that allows us to appear and interact with one another. 'Action' is the activity that does not involve an intermediary but takes place directly between human beings. It is speaking and doing things in public in such a way that they are noted and talked about, creating a memory and a history that connect and unite us as a people. For Arendt, action is ultimately related to the condition of plurality, and without action, we cannot fully participate in what it means to be human.

To act, for Arendt, is to begin something new, to set something in motion. It is the capacity to initiate, without the ultimate aim to achieve something or without the expectation of a particular outcome. It is to do something that begins a process that could not have been predicted on the basis of what came before. Every human being has this capacity although it may lie dormant, may be suppressed or destroyed by total domination. It is grounded in what Arendt called natality, meaning a new beginning inherent in every birth. By engaging in the public realm by speech and deed and gesture, we bring about a new beginning, a 'second birth'. Although action is grounded in the human capacity to bring about something new, we do not act in isolation or in a historical vacuum. Every action occurs in a context of plurality and in a web of already existing and emergent relationships. In other words, it takes place in the 'in-between'. Moreover, it always goes further and puts in relation and motion more than the acting agent(s) can predict. Arendt's point of view is characterized by taking seriously the fact that when we act, we never know the results of our actions; if we knew, we would not be free.

Political action, for Arendt, is performance *par excellence:* it does not subscribe to means-ends rationality; it is an end in itself. In that regard, it is similar to a virtuoso performance where one enjoys acting for its own sake. As the courses of action are irreversible and unpredictable, this 'treasure' can get lost in the murk of history. Establishing a common world and carrying forth the legacy of revolutionary moments requires skilled 'pearl divers' who memorialize this 'lost treasure' through stories, artworks, poetry and historiography. And, for these to be able to appear, to be looked at and talked about in ways that matter, depends, of course, on the existence of spaces of appearances, which is precisely that which authoritarian regimes and tyrannies aim to eradicate.

Unlike fabrication or work, action does not follow an instrumental, i.e. a means-ends rationality: it is sheer actuality. That is, there is nothing to achieve, no 'work' or 'product', but the deed itself. In that regard, for Arendt, there is an affinity between politics and the performing arts. In the section titled 'Power and the Space of Appearance', Arendt elaborates on how action is related to performance as *energeia,* i.e. 'sheer actuality'.

Another text in which Arendt discusses politics as performance is the 1961 essay 'What Is Freedom?'. Action, which is spontaneous, unexpected, not following rules or means-ends rationality, cannot be judged by moral rules but by standards of greatness, and this greatness can lie only in the performance itself. For Arendt, freedom is a performance, and to be free and to act are the same. Human beings are free as long as they act and not before or after. Furthermore, action is guided not by intellect or will preceding action, but springs from a principle, which becomes only manifest in the action itself (150–51). In that regard, Arendt considers the performing arts as closest to action, unlike other creative arts that make things, objects. The accomplishment is in the action itself and not manifest in the end product. As she writes:

> The performing arts… have indeed a strong affinity with politics. Performing artists—dancers, play-actors, musicians, and the like—need an audience to show their virtuosity, just as acting men need the presence of others before whom they can appear; both need a publicly organized space for their 'work,' and both depend upon others for the performance itself. (152)

Not only does Arendt consider freedom as performance, but she also conceives it as a 'virtuosic performance' by drawing on Machiavelli's concept of *virtù,* the effective, skilful and strategic exercise of power. As Arendt writes:

> Freedom as inherent in action is perhaps best illustrated by Machiavelli's concept of virtù, the excellence with which man answers the opportunities the world opens up before him in the guise of fortuna. Its meaning is best rendered by 'virtuosity,' that is, an excellence we attribute to the performing arts (as distinguished from the creative arts of making), where the accomplishment lies in the performance itself and not in an end product which outlasts the activity that brought it into existence and becomes independent of it…. The virtuoso-ship of Machiavelli's virtù somehow reminds us of the fact, although Machiavelli hardly knew it, that the Greeks always used such metaphors as flute-playing, dancing, healing, and seafaring to distinguish political from other activities, that is, that they drew their analogies from those arts in which virtuosity of performance is decisive.' (151–52)

So, why would anyone, then, act at all, if we cannot control the outcomes of our actions, and if we are not the sole agents of history? If action is boundless, irreversible and unpredictable, and if we cannot control how things work out, how do we deal with it? Why do we 'appear' at all?

For Arendt, the consequences of action are boundless: 'The smallest act in the most limited circumstances bears the seed of the same boundlessness, because one deed, and sometimes one word, suffices to change every constellation' *(Human Condition,* 190). In 'The Arts, Radical Politics, and Social Hope' I argued that this is the precondition of being hopeful, that is, to accept that we may never see the fruits of our endeavours in our lifetime. As Benjamin wrote in 'Theses on the Philosophy of History', 'nothing that has ever happened should be regarded as lost for history' (1940, Thesis III).

It is one of Arendt's most important claims that the meaning of action itself is dependent on the articulation retrospectively given to it by historians, narrators, poets, artists and storytellers. And herein lies the complementary nature of action and work, *praxis* and *poeisis*. Action always produces stories, intentionally or unintentionally. For Arendt, the perpetuation of memory in the story is the remedy for the frailty in acting. As we have said, the agent cannot control the results of his/her actions. Only when it's too late will he/she know what he/she has done: 'the light that illuminates processes of action, and therefore all historical processes, appears only at their end'. What distinguishes the meaning of an act can only be revealed when the action itself has been completed and has become a story susceptible to being told.

While Arendt wrote about political action from the perspective of the actor, in her later writings, such as *The Life of the Mind* (1978), she writes from the perspective of the spectator, wherein she underscores the significance of appearing for worldliness and public life. For Arendt, the world, the common, intersubjective, shared world is, first and foremost, a space of appearance. It is a space that provides human beings with a kind of stage, a polis, where they can appear to others. A passage from *The Life of the Mind* clearly illustrates this:

> In contrast to the inorganic thereness of lifeless matter, living beings are not mere appearances: To be alive means to be possessed by an urge towards self-display which answers the fact of one's own appearing-ness. Living things make their appearance like actors on a stage set for them. The stage is common to all who are alive, but it seems different to each species, different also to each individual specimen. Seeming—the it-seems-to-me, dokei moi—is the mode, perhaps the only possible one, in which an appearing world is acknowledged and perceived. To appear always means to seem to others, and this seeming varies according to the standpoint and the perspective of the spectators. (21)

To conclude, with Lecture for Every One, Sarah Vanhee achieves several things at once. She illuminates the possibilities of art as political action. Also, she demonstrates how, with the performance itself and its aftermath—for instance, with this book project—artists as both political agents and storytellers can and do bear witness to the history of the present.

References

Arendt, Hannah. 1998. *The Human Condition*. Chicago University Press.
Arendt, Hannah. 1978. *The Life of the Mind*. Harcourt Brace Jovanovich.
Arendt, Hannah. 1961. 'What Is Freedom?' In: *Between Past and Future*. Penguin Classics.
Benjamin, Walter. 1940. 'Theses on the Philosophy of History.' In: *Illuminations*. Pimlico.
Ertem, Gurur. 2018. 'The Arts, Radical Politics, and Social Hope.' www.gururertem.info/uploads/8/8/7/6/88765342/the_arts_radical_politicsand_social_hope_engaging_histories.pdf.

The artist who stole the microphone

Memories of Sarah Vanhee

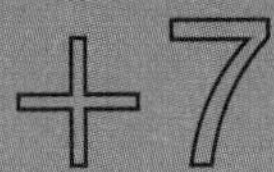

AMSTERDAM

28.10.2014
1:30 P.M.

DIKS car rental. Meeting of the management team.

S

At the meeting of the management team of DIKS car rental, there are, as expected, only men around the table. More blue collar than in a usual management meeting, that's true. They listen carefully but distantly. I feel fragile and also a bit too soft for this male environment, especially because I'm visibly five-months pregnant. After a few minutes a man enters, late. He just pulls up a chair, doesn't seem to ask himself what is going on, simply puts up with the situation. When I ask the question 'Do you think you're stronger than I am?', he answers, spontaneously, that you can be strong in different ways, that physical strength isn't everything. Something changes in the room. It relaxes, warms up. He reacts to everything I say, with very precise answers, based on careful listening, and involves the others. What do they think? When I talk about 'care', he says something like, 'We all have to take care of each other, it's the most important thing in life. It's something to *do,* you should never forget that.' A man like that in blue overalls, with big hands, tender and generous, on a Tuesday morning, in front of his tough colleagues. I have, I think, met the heart of DIKS car rental.

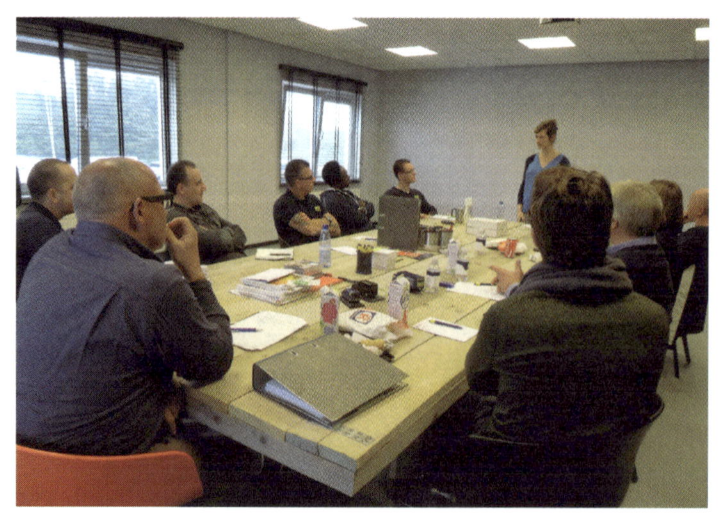

GHENT

09.04.2013
9:00 P.M.

Lions Club, gentlemen's club. Dinner-debate.

S

Every fortnight, the Lions Club comes together in order to dine, network and discuss what good causes they're going to spend their money on. Right before dessert is served, I arrive in an elegant reception hall. About eighty white men are seated at round tables, having already dined and wined. The man who introduces me is MCing for the first time. He is nervous and chaotic. After his introduction, I have to make an effort to capture the attention, to address people individually. After about three minutes, my effort pays off, they're on board. They even chant 'We are before' with me cheerfully. Towards the end, things quieten down.
As I leave, amidst applause, the MC chases after me. He can't find his mic anymore and accuses me of stealing it. The cliché of the poor artist taking advantage of the situation... He won't let it go, won't let me go, until our friendly contact person intervenes and, in an apologetic tone, says that they 'really are very expensive microphones'. Later he lets me know that he thought it was a 'wonderful presentation' and whether I'd like to do it again for a Lions Club? I tell him that it's not a service I offer, we only invite ourselves.

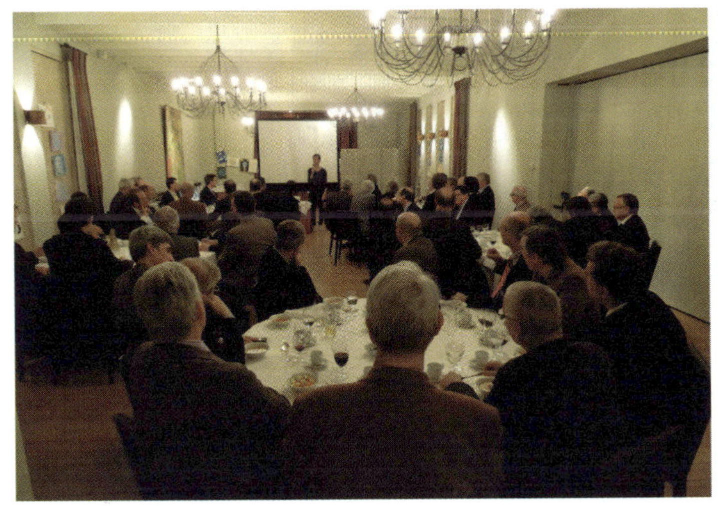

GHENT

23.10.2013
1:00 P.M.

Psychiatric Centre Dr. Guislain, department De Klip. Meeting of the residents with some staff members to discuss the practical issues of the next day.

S

The room is full, people are seated around the table and beside it, in the corners. In some environments, like this one, I find it difficult to say: 'Here we are. Some of us more damaged than others, some of us more troubled, some of us more wounded than others.' I say it almost hastily, formally. When I ask, 'Do you think you have more or less money than I have?', a man answers: 'Money is the sin of the world'. He keeps repeating it throughout the lecture, roughly every minute: 'Money is the sin of the world.'

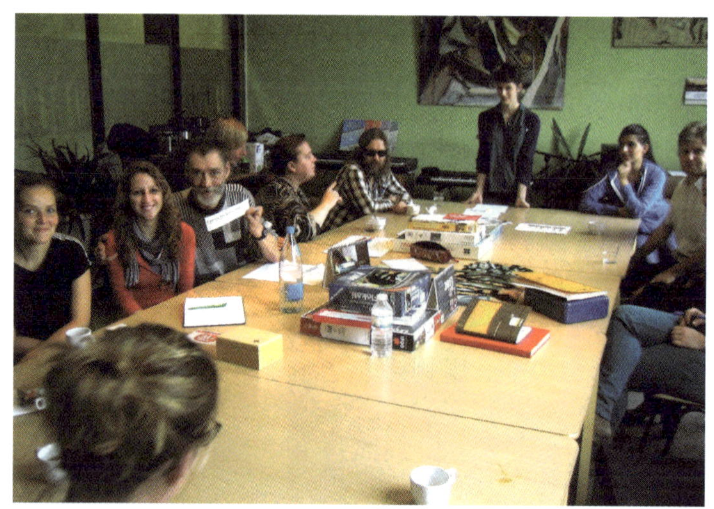

KORTRIJK

26.04.2014
2:00 P.M.

Police. Daily briefing of the intervention team, late service.

S

Edith and I are too early, we wait in the car park in front of the police station. A tragedy is unfolding: a car arrives with screeching tyres, a mother and two children jump out, they want to run inside. An officer stops them, 'You can't park there, Ms'. The woman is hysterical, 'My ex, my ex, he's been released and he's coming for us'. The children at her side are trembling. 'He has a knife, he wants to kill us all!' The officer is not impressed. He says she first has to move her car. Then they dash into the station. Edith and I end up in the same waiting room as them. 'Living alone. Living with others. Here we are…' I can now deliver the lecture to the intervention team. Half the team is out answering calls, about six uniformed officers are seated around the table. We constantly hear calls and alarm bells, from an intercom and their own walkie-talkies. The officers are clearly used to the constant interruptions so I decide to ignore them too. It surprises me how, despite all the commotion, they can really listen. They look surprised, a bit bewildered too. Just after I say, 'We are before', a call comes in. There's been a break-in. Two officers jump up immediately. The voice in the intercom says something else that I can't understand. 'Ah, the thief's gone already', the officers say, and sit down casually again to listen. The emergencies in the lecture are of a totally different order than those which these officers face on a daily basis. What world do we share?

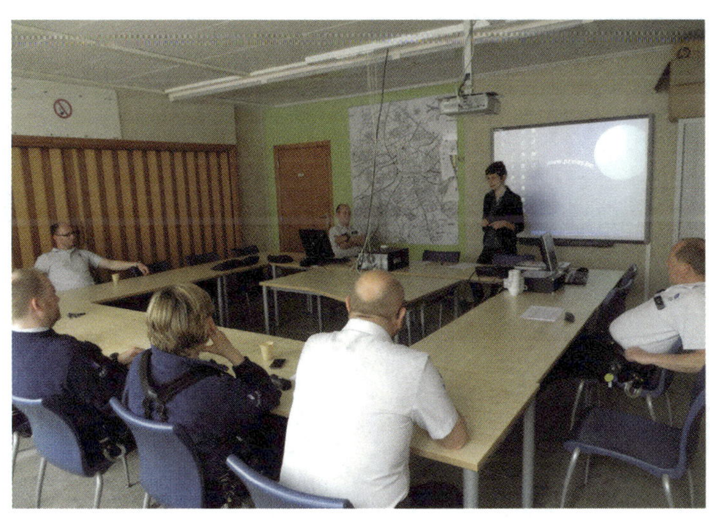

GHENT

17.10.2013
1:30 P.M.

Children's house De Sloep. Group session on educational support for Turkish mothers.

S

I generally stand at the head of the meeting table. This feels out of place here, it's so cosy with the coffee and the tea and all the mums gathered together. So I sit among them, with a Turkish interpreter at my side. I feel comfortable in this company. The women are attentive and look at me warmly. After only six sentences, the young woman sitting next to me interrupts me. 'Your words are very nice', she says, 'but they're also painful to me'. I hear her, I feel her, I try to continue as softly as possible. The women answer, react, often emotionally. When I tell the story of the taxi driver, they are shocked; when I talk about the widespread fear of the other, they nod seriously. The lady at my side continues to comment, I'm grateful to her, it is as though she can translate emotions. She too is a parrhesiast.

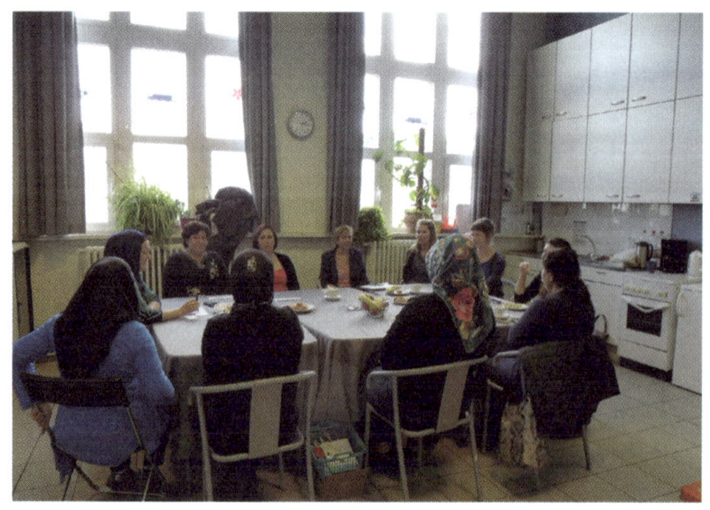

LISBON

06.12.2013
8:15 P.M.

Goethe-Institut. Farewell party for the director.

S

At the Goethe-Institut in Lisbon, I deliver the LFEO as a surprise during the farewell party of the director. It's not that easy to do from a raised stage, with an audience that is downing champagne. At the end a man comes up to me. The lecture moved him, he says, and he absolutely wants to introduce me to the work of a Portuguese writer (whose name I'd never heard). I remind him so much of her. A few days later I receive a package with two books by Maria Gabriela Llansol. And an email: 'We talked briefly at the Goethe-Institut after your "Lecture for every one", and I promised you I would leave you at the Teatro Maria Matos one or two books by that woman-writer who lived 20 years in exile in Leuven, and whose universe has so many affinities with your (and my) way of seeing the world today. I left you two of Llansol's books in French translation today at the artist's entrance of the Theatre. If and when you find some time to read them, I suggest you start with *Le jeu de la liberté de l'âme.* I am sure you will be startled by the powerful beginning of this book. The other one, *Finita,* is her second diary, dealing with experiences of the 70's and 80's in Belgium.'

I leaf through the book. Llansol coined a word, *'legente'* which means: the one who reads, but then in an active, intervening manner. A bit further I read another sentence that reminds me indeed of LFEO: *'Et j'ai pensé que la communicabilité des arts — et aussi bien celle d'aimer — n'avait aucun pouvoir.'*

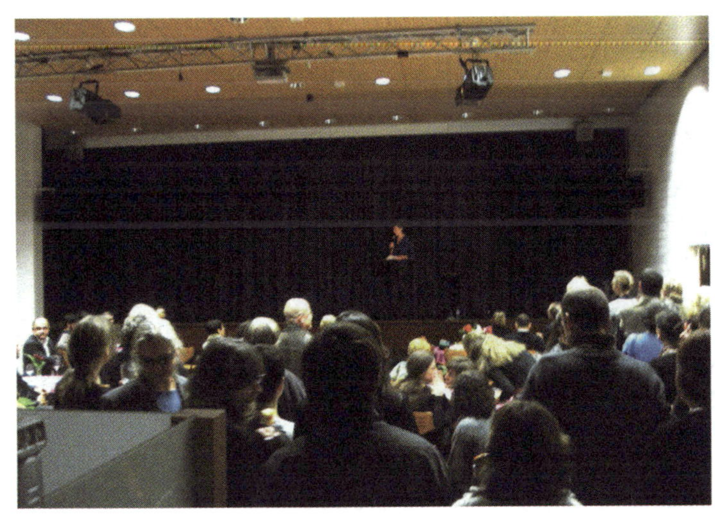

ROTTERDAM

17.09.2013
1:00 P.M.

Hogeschool InHolland. Consultation of the Board of Examiners of the Media & Entertainment Management section.

S

I never forget this intervention because there was someone who became so terribly angry. He won't say it out loud, I can just tell from his face that is slowly turning red, his energy, he seems to be trembling with rage. It is an unpleasant environment, such a context in which everything has to be conceptually transparent, and which makes you feel unsafe. Everything is of glass here, but there is in fact too little space, space that is constantly flooded by sounds from next door or above or below—so transparent in fact that you can't actually say anything anymore really. In the beginning, the man just looks on with a grumpy expression, but the more I read, the angrier he gets. I focus on other faces, quite friendly, quite soft, but that man, it's as if his veins were about to pop. I'm relieved to be able to leave, and when I go out, I almost feel pity for the man, for having tortured him so terribly with my 15-minute lecture.

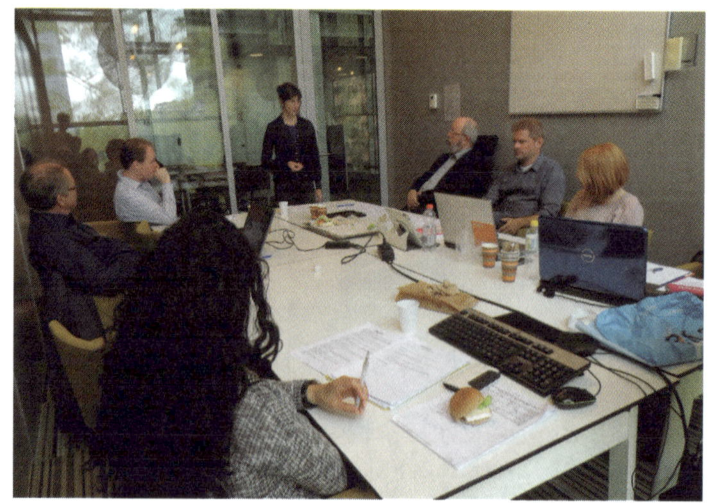

ROTTERDAM

19.09.2013
12:30 P.M.

St Paul's Church, church café. Meeting where recent events with regard to Bible stories are being discussed.

S

This is such a stark contrast with the Rotterdam concern management that I visited in the morning, where powerful people gather, people who know they hold the strings. These people, the drop-outs, former addicts and homeless people who come to St Paul's Church, find themselves on the other side of the company called the city of Rotterdam. Half a dozen people are seated here. Even before I open my mouth, someone starts sniggering. Later I learn that he recently tried to kill himself. While in the morning I had to show that I knew what I was doing, had to direct my gaze and text in a clear direction, it now feels as though just thinking the words is enough. The people's fragility disarms me. Reading the faces and the bodies demands not the least effort. Where I initially thought that it would be cynical to talk about the system with these people, it strikes me now that they're in close contact with that system, and know exactly what I'm talking about. But when I talk about fear and love and care, they also listen with their open, almost tender faces, nodding and smiling. And crying. When at the end I say the word 'power', and 'this is for you', I mean it from the bottom of my heart. To me, they have the power to make me feel completely safe, gentle and vulnerable. That is a power the concern management doesn't have.

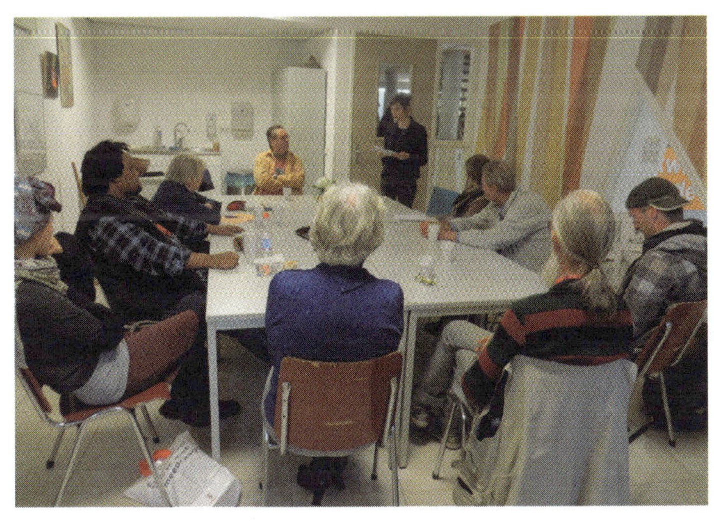

ROTTERDAM

21.09.2013
6:00 P.M.

Wi Masanga, meeting centre of the Surinamese community in Rotterdam.

S

I enter and see that no 'meeting' is in fact being held in the meeting centre. Normally we go to meetings where there is already a certain measure of focused concentration. Not in this case, the space is divided into two parts and about 70 men are playing cards, talking, drinking coffee. They are all black persons of colour, except me. To heighten the contrast even more, our contact person announces me in a loud voice: 'We have a lecture for every one here by a lady from Belgium. They always say that the Surinamese have loud voices. Let's see if this white lady can also raise her voice.' She means well. I begin carefully, at my regular tempo. At best, five men turn around. Just as I think, this isn't working, I need to draw on a different energy, the woman grabs me and drags me to the middle of the hall. Together, her drive and mine ensure that, very intuitively, I shout out my text and convey it with a lot more expressiveness than elsewhere. It works. They all stop playing cards and look at me. They answer, call to each other. When I ask, 'Imagine a catastrophe', someone says, 'The closing of this centre'—which is coming near, apparently. Something is happening, people are talking. There is some applause. Once I've finished, a large, older man shakes my hand and says, 'Well, how brave of you to come and do that here. I myself write poems, but they never listen to me. Respect.'

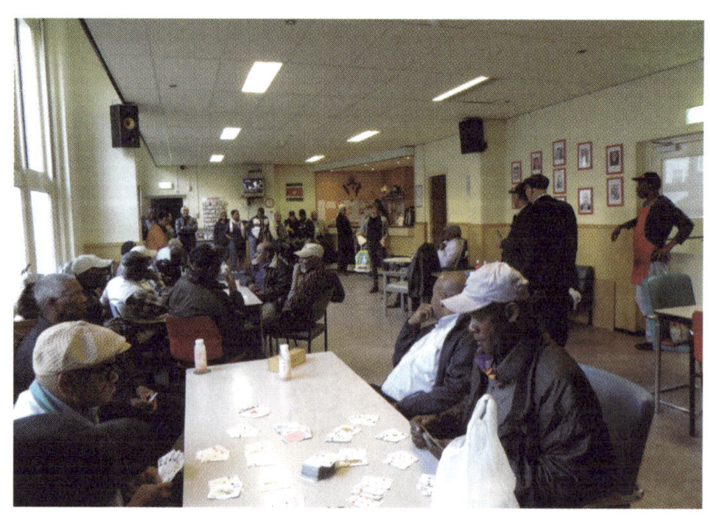

TALLINN

27.08.2014
9:00 A.M.

Swedbank. Biweekly meeting of the private banking department.

S

I still find it exciting to do LFEO for banks. Our contact, the director, is tremendously affectionate when receiving us. Upon leaving, he gives me a hug. A hug! From a bank director! Subsequently I hear that, not much later, he resigned because he wanted to start a different life.

BRUSSELS

29.10.2019
3:15 P.M.

La Bellone.
Writers' residency.

S

October 2019. I'm working on this publication with Marika Ingels in the writers' residency of La Bellone. Elise Simonet—an artistic acquaintance from France—is in town and drops by to say hello. She asks what we're doing. When I explain she says, 'Let me know when the publication is ready, I'll give my Dad a copy as a present.' 'Why your Dad?', I ask, surprised. 'My father's a truck driver', she explains. 'When Lara Barsaq did LFEO in Bordeaux, she stayed in my parents' home. During the public presentation of LFEO, my father cried. He didn't understand why. He said: "It's such a simple text—nothing earth-shaking, nothing new, and it's conveyed in such an ordinary way, why then does it move me so? Probably because it's so simple precisely, for every-one."'

A broken bone: facilitating a void where other things can happen

A conversation with Daniel Blanga Gubbay

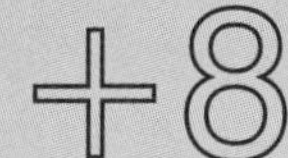

Daniel Blanga Gubbay is a researcher, teacher and curator in the performing arts. Since 2019 he is one of the three directors of the Kunstenfestivaldesarts (KFDA) in Brussels.

The KFDA co-produced LFEO in 2013 and is now co-producing this publication as well as a new version of LFEO with Brussels teenagers, to be presented in May 2020.

The following text is the result of a conversation between Sarah Vanhee and Daniel Blanga Gubbay that took place in Brussels on 20 October 2019.

S

You've seen a lot of my work, both the black-box works and the ones outside art institutions.

D

Yes, I've had the chance to follow your work over the past eight years; it's a path characterized by many different formats and media. When you shift from one project to another, you're in a completely different—not only universe, but also way of working. That's been very fascinating to me, especially because in contemporary artistic practice there is very often the tendency to turn the artist's signature into a recognizable tool. You, on the contrary, have withdrawn from this and try to enter and investigate completely different fields. But at the same time, even if the result is different, it's interesting for me to understand how, in these different areas, you use similar strategies, in the way you operate and the gestures you make. So, I was thinking, what's the continuity in your practice? Is there a common lens through which you look at what you are doing, or a filter through which you transform the material?

There are three different elements I recognize.

The first is the notion of generative fiction. You make use of fiction, but always escaping the classical mode of fiction as a fixed, constructed place. Instead, while you work on some conditions of the reality that we share, you use fiction as a tool that reveals something that otherwise wouldn't be revealed, that can activate something. Last year, while reading a text by Anne Michaels, I found an expression in which she speaks about fiction in a beautiful way: she says fiction does not represent reality but 'operates as a broken bone that you insert in the body of the present'. It's something you put inside, and then it transforms the body into which it has been inserted. I love this image; it breaks down the modern opposition between fiction and reality that is at the basis of Western theatre. It presents fiction, not as a frame, but as a tool to reveal or transform something that is there. The term 'generative fiction' starts from here. I got to use the term while in conversation with Lebanese artist Rafat Majezoub. Fiction generates something that exceeds the frame of fiction, that has consequences on so-called reality. What you do are very often gestures that live in this ambiguity between fictional and non-fictional space. At the same time, it's not simply about blurring the space, it's more like an affirmative gesture that produces something that otherwise would not be there.

This is present in LFEO, the gesture itself, which we can also consider as a kind of fiction, invading a space. The focus is on the gesture itself but even more on what is generated by the gesture: what it reveals, activates, how people react, and other elements that potentially were already there but were in need of this 'broken bone' to be revealed. When I saw 'The Making of *Justice*', I had exactly the same feeling. The way you used the text and the very explicit use of fiction, not as a form of escapism from reality, but to reveal a discourse that was potentially there. It's a very specific form of practice. I find it very strong; somehow it has to work with very sharp gestures but it also has to acknowledge that the focus is not the gesture itself but what will be generated by it.

S

I like this 'broken bone inside the body'. In the beginning when you were saying that my work does not have a continuity in its format, but rather in tools or in strategies, I was thinking, no, it's not that—that already sounds so much like something outside myself. When I think about my work, it's something that at the same time is inside me, but that always transforms me. In a way, it's always a crisis. So yes, I would rather agree with the words 'attitude' and 'gesture', words you used later. Those words are connected to the body that is life, real life. So strangely, even if I work so much with words, I recognize something of the somatic in there: through these works, I put myself into something, I am myself the bone, in a sense.

What I bring in then has to be sharp. Because otherwise, it can't generate. I'm aware that I often touch on very vast topics or worlds, and that can only be when the gesture is extremely sharp. Often there is something unsettling about it, or even violent, like in the case of LFEO. But it has a generative potential that hopefully feeds into the imagination.

I'm more curious about what it's going to generate or produce than *what it is*. That's why I'm only making a publication about *what* it is after seven years—by now it has become something else already.

D

In the idea of generative fiction there is no opposition between being sharp and being open. These two elements are connected somehow, which is why I referred several times to an affirmative gesture. It's not the idea of 'let's see what's going to happen'. I like this image of the broken bone, because it's not simply about opening the body or producing a wound and then seeing what happens; it is a very sharp gesture, something really is placed there, and once it's there—it still generates something that is not completely under your control, the consequences of which are still open. This is very strongly present in LFEO. Also, when I experienced 'The Making of *Justice*', so much was coming out of those prisoners in the desire to speak… The way you brought fiction, as a kind of field or a meeting place, that was the key that opened up a very important discourse. But what is disclosed is not fictional at all. It's something that was already there, that somehow needed to be revealed.

S

Fiction itself is important to me, more important than art. It produces a state of affirmation in me, a belief. I think that through fiction everything is possible, even if you don't know yet what this everything is. In my mind, everything is possible! I'm puzzled by the metaphor of the 'broken' bone. It's not a bone, a new bone, or another bone. No, it's a bone that has been broken already. It somehow makes a lot of sense that it's broken. But why? *(laughs)*

D

I think that in Anne Michaels' idea it's a broken bone that can solidify in very different ways. It's not a gesture that is done out of efficiency. It's not that you are inserting the bone because the body needs the bone, or because the body was in demand of this bone. It means reopening a kind of configuration that was not consciously asking to be opened.

S

One could think of science—'OK, you do an experiment and you don't know what the outcome will be'—or alchemy. But it's not that. It's not about throwing in an element and seeing what happens. It's not that I 'set' the conditions—it's not so formal. But more like, in what kind of space does this happen? What kind of 'being together' are we creating here? And that has much more to do with attitude, or even performing. In 'The Making of *Justice*', there are passages in which I appear. When I now look at that, I ask myself, what am I performing? Who am I there? How does my attitude influence the situation?

Another very clear example is *The Miraculous Life of Claire C,* the novel I published in 2009. What I'm basically doing there is invoking fictions. Maybe over the years, I've become much more sensitive to how my own presence or attitude influences the kind of space that is being generated. What does your presence evoke, your way of speaking? How is your own belief in fiction packed into who you are there? Because I could script the work and give it to someone to do it, but I feel there is also something with *how.*

D

So, generative fiction was the first term I had in mind. Then there is the second one: a politics of listening. This might appear to contradict this idea of the affirmative gesture, or the act of speaking. But for me it doesn't. Listening is not a passive act, but an active act that creates the condition for something to happen. You often set the conditions to invite the audience, or the viewer, to expend their awareness about listening as a political act. Like in LFEO, in *Untitled* too, it starts from this act of listening. Also in *Unforetold,* where it is a lot about accepting that the first thing you have to do is not the active gesture of understanding, but first of all the act of listening, facilitating a void where other things can happen. Sometimes I have the impression that you expand this beyond anthropocentricity. Like in *Oblivion:* how you listen to objects and materials. Discovering that our life is made up of so many potential voices that are there. It becomes a political exercise of listening as a relational attitude, with both the human and non-human. And for me, again, it's not an *element* of your work but more an *attitude* that I detect. It is also part of a historically fundamental feminist practice of reclaiming the politics of listening, which has been put forward from Pauline Oliveros onward as a political and feminist practice.

S

This idea of creating a void has always been there. In *Turning Turning,* for instance, it's like becoming empty myself in order to receive. I don't have to manifest myself. I rather become a vessel through which something else can translate or manifest itself, mostly some 'things' else. And I lend myself to that. That, for me, is the pleasure of making work—to be able to transgress, transform yourself constantly and in that sense to feel connected with yourself and with your environment. With *Oblivion* I had the chance to work for a long time in a quiet, focused and isolated way with the material, not distracted by a lot of social conditions, so I could really examine my relation to these things here, to all the 'things'. A word I worked a lot with is 'investment'. Listening is about investing. In that sense, it doesn't differ much from speaking. They're the same, just kind of upside down. That's another pleasure, strangely, together with 'being empty'; simultaneously, it's about investing yourself again. You have to empty yourself in a way to be able to invest into? something else, someone else, to say yes to that potential fiction. That's why indeed it doesn't matter what the outcome is. Rather, I like to invite other people to collaborate, to join this process of investment. Like in *Untitled,* when you as a visitor, go to the front door of unknown people and ring the bell and are invited into their home. You are invited to look at something that someone else calls 'art' in a way that is the radical opposite of market 'investment'; it's through affection, words, context that you are invited to invest in it, maybe attribute value to something that you would normally not give value to. And this is the same in 'The Making of *Justice*' when you listen to the inmates speaking, all of them convicted murderers. A lot of people say they're confused when they watch the film, because they find themselves struggling with their own prejudice. So it's also about suspending judgement. Which is unsettling, not always pleasant. The act of listening as investing and empathizing—temporarily suspending the ego, in fact.

D

There is no contradiction between the affirmative action of speaking and the one of listening. They are part of this cycle of how to be in relation.

S

There's a notion of listening that is just so much wider. Even from a perceptual point of view, it's like this all-around thing. Listening is non-discriminatory. With my eyes I can choose to look at that window, and not to look at that paper. But with my ears I can't filter out sounds, so I also get what I don't want to hear. That, again, is, I don't know whether feminist, but feminine for sure. This envelopment, enveloping. You can't choose so much. So therefore it's hard to grab hold of *what* then is generated precisely, hard to pin that down.

When you were speaking of generative fiction, I was thinking of Wallace Stevens, a poet who coined this idea of the 'supreme fiction', which is a fiction that we all know is a fiction but nevertheless decide to believe in. And there again there is this idea of investment: to *invest* in a fiction. Maybe that's kind of the spell I like to work with: an invitation to step into a 'supreme fiction'.

D

Then there is a third term I associate with your work. I sum this idea up in the term 'unproductive'. In different works of yours we can see the 'unproductive'; your work clearly questions some values of efficiency or productivity—values that are very strong in the neoliberal present. Somehow the spaces you open up suspend themselves from this trajectory. The linearity of time, the goal-oriented or production-oriented arrow, in which we all are, is halted for a moment, suspended to open up multiple directions that somehow broaden our perspective of the linearity of time. This was very strong in *Oblivion,* where what you were doing indeed was 'to bring back', as you often say, 'everything that we usually disregard in order to be more efficient'. That's everything that we throw away, like spam, or everything that has a potentially distracting influence on our clear path towards our journey or goal. What does it mean to bring this back materially? Not simply as an obstruction, but also to remind us about the amount of work we do to focus on one direction. And how much this one direction is linked with the idea of productivity and reducing non-efficiency, leading to riskless alternatives.

We could say that artistic creation always has to be more complex than productive. But in your case, this is brought to the surface as a clear need to speak about the value and importance of our productive time. It's really dealing with, listening to the unproductive, cherishing this unproductive and remembering the importance it has in what we are and what we can be, each of us in the future. It might be a term related to the generative fiction: somehow to produce a gesture without knowing exactly what it will be, leaving space for something unproductive to emerge, and listening to it.

In LFEO, for instance, your gesture was to open up a moment that was not an immediate productive one, but on the contrary, was kind of suspending time in situations that are supposed to be productive ones: meetings, assemblies where people have to take decisions or reach conclusions. And then LFEO arrives as a kind of unproductive time that reveals the productivity of unproductivity. It's really the gesture of suspending the production-oriented or the efficiency of what it means to 'be together'. LFEO opens up the question of why we are together. Are we together because it's more efficient? Or are we together beyond the notion of efficiency? Do we meet in meetings because it's the most efficient way to achieve work? Or do we meet because we need to meet? And we don't have a goal and somehow what we are going to do exceeds this notion of productivity. I found this a rather urgent value to bring back in our society.

S

That's very nice. In LFEO there is also a lot of silence. There is this literal creation of the moment, upon which follows a silence. When I return now to some people who received the lecture maybe seven years ago, hardly any of them remember the text, but everyone remembers the silences. And the kind of space it generated, the kind of affects and emotions—everything between the words actually.

The problem with this whole drive to what you call productivity—maybe even more efficiency—is that it creates poverty rather than richness. It sells us the myth that it will makes us rich, but we are only heading in one direction and we don't see or perceive anything around there. It makes us feel like we have to run after things that are not there yet, whereas there is so much already. Not only are we not looking at what is around us, but neither are we looking at what is behind. I recognize the kind of spaces you describe that are there in my work, and that's why I like to be there. I like to be that person, creating those spaces. But at the same time to reach that I have to be very efficient and productive. Over the past two years, I also started to question that for myself: whether it's enough to serve the creation of those temporary spaces with an attitude that is in itself very efficient and productive. With *Oblivion* at some point I felt like the happiest person on Earth, because I felt like, 'Everything is there already, I don't have to produce anything, I just have to invest in what is already there'. That was an extremely peaceful thought. My underlying quest now—as both an artist and a person—is how to dare to do that. You know, when I think about producing efficiency—I can't show it now—but it's like in the chest, it's something hardening.

D

It's also about this question of 'what is new'? It's not about rushing toward something that's not yet here, so as to conquer it, reproducing a myth at the basis of capitalism and the colonial project. It is about abandoning the model of conquering the new, the new! This can only be done while stepping out of the paradigm.

S

That's why it's a big life question! *(laughs)*

D

What kind of model of research do we allow ourselves to have?

S

I do have a strong desire, but this desire is deeper, it's more from the belly or the cells—to create, to create maybe rather than to produce. Creation has to do with what is already there, it's not necessarily out of the blue. I was reading Tagore who wrote that 'children are in love with life, and it's their first love'. For me, creation also has to do with this kind of love for life. Where can we feel love? How can we generate the spaces where we can feel love, which means connection? This doesn't necessarily mean an affirmation of yourself but rather an extension of yourself and that has to do with this richness rather than with poverty. How to stay loyal to that?

To say yes to a fiction, to a connection, to say yes to 'investing', because you always make yourself fragile.

And that would be really interesting, to think even less efficiently. This is something you must also be confronted with when making a yearly festival!

D

For me, all these questions are connected: what does it mean to be productive, to be efficient? But also, in my practice, what does it mean to be 'new'? Because I work in a system where novelty is a value that is so much appreciated. I think it's very important to support new things, new artists, but I am also interested in you going back to LFEO. And what does it mean, as a festival, to present again a project that has already been presented and produced by the festival, but that now is different. It's an important element in reclaiming or thinking about the sustainability of the artistic practice: do we have to follow the pattern of extreme novelty where we always ask about new projects? Even if it is important to support new artists and new practices, this can't be the only parameter, because then you're reproducing the dynamic of the market: the continuous rush towards the new.

S

The arts sector is not very 'progressive', in that sense. Perhaps we talk about it, about how to break with this cultivation with the 'ever new', but then to really practise that…

D

Yes, it seems to be a question that is also very practical. I'm speaking from the side of a festival that has a history of mainly creating new works. And this is still part of the festival's mission today. But it's important to understand, 'OK, but what are the possibilities for artists?' It's more a question of the ecology of the artistic practice.

S

Indigenous peoples have a strong capacity to look back, to go back. It's important to know the stories of your community, the traditions, what you relate to. There—and that is opposed to the alt-right's nostalgia here—it also means to go back even if something has been completely ruined or spoiled or destroyed. It means sticking to something and not just abandoning because it's not working anymore.

D

That brings up another very important value for me, commitment. That means you stick to something, even when things are not efficient.

S

Yes, how can something ever be generated if not from an instance of commitment? I think people want to commit. There is deep pleasure and joy only when there can be commitment. I just finished reading *Why Does Patriarchy Persist?*, a psychological analysis of patriarchy. Basically it says that in patriarchy, our real human need for authentic relations has been replaced by hierarchies. And hierarchy presupposes a power pyramid, a set of power relations, through which we don't have to make up our own relations anymore. Because the hierarchy dictates what the relations are going to be. And to be able to set aside—which initially comes along with resistance—our real need for relations, to comply with the hierarchy, boys have to cut off their feelings, and girls have to refrain from voicing their needs. That's the model. And I think a lot of work has to be done to rediscover these broken relations—back to the 'broken bone'. Not to heal, maybe—I can't do that—but to offer, to create a possibility of reconnecting with the other, or with oneself, with an object, with the Earth, with a story maybe. But to deal with the need for real connection.

D

I think this happens in creating situations that allow to voice out. That's something very present in the work. It's also the possibility in your work to reconnect with the presence of feeling—both for males and females. In 'The Making of *Justice*', this was very present. How do you open up possibilities of being heard outside the traditional construction of gender?

S

How can you hear yourself again? That's also what we did in *undercurrents* with the screaming: we invited people to scream, to hear their own voice. Very unspectacular in a sense, and so big actually. The massiveness, the complexity… and yet again, it's not about expressing something. Rather the opposite: it's creating a room through which *something* can be expressed but we don't know what. The voice has a very specific role in that, as exactly this place where so much feeling, emotion, affect is gathered, that we can't control, that we can't mould, that is not in our power. I think a lot in terms of resonance in that sense, which brings us back to the listening. How something resonates…

D

That's the principle of the generative fiction. It's not the sound itself but what it generates in the echoes, etc. How it reverberates in a very concrete way. I like this image because, in this theory of reverberation, the sound is potentially already present *in* the material, as a latent sound. It's not something that you are creating, but you create the conditions for the sound to be heard again.

DIY

Suggestions for writing, organizing and performing your own Lecture For Every One

+9

GENERAL

Don't be alone.

WRITING

What do you really want to say? What are the stories, thoughts, questions, words, observations and sensations you want to share?

The text needs to be said live, from person to person. Publishing it online would maybe make it for everyone, but not for every one.

Read. Listen. Look. Talk with people. Get inspired. Write down important thoughts you want to pass on. Try to articulate them in different ways. Find essence without reducing your message. Say it in words every one can understand.

Gather elements of meaning, rhythm, atmosphere. Write it all down—in shorter or longer units. Play with them: extend, shorten, transform. What do they do? Experiment with what they mean when you place them together, in different combinations. You are composing an experience in time.

Invite other people to play and think along. Listen to what resonates in you.

Dare to use words that are simple yet not cliché. If the words are too empty, flat or highbrow: don't use them. If words feel right, they will charge you as you say them.

Try to imagine that you are the listener: where would you disconnect? Leave out those words, passages, tones, attitudes and gestures.

Try to make it of interest to everyone. Start out from us being together as human beings.

This is an open moment in time for people to feel and think on their own, while also being and thinking together. This is a moment that you create with them.

No stress. You are not writing THE Lecture For Every One. You're only writing A lecture for every one.

The words will be heard the moment you speak them. So try to be with the listeners, alongside them—not before or behind—as if you were making it up in the moment. You, just like them, don't know where it's going. The words are fixed but their resonance will be different each time.

Try it out several times, with different people.

ORGANIZING

See 'Logistics' (+3) and 'Conversation with collaborators' (-3).

Use your imagination. Use your networks, your perseverance, your charm.

PERFORMING

Acknowledge how you are today. Acknowledge the space, the people, the situation. Accept. No one asked you to be there. However, you are responsible for your presence. You're an uninvited guest.

You can not but say this text. The words will guide you. Just start and then it will roll by itself. When saying the words, they will resonate and feed into what you will say next.

It's more a 'thing' than a lecture. It's only called a 'lecture' because it has a recognizable shape. The papers in your hands are a prop, an excuse to be in the meeting.

You will never get any message through unless you first connect with your interlocutor. Try to find the sound, the energy, the vibe, the presence that allows for connection.

Don't assume anything from anyone. You don't know what your interlocutors just went through this morning, this week, this year. You don't know anything about their traumas, sadness, obsessions, doubts, background, thoughts, feelings. You don't know what the relations between these people are.

You're just someone saying a lecture for every one. Let go of expectations. You're just a messenger.

Breathe. Smile. Move. Don't forget your sense of humour.

You're an interrupter, a saboteur. Speak from a place of softness, vulnerability, empathy, where a constant searching and transforming is happening. Nothing ever establishes there.

Vulnerability can come with firmness, with power.

Everything that happens is okay, nothing can go wrong.

There is no closing. Something is being opened.

Sources

Works mentioned in this book:

Arendt, Hannah, *Truth and Politics,* 1961
Badiou, Alain, *Saint Paul,* 2003
Critchley, Simon, *The Faith of the Faithless,* 2012
De Zegher, *Catherine, Women's Work Is Never Done,* 2014
Foucault, Michel, *Fearless Speech,* 2001
Gilligan, Carol & Naomi Snider, *Why Does Patriarchy Persist?*, 2018
Hobbes, Thomas, *Leviathan,* 1651
Kelleher, Joe, *Virtuosi of Exposure,* 2011
Llansol, Gabriela Maria, *Finita,* 2012
Llansol, Gabriela Maria, *Le jeu de la liberté de l'âme,* 2009
Lorde, Audre, *Sister Outsider,* 1984
Mandelstam, Nadezhda, *Hope Against Hope,* 1972
Michaels, Anne, *Infinite Gradation,* 2018
Piketty, Thomas, *Capital in the Twenty-First Century*, 2013
Plempius Vopiscus Fortunatus, *Ophthalmographia,* 1632
Rose, Gillian, *Love's Work,* 1995
Rose, Gillian, *The Broken Middle,* 1992
Rousseau, Jean-Jacques, *The Social Contract,* 1762
Stengers, Isabelle & Philippe Pignarre, *Capitalist Sorcery: Breaking the Spell,* 2007
Stengers, Isabelle, *Cosmopolitics,* 2010
Stevens, Wallace, *Notes Towards a Supreme Fiction,* 1943
Tagore, Rabindranath, *Chakravarty,* 1961
Vanagt, Sarah, *Dust Breeding,* 2014
Vanagt, Sarah, *In Waking Hours,* 2015
Vanhee, Sarah, *Oblivion, 2015*
Vanhee, Sarah, *The Making of 'Justice',* 2017
Vanhee, Sarah, *The Miraculous Life of Claire C, 2010*
Vanhee, Sarah, *TT, 2012*
Vanhee, Sarah, *Turning Turning (a choreography of thoughts), 2011*
Vanhee, Sarah, *undercurrents, 2019*
Vanhee, Sarah, *Unforetold, 2018*
Vanhee, Sarah, *Untitled, 2012*
Waddington, Laura, *Are You a River?* M's Story, 2020

Other works that inspired LFEO:

Arendt, Hannah, *The Promise of Politics,* 2005
Arendt, Hannah, *Vita Activa,* 1994
Badiou, Alian, *In Praise of Love,* 2012
Bishop, Claire, *Artificial Hells,* 2012
Borges, Jorge Luis, *The Craft of Verse,* 2002
Butler, Judith & Sunaura Taylor, *Examined Life,* 2010
Butler, Judith, *Notes Toward a Performative Theory of Assembly,* 2015
Cage, John, *Silence*, 1968
Carrère, Emmanuel, *Limonov,* 2011
Coates, Ta-Nehisi, *Between the World and Me,* 2015
Critchley, Simon, *Infinitely Demanding,* 2012
Curtis, Adam, *The Century of the Self,* 2002
Fisher, Mark, *Capitalist Realism,* 2009
Hessel, Stéphane, *Indignez-Vous,* 2010
Holquist, Michael, *Dialogism: Bakhtin and His World,* 1990
hooks, bell, *all about love,* 2000
Illouz, Eva, *Cold Intimacies,* 2007
Invisible Committee, *The Coming Insurrection,* 2008
Klein, Naomi, *The Shock Doctrine,* 2008
Kobayashi, Masaki, *The Human Condition,* 1960
Lababidi, Yahia, *Daring to Care: Notes on the Egyptian Revolution,* 2011
Le Guinn, Ursula, *The Left Hand of Darkness,* 1969
Luyendyk, Joris, *Swimming with Sharks,* 2016
Nancy, Jean-Luc, *Being Singular Plural,* 1996
Nietzche, Fri*edrich,* Human, All Too Human, 1878
Nussbaum, Martha, *Not for Profit,* 2016
Rancière, Jacques, *The Politics of Aesthetics,* 2013
Senneth, Richard, *Together,* 2012
Steyerl, Hito, *Freedom from Everything,* 2013

Speeches and songs by:

Alexandria Ocasio-Cortez, Audre Lorde, Bernadette Devlin, Buckminster Fuller, Charlie Chaplin, Chimamanda Ngozi Adichie, Cornel West, Emma Gonzalez, Greta Turnberg, Idle No More, John Cage, Kate Tempest, Malala Yousafzai, Malcolm X, Martin Luther King, Maya Angelou, Naomi Klein, Rosa Luxemburg, Sojourner Truth, Starhawk, Subcommandante Marcos, Xiuhtezcatl Martinez and many others

Credits LFEO & Places

Credits LFEO

Concept & text
Sarah Vanhee

In collaboration with
Juan Dominguez Rojo, Berno Odo Polzer, Dirk Pauwels & Kristien Van den Brande

Management host organizations & website
Edith Goddeeris, Marika Ingels, Linda Sepp & Kristien Van den Brande

Performance Flemish version
Sarah Vanhee
Christine De Smedt (Evergem)

Performance English version
Sarah Vanhee

Performance French version
Mylène Lauzon
Lara Barsacq (Bordeaux & Gennevilliers)

Performance Finnish version
Elina Pirinen

Performance Portuguese version
Anabela Almeida

Performance German version
Katja Dreyer (Darmstadt)
Deborah Hazler (Vienna)
Mariel Jana Supka (Berlin)

Performance German & Swiss German version (Bern)
Carola Bärtschiger

Performance Swedish version
Tove Wiréen (Gothenburg)
Salka Ardal Rosengren (Stockholm)

Performance Italian version
Sara Masotti

Performance Estonian version
Iiris Viirpalu

Performance Greek version
Matina Pergioudaki

Performance Icelandic version
Bryndís Bergmann

Thanks to
Anne Watthee, Berthe Spoelstra, Saar Vandenberghe, Ibelisse Guardia, Bojana Cvejic, Jakob Ampe, Pol Heyvaert, Joanna Bailie, Bert De Geyter, Arts Centre BUDA (Kortrijk)

Special thanks to everyone who helped us to spread Lecture For Every One

Production
CAMPO (Ghent)

Co-production
Kunstenfestivaldesarts (Brussels) & Frascati Producties (Amsterdam)

Supported by
STUK House for Dance, Image and Sound (Leuven)

Host organizations
Lecture For Every One was hosted by:

Kunstenfestivaldesarts – Brussels (BE)
Urb Festival – Helsinki (FIN)
Festival de Keuze – Rotterdam (NL)
STUK Start – Leuven (BE)
Possible Futures (Vooruit & CAMPO) – Ghent (BE)
Maria Matos Teatro Municipal – Lisbon (PT)
VIRUSfestival/ De Spil – Roeselare (BE)
Imagetanz 'Who Cares'/ BRUT – Vienna (AT)
BUDA – Kortrijk (BE)
Göteborgs Dans & Teater Festival – Gothenburg (SE)
Théâtre de la Cité internationale (in collaboration with Théâtre de la Villette) – Paris (FR)
Santarcangelo Festival – Santarcangelo di Romagna (IT)
Augusti TantsuFestival – Tallinn (EE)
Biennale Bern – Bern (CH)
Thinking Together – Darmstadt (DE)
Espace Malraux, festival A Nous – Chambéry (FR)
Hebbel am Ufer – Berlin (DE)
Frascati – Amsterdam (NL)
MIR Festival – Athens (EL)
Materiais Diversos – Minde (PT)
Théâtre de Gennevilliers – Gennevilliers (FR)
Chahuts Festival and TnBA – Bordeaux (FR)
MDT Stockholm (SE)
Cultuurcentrum Evergem-Sleidinge – Evergem (BE)
Komm'n Act, Festival Parallèle – Marseille (FR)
Extra City – Antwerp (BE)
Everybody's spectacular – Reykjavik (IS)

Places
Lecture For Every One was performed at:

REYKJAVÍK:

– City of Reykjavik, Department of Education and Youth. Executive committee meeting.
– Gardabaer Comprehensive Secondary School. Mathematics class.
– Matís, Food Production, Biotech and Food Security. Executive and administration meeting.
– Icelandic Red Cross. Teenage asylum seekers' meeting.
– Reykjavík Energy. Quality and security organization meeting.
– Sports club Fylkir. Cheerleading team, Valkyrjur, training session.
– University of the Arts in Iceland. Laugarnesvegi 91. Consultative meeting with department heads.
– University of the Arts in Iceland. Laugarnesvegi 91. Public presentation of the project in the context of Everybody's Spectacular.

ANTWERP

– Argenta. Belgian banking & insurance group. Meeting of the risk committee.
– Kunsthal Extra City. 'Stadsraad'.
– Open School within the framework of Inside Out (a programme of the OCMW public social-welfare centre). One of the classes in a tenfold course of communication.
– PROGRESS Lawyers Network Antwerp. Law office. Weekly team meeting.
– Public maintenance, Deurne Zuid, Berchem & Borgerhout. Lunch break.
– Redeemed Christian Church of God. African Pentecostal Church. Sunday service.

MINDE

- Atlético Clube Alcanenense, 3rd division football club. Daily team practice.
- Centro Hospitalar do Médio Tejo. Administration and chief physicians' board meeting.
- Escola Secundária de Alcanena. Teachers' general meeting for the school-year beginning.
- Escola Secundária Maria Lamas, Torres Novas. Secondary-school class.
- União de Freguesias de Malhou, Louriceira e Espinheiro, community council. General assembly.

GENNEVILLIERS

- CSM-Gennevilliers Rugby. Preparatory meeting for the club's annual party.
- Cultural centre Aimé Césaire. Sewing workshop.
- Europ Assistance, international insurance company. Meeting of the internal communication team.
- Mosque Ennour. Inter-religious meeting at the mosque's cultural centre.
- T2G. Public presentation of the project in the context of Le festival (tjcc).
- Town hall of Gennevilliers. Meeting of the environment department.

STOCKHOLM

- Bontouch, a company that develops apps. Presentations of ongoing projects.
- DCC. A secondary school. Planning day for the teachers.
- Environment department. Informal staff meeting.
- Hagsätra library. A weekly Swedish-language café for newly arrived immigrants.
- Karolinska University Hospital. Meeting of the doctors specializing in gynaecology & childbirth.
- MDT (try-out). Weekly staff meeting.
- POOL. An advertising company. An after-work.

BORDEAUX

- Aquitanis. Public housing office in Bordeaux. Meeting on the BTP archi site.
- EDF. French electric utility company, purchase department for nuclear energy of ARAP (Agence Régionale Achat Production) Grand-Ouest. Meeting of the purchase staff.
- La Bellone (try-out in Brussels). Staff meeting.
- InCité. Constructor, social landlord and developer. Budget meeting.
- Many Vigier Équipements. Regional enterprise specializing in the adaptation of utility vehicles. Planning meeting.
- Town hall of Bordeaux. Meeting of the communication department.

EVERGEM

- Calcutta, a textile company. Monthly staff meeting.
- City Council Evergem. Public hearing.
- Comeet, an intermediary joint venture—together with the 14 municipalities of the region 'Meetjesland'—taking care of the regional dimension of its cultural policy. Board of directors.
- Cultural Board of Evergem. A communal entity looking for cohesion among all of the sociocultural, amateur arts and heritage associations. General meeting.
- Femma, a women's organization. One of the ten lessons of the course 'Arranging flowers all year round'.

– Global Services, a company specializing in supporting end users in the context of change management, mainly in SAP implementations, Office applications and custom software. Staff meeting.
– Maldex, a family company that makes doors and (car)ports. Weekly meeting of the sales team.
– Municipal Elementary School Belzele. Monthly meeting of the management and the teachers of the nursery and primary school.

MARSEILLE

– AFPA. Training centre. Computer course.
– Ballet National de Marseille. Rehearsal for a dance piece named 'Le corps du Ballet National de Marseille'.
– EDF/CMCAS. Electricité De France/ Caisse Mutuelle Complémentaire d'Action Sociale. Meeting of the management team about the content of the activities, the finances of the activities and the coming projects.
– Olympique Marseille. Evening activity for the players in training.

ATHENS

– An investment research company. Weekly market review meeting.
– Batala Atenas, drumming group. Weekly rehearsal.
– Choir of the musical department of the National Technical University of Athens. Weekly choir rehearsal.
– Greek in the Agora, association for foreigners run by volunteers. Greek class.
– Holargos.bc, basketball team, 2nd league. Training.
– National and Kapodistrian University of Athens. Postgraduate class of the Communication and Mass Media department 'Political Communication and New Media'.
– Poetry group. Weekly meeting at the British Council.
– Seascape Group of Companies, Deck Equipment Supplies & Shipyard Services. Weekly meeting.
– Stone Soup, start-up company for online marketing, communication and development. Search engine optimization meeting.
– Warply, app design. Weekly team meeting for all employees.

AMSTERDAM

– Both ENDS. An NGO. Meeting of the directors of different NGOs and Fossilfree NL.
– DIKS car rental. Meeting of the management team.
– Thalassa diving club. Weekly training.
– Netherlands Institute for Neuroscience. Weekly meeting of the Sleep & Cognition research group, at which a researcher each time makes a presentation.
– Ondernemershuis Crataegus. Club house for entrepreneurs from Amsterdam. Entrepreneurs' dinner.
– PopUpChurch, an alternative Christian church. PopUpKerk @ white label coffee.
– Sajet Telting & Partners. Tax lawyers. Consultation meeting with another fiscal office.
– Qelp. Provider of multichannel customer-care products for smartphones. QelpTalk, a regular employee meeting.

BERLIN

– ASA-Program – Engagement Global gGmbH, Service for Development Initiatives. Learning and qualification programme, project meeting.
– betterplace.org, donation platform. Organizational meeting.
– Café Anna Blume, culinary and floral specialties. Monthly staff meeting.

– Café Wippe, Berlin support for gay men. Weekly open-meeting point and café.
– Craftspersons regular table Kreuzberg. Monthly meeting.
– Deutschlandradio Kultur. Editorial meeting for the programmes 'Gespräch'/'Kompressor'/'Fazit'.
– Eitner Security, security service/ protection of property, watch-keeping, construction sites guards. Team meeting.
– Federal Foreign Office, department of Culture and Intercultural Dialogue. Team meeting.
– Funk Gruppe, international insurance brokers and risk consultants. Meeting of the customer consultants.
– Goethe-Institut, Visitors Programme department. Team meeting.
– Jazzchoir Blue Wednesday, amateur choir. Weekly rehearsal.
– KHSB, Catholic University for Social Sciences Berlin. Introduction session for first-year students.
– LFS Financial Systems GmbH, consulting and management company. Argumentation training for international junior managers.
– LKJ, state umbrella association for cultural youth education. Monthly team meeting.
– MSC, Marine Stewardship Council. Lunch for employees of the fishing, communication and commercial management departments.
– Neighbourhood management Kreuzberg, urban development and environment in Kreuzberg. District council meeting.
– NHU, Neighbourhood Centre Urbanstrasse. Project meeting with long-term unemployed people.
– Organiced Kitchen, bio catering. Staff meeting.
– Otis Elevator Company. Development centre meeting.
– Residents Initiative Ernst-Thälmann-Park, association of residents living in the vicinity of Ernst-Thälmann-Park. Co-ordination meeting.
– Saint Elmo's, communication and marketing agency. Weekly team meeting.
– St Mary's Church. 'Celebration of the senses', evening service with Holy Communion.
– Tango Art 13, tango dance school. Practica, open training for beginners and intermediate level.
– taz, daily newspaper. Daily editorial meeting of the department heads.
– Trauma Hospital Berlin. Monday lecture for the entire hospital staff.
– VHS, adult education centre. German course level B2.
– Women's Network Meeting, HAU1 Foyer. Monthly meeting.

CHAMBÉRY:

– Atelier Porraz. Packaging company. Annual review meeting with the entire staff.
– Espace Malraux. Staff meeting.
– Louis et Perino. Architectural firm. Weekly meeting on current affairs.
– Maison des Adolescents. Open meeting for the entire staff.
– Orchestre des Pays de Savoie. Monthly meeting of the administrative staff.
– Ramus. Carpentry. Quarterly general meeting with the entire staff.

BERN:

– Administrative Office for Education Canton Bern, Department of Culture. Board meeting.
– BEKB Region Bern, Berner Kantonalbank. Board meeting of different departments.
– Bern University of Applied Sciences, Department of Agricultural, Forest and Food Sciences. Meeting of the communication department.

- BFH, Bern University of Applied Sciences, Health Department. Board meeting.
- Der Bund, daily newspaper. Editorial staff meeting about the layout of the newspaper's front cover.
- DOK, Bern's umbrella association for social work with children. Meeting of social workers from different institutions.
- Inselspital, University Hospital. Weekly meeting of the PR and communication department.
- Rotary Club. Weekly lunch meeting.
- Salsadancers, salsa dance school. Salsa Cubana for beginners.
- Schlachthaus, Biennale Bern. Team meeting.
- Women's choir of the cultural centre Reitschule. Weekly rehearsal.

TALLINN

- August DanceFestival. Team and volunteers' meeting at Kanuti Gildi SAAL.
- BDA Consulting, project management and consultancy company. Weekly team meeting of the entire staff to discuss current projects.
- Estonian Parliament. Meeting of the Social Democratic Party's ministers and chancellors.
- Estonian Public Broadcasting. Weekly meeting of the radio programmes board and the chief editors.
- KAFO, coffee enterprise. Weekly team meeting of the sales department.
- RSA Estonia, General Insurance Company, part of the multinational Insurance Group. Management and key stakeholders meeting.
- Swedbank. Biweekly meeting of the private banking department.
- Toggl, time-tracking software development. Weekly informal 'kitchen talk' of the team.
- Viimsi Cinema. Cinema team and workers' meeting.

DARMSTADT:

- Committee on Culture. Informal meeting.
- Concert choir. Last rehearsal without the orchestra before the upcoming Stockhausen concert.
- Darmstadt Marketing. City, Tourism and Event management. Meeting about barrier-free events in the city.
- Eumetsat (European Organisation for the Exploitation of Meteorological Satellites), intergovernmental organization supplying weather and climate-related satellite data, images and products. Monthly meeting of the HR department.
- HEAG Mobilo, public transport company in South Hesse. Biweekly meeting of the company's management.
- KAO. A chemical and cosmetics company, European HQ. Kick-off meeting of the R&D department (chemical research and marketing) concerning the topic 'permanent wave'.
- Palaterra. Public meeting around the topic of gardening and Palaterra technology.
- Planquadrat. Architects and city planners. Monday meeting for the presentation and discussion of current projects.
- Rotary Club. Regular meeting for dinner, followed by a speech.

SANTARCANGELO:

- Associazione micologica. Association of mushroom collectors. Board meeting to discuss the future activities of the association.
- Boxing club Santarcangelo. Weekly training starting with a run through the city.
- Municipal council. The newly elected mayor convenes the first council of Santarcangelo's new administration.

– Convento Frati Cappuccini. Moment of prayer and encounter of the Novices with the Friars of the Convent.
– Coro Magnificat, a choir. Rehearsals before mass.
– JUST cosmetics. Product presentation and demonstration in a private home.
– Lions Club. Summer party and ceremony of handover (investiture of the new president).
– Maggioli Editore, publishing company. Internal business meeting on the results of the previous months' sales.
– Polizia. Monthly meeting of the traffic department.
– Santarcangelo. 14 Festival Internazionale del Teatro, festival canteen. Meeting after lunch for the festival's office staff.
– Studio Battistini, housing association. Yearly meeting of apartment owners.

PARIS

– Caisse des Dépôts. Breakfast meeting gathering the departments of Finance and Strategy.
– CDC Climat. Weekly management meeting. A 100 per cent-owned subsidiary of Caisse des Dépôts dedicated to furthering the energy and environmental transition.
– HLM, organization for social housing. Team-building meeting.
– Espace 19. Meeting for knowledge exchange.
– Fnas. Weekly team meeting on current issues.
– La Villette. Board meeting.
– Parti de Gauche. General meeting of the 20th district of the Parti de Gauche.

GOTHENBURG

– Bokmässan, Gothenburg's annual book fair. Celebration meeting for the staff, on the occasion of the upcoming publication of this year's seminar programme.
– CBG, a translation agency. Weekly informal meeting for all employees.
– Eskulapius, an association for apartment owners. Monthly meeting.
– Ferrum architects. Weekly informal meeting.
– Gärde Wesslau, a lawyer's office specializing in Swedish and international commercial law. Weekly team meeting for all employees.
– Göteborgs Dans & Teater Festival. Staff meeting for volunteers.
– Göteborg & Co, a destination development agency for Göteborg as a tourist, meeting and event destination. Meeting of the leading team.
– Intermezzon, a company for performance management, change management and practical competence development offering e-learning, e-simulation and classroom training. Weekly 'inspiration time' meeting.
– Lundalogik, IT company and one of the largest providers of Customer Relationship Management in the Nordic region. Weekly informal meeting for all employees.
– Steget Vidare, HBV Donau. A home welcoming children with a residence permit, coming to Sweden on their own. Staff meeting.
– Volvo AB, one of the world's leading manufacturers of trucks, buses, construction equipment and marine and industrial engines. Farewell celebration for a member of the invoice & cost-control department.

KORTRIJK

– ACV South-West Flanders. Political debate leading up to the elections.

– Intercommunale Leiedal. Board of Directors.
– Rotary Groeninge. Statutory assembly celebrating the club's 30th anniversary.
– The police. Daily briefing of the intervention team, late service.
– Voka. Speaker's corner. Six-weekly meeting where a number of Voka employees introduce a new project or idea to their fellow colleagues.

VIENNA

– Austrian Parliament. Weekly meeting of the European Relations department.
– Best in Training, language school. German class.
– Boehringer Ingelheim, pharmaceutic research and production company. Weekly meeting of the laboratory's unit of quality control.
– brut im Künstlerhaus. Weekly meeting of the staff.
– Caritas' Haus Daria, home and assistance for asylum seekers. Weekly staff meeting.
– ERSTE Group. Quarterly networking event for ERSTE Group's 'Innovation Lab' and employees from different departments.
– ERSTE Stiftung, main shareholder of Erste Group, savings bank foundation for projects in culture and social development. Biweekly jour fixe of the foundation's staff.
– Gebietsbetreuung Stadterneuerung, public service for the 'soft development' of Vienna's city districts. Meeting of the 'artists network' group.
– Haus Rossau, home for the elderly. Before a mandolin concert for the residents and staff.
– MSC, Mediterranean Shipping Company, agency engaged in worldwide container transport. Biweekly meeting of the management department.
– Josefstadt Prison. Informal meeting of the prison board.
– The Gap, magazine for pop culture and music.Weekly meeting of the editorial department.
– Umweltdachverband, umbrella association for environment, nature and sustainable development. Biweekly meeting of the direction and management department.
– VinziRast, shared house for students and former homeless people. Monthly meeting of the residents and the executive team.

ROESELARE

– Dominiek Savio. Special needs secondary education. Evaluation of the students.
– Fire brigade. Training for firemen, concerning traffic accidents with jammed people.
– OCMW. Service centre Ten Elsberghe. Meeting on the reform of the rehabilitation centre.
– Roularta Media Group. A key player in Belgium in the publishing and printing of news and niche magazines, of newspapers and publicity. Board meeting.
– Soubry. Weekly operations & planning meeting.

LISBON

– Academia de Música de Santa Cecília. Teachers' reunion to discuss student grades.
– Canal Q. A television channel. Editorial meeting.
– Centro de Acolhimento para os Refugiados. A non-governmental refugee organization. Team meeting to analyse the 2013 activities and to prepare the New Year's party.
– Coro Gulbenkian. A choir. Rehearsal of Bach's *Weihnachtsoratorium*.

- Faber. A product/venture development company that explores opportunities to build, launch and scale early-stage digital businesses.
- Fundação do Gil. Organization that helps children return home after long hospital stays. Weekly team meeting.
- Goethe-Institut. Germany's global cultural institution. Farewell party for the director.
- Hospital Santa Maria. A clinic session for the Medicine Service ID.
- Hotel Lutécia. Employees' meeting to organize the staff Christmas dinner.
- Lisbon municipal council. Presentation of the new mandate for culture 2013–17.
- Maria Matos Teatro Municipal. General co-ordination meeting.
- Moinho da Juventude. A community project formed by the local inhabitants to help and work with the Cape Verdian community. Weekly intergenerational project uniting people of different ages.
- Nova School of Business & Economics. Seminar of research group—PhD students.
- Social Work Irmãs Oblatas Santíssimo Redentor. A religious congregation that seeks to assist women in the context of prostitution or sex trafficking, to promote justice and develop a process of dignity for women.
- Vodafone. Telephone company. Meeting of the staff of the OSS group Portugal.

GHENT

- ABVV East Flanders, meeting of the judges of the Labour Court.
- ACV, Christian union. Propagandists meeting.
- Amsab Institute of Social History, the Heritage Centre for social, humanitarian and ecological committed movements. Team meeting.
- Arteveldehogeschool, faculty of Business Management. Biweekly meeting of the core team.
- Bostoen. Building company. Monthly meeting of the Strategy Group 2.
- CY Sales & Marketing. Weekly evaluation meeting with the call agents.
- De Sloep. Group session on educational support for Turkish mothers.
- GE Industrial Solutions. Weekly staff meeting.
- Ghent University, Faculty of Physics and Astronomy. Mechanics class.
- IKEA. Three-day training for the Sales, Logistics & Communication managers.
- Intercultureel Netwerk Gent. Monthly staff meeting.
- Lodge De Ruwe Kassei. Weekly session.
- Psychiatric Centre Dr. Guislain. Department De Klip. 'De Zotte Morgen': meeting of residents with some staff members to discuss the practical issues of the next day.
- Sint-Michielsgilde. Annual meeting of the board members.
- Vooruit, bar & catering team. Periodical meeting.
- Vtax, a taxi company. Switching from the day shift to the night shift.

ROTTERDAM

- Gemeente Rotterdam. Meeting of the executive board and the municipal secretary.
- Grannys Finest. Knitting class for seniors under the guidance of a fashion designer.
- Hogeschool InHolland. Consultation of the board of examiners of the Media & Entertainment Management section.
- Kooijman Lambert Notaries. Daily morning meeting.
- Leeszaal Rotterdam West. Breakfast for freelancers.

– St Paul's Church. Church café. A team discusses recent events with regard to Bible stories.
– Rotterdam Running Ambassadors. Meeting after weekly training session.
– Rotterdamse Schouwburg, opening Festival De Keuze.
– Unique Interim. Consultants and managers' work meeting.
– Wi Masanga. Neighbourhood activity of the Surinamese community in Rotterdam.

LEUVEN

– Acerta, a service provider for entrepreneurs, specialized in HR advice and social administration. Meeting of the Change Management consultants.
– ALMA, restaurant for students and employees of the University of Leuven. Management meeting.
– Cinema Zed, before the screening of *Lars and the Real Girl.*
– de Ark, primary school. This school year's first meeting of the parents' council.
– De Warande, cultural centre in Turnhout. Guided tour in STUK for the logistic and technical staff.
– European Parliament, Socialists & Democrats (S&D). Meeting of the Transport work group on the 4th European Rail Package.
– Filipiniana-Europa vzw, multicultural associaton for Philippine women and other nationalities. Meeting to prepare the Dinner-Costume Party to celebrate their 15th anniversary.
– Imec, a research institute for nano-electronics and nano-technology. Team meeting external communication.
– Landelijke Gilden, organization that arranges sociocultural activities for people living in the countryside. Team meeting 'Planning and Education'.
– Leuven: the mayor and the councillors in the city of Leuven. Weekly meeting.
– Museum M, museum for classical and contemporary art. Staff training on 'working with volunteers'.
– Leuven prison. Training for the guards.
– Vormingplus, sociocultural centre for adult education. Meeting of the education team.

HELSINKI

– Bore, shipping company. Meeting between Bore's communication and HR manager, and an external team of web designers.
– CGI, local and global end-to-end IT and business process services. One of the weekly team meetings.
– Helsinki University Central Hospital Emergency department, medical staff meeting following the night shift.
– Institut Français. Weekly meeting of the administration team.
– ISS (International Service Solutions), a global provider of facility services. Monthly staff meeting of the Kiasma cleaning team.
– Kiasma Museum of Contemporary Art.
– Kinapori Service Centre for the elderly. Weekly meeting of the social and health instructors.
– Minerva Foundation Institute for medical research in biomedicine. Weekly meeting including a scientific lecture for laboratory researchers.
– Ministry of Social Affairs and Health. PR department meeting.
– Stockmann department store. Morning meeting for the store's salespersons.
– Tsto, a design agency active in the fields of graphic design, art direction and consultancy in both digital and printed media. Weekly team meeting between the designers.

BRUSSELS

- African Joys, a gospel choir, weekly rehearsal in church.
- ASCO Industries, a high-tech company active in the aerospace industry, works council (union & management).
- BECI, Brussels Enterprises Commerce and Industry (represents and supports the interests of businesses in Brussels in their dealings with local, federal and international authorities), executive committee.
- BNP Paribas. Conversation table.
- Café Marché, a music orchestra. Rehearsal.
- Le Cercle Gaulois, a gentlemen's club, during a lunch-debate on urbanism.
- COMOPSAIR, Belgian Defense. Division Commanders Meeting.
- Conservatoire royal, a French theatre school. Bachelor class physical theatre. (try-out)
- Davidsfonds, a Flemish cultural association, regional administration meeting.
- Euroclear, Central Securities Depository of Belgium. HR management meeting.
- European School of Administration.
- European School for Podology. Bachelor class English. (try-out)
- Feza, a French course for immigrant women.
- Flemish Government, Work and Social Economy department. Staff meeting.
- Foyer, an integration centre in Molenbeek. Wood workshop.
- German Embassy. Staff meeting.
- HOBO. A football club for people in precarious living situations.
- Huis van het Nederlands, Dutch-language house of Brussels. Staff meeting.
- IBM, a multinational technology and consulting corporation that manufactures and markets computer hardware and software. Team meeting of the Client Unit.
- Ixelles, municipality. Prevention department. A council meeting.
- KBC, a Belgian bank. Meeting of HR staff and legal advisors.
- Lhiving. Discussion group for deprived people with a chronic disease. (try-out)
- Lydian, a Belgian business law firm. Meeting of lawyers working in the Employment department.
- Metro, a free daily newspaper. French editors' meeting.
- Molenbeek, municipal council. Monthly public hearing.
- Natagora, a nature protection organization. Communication department meeting.
- NEOS Wommelgem. A group of active seniors on a guided tour on the Tour & Taxis site, organized by Korei vzw.
- Nestlé, European Affairs meeting
- NMBS/SNCB Holding, Belgian Railways. Factory meeting in the ICT department ICTRA.
- RTD Chorale, choir of people working for different European Institutions in Brussels.
- RVA/ONEM, National Employment Office. Meeting of Top 6 and the Organisational Development department.
- RVP/ONP. National Pensions Office, direction committee.
- Saint Jacques, district assembly. Monthly meeting of traders and residents of the District Saint Jacques.
- Securex, international company in the social administration and human resources field. Staff meeting.
- SeGEC, an umbrella organization for the Catholic schools in the French-speaking community. Internal meeting.
- Church of St Roch, Sunday mass, right after communion (parts of LFEO were translated into Lingala by the priest).
- Syntra. An evening course for electricians.

– The Dominican, a 4-star luxury hotel, sales meeting.
– Total. Meeting of the External and Professional Communication department.
– Umicore, a global materials technology group. Executive committee.
– Union des juifs progressistes, a Belgian-Jewish organization. Internal meeting.
– Volvo Trucks. Staff meeting.
– VOKA committee Brussels, a Flemish employers' organization, during a guided Art Deco and Art Nouveau tour through the city of Brussels, organized by Bruksel Binnenste Buiten.
– VRT, Flemish public radio and TV. Chief editors' meeting.

In April 2013, we organized
TRY-OUTS in GHENT

– IP Hills. Seminar on the 'Cycling Economy'.
– KISP cvo, centre for adult education. Evening sewing class.
– Lions Club, gentlemen's club. Dinner-debate.
– Sint-Lievenscollege, secondary school. Works council.
– Ghent University. Bachelor class in Dutch Language.

Colophon

APE#168
Lecture For Every One
Sarah Vanhee

ISBN 9789493146501
www.artpapereditions.org
www.sarahvanhee.com
www.lectureforeveryone.be

First edition of 500 copies
April 2020

Design: 6'56" (www.6m56s.com)
Printed and bound in Tallinn

Concept, text and editor:
Sarah Vanhee

With texts & contributions by:
Adinda Van Geystelen, Anabela Almeida, Anne Thuot, Anton Wilsens, Bojan Djordjev, Carola Bärtschiger, Christine De Smedt, Christophe Slagmuylder, Daniel Blanga Gubbay, Deborah Hazler, Edith Goddeeris, Elina Pirinen, Evelyne Coussens, Gurur Ertem, Iiris Viirpalu, Jan De Brabanter, Jan de Zutter, Joe Kelleher, Katja Dreyer, Kristien Van den Brande, Kristof Blom, Lara Barsacq, Lex Bohlmeijer, Linda Sepp, Mariel Supka, Marika Ingels, Matthieu Goeury, Mylène Lauzon, Robin Vanbesien, Salka Ardal Rosengren, Sarah Vanagt, Silvia Bottiroli, Taziana Pyson

Transcriptions:
Flore Herman, Nadia Mharzi

Advice:
Ilse Ghekiere

Thanks to:
Marika Ingels, Clara Beel

Translation:
Patrick Lennon

Copy-editing
Patrick Lennon, Cillian O'Neill, Maya Wilsens

Production:
Manyone
(Eva Wilsens, Cillian O'Neill)

Co-production:
Kunstenfestivaldesarts (Brussels), CAMPO (Ghent), Vooruit (Ghent), STUK (Leuven), Arts centre BUDA (Kortrijk), BIT Teatergarasjen (Bergen), SKOGEN (Gothenburg), La Bellone (Brussels)

All pictures were taken by LFEO collaborators during the intervention. They are published here with the permission of the places.

When there is an empty frame instead of the picture, it is because we did not obtain permission to publish the image in this book.

Header image
© x-ray delta one (cc by-nc-sa 2.0)

Supported by:
Flanders State of the Art

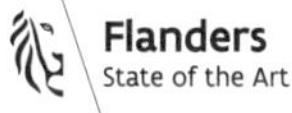

Sarah Vanhee is supported in the frame of apap—Performing Europe 2020—co-funded by the Creative Europe Programme of the European Union

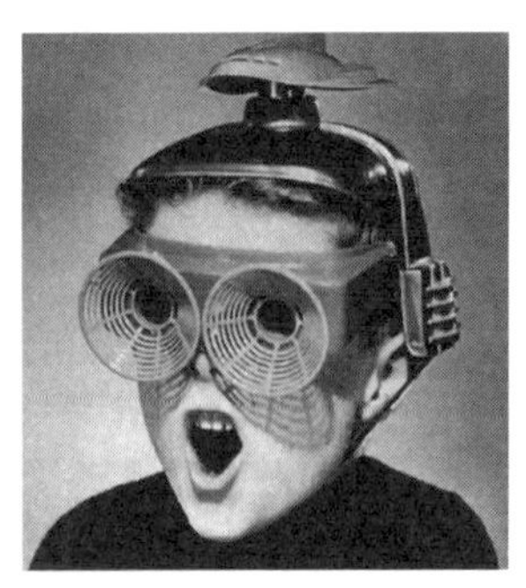